IN THE WORDS OF THE
PRESIDENTS

IN THE WORDS OF THE
PRESIDENTS

IAN CROFTON

Quercus

✳✳✳ CONTENTS ✳✳✳

INTRODUCTION

'Ask not what your country can do for you ...', 'The only thing we have to fear is fear itself', 'Government of the people, by the people, for the people' – these quotations from US presidents are deeply familiar to all Americans, and, indeed, to hundreds of millions of people around the world. But fewer people, perhaps, are aware of the context in which these famous words were spoken – or of the many other fine words uttered by Kennedy, FDR and Lincoln, or the forty presidents that came before and after them. This collection aims to present the best – the loftiest, most moving, wittiest and even the dumbest – words ever uttered by the presidents of the United States, from the 1st to the 44th.

Here are stirring flights of oratory, from Lincoln's Gettysburg Address to Lyndon Johnson's Great Society speech, from Woodrow Wilson's request to Congress for a declaration of war to George W. Bush's broadcast to the American people on the evening of 9/11. This book does not aim to reproduce any speech in its entirety (with the exception of all 268 words of the Gettysburg Address); only the most memorable extracts are included. Sometimes these are just a few short words; in other cases a paragraph or two, where the effect depends on rhetorical build-up. But this is not just a collection of extracts from presidential speeches: here also are letters, statements, passing remarks, loaded exchanges, witty quips and biting ripostes. There is even a handful of anecdotes, though for a real banquet of such stories, the reader is referred to Paul F. Boller's *Presidential Anecdotes*, which manages the enviable feat of being at once scholarly and enormously entertaining.

In the present volume, the chapter on each president begins with a number of key facts and then a brief biography, to help put the quotations in context. In addition, each quotation or group of quotations is preceded by a brief explanatory or contextual note, and is followed by a note of the source, wherever it has proved possible to trace one. The arrangement of the quotations is broadly thematic, rather than strictly chronological, so that the reader may more easily compare each president's thoughts on a range of topics.

Such topics include big government vs small, the scope of the Constitution, states' rights vs federal power, slavery and civil rights, democracy and civic duty, isolationism vs international engagement, unilateralism vs multilateralism, pluralism vs homogeneity, individualism vs collectivism, the lessons of the past and the dreams of Americans for the future. Less loftily, there are also scandals and skulduggeries, from the excesses of the spoils system ('All patronage is perilous') to Watergate ('There can be no whitewash at the White House') and the Lewinsky affair ('It depends on what the meaning of the word "is" is'). There are many glimpses of the more human side of the presidents, including their estimations of themselves: 'I am a man of reserved, cold, austere and forbidding manners: my political adversaries say, a gloomy misanthropist, and my personal enemies, an unsocial savage' (John Quincy Adams); 'I am more of a farmer than a soldier' (Ulysses S. Grant); 'I am as strong as a bull moose' (Theodore Roosevelt); 'I am not fit for this office and never should have been here' (Warren Harding); 'I'm not a crook' (Richard Nixon); 'I'm a better ex-president than I was a president' (Jimmy Carter).

Additionally, the opinions of others, whether favorable, antipathetic or historically detached, are given due weight. Thus we find Washington's contemporaries describing him either as 'One of the greatest captains of the age' (Benjamin Franklin) or 'That dark designing sordid ambitious vain proud arrogant and vindictive knave' (General Charles Lee, who thought he, rather than Washington, should have been put in command of the Continental Army). While he lived, and before the hagiographers got to work, Lincoln was 'a slang-whanging stump-speaker' (*Albany Atlas and Argus*) and 'incapable of any grand or noble emotion' (*New York Post*) and 'a damned fool' (Edward Stanton, Lincoln's secretary for war'); after his death he was 'the most perfect ruler of men the world has ever seen' (Stanton again). A particular feature, scattered through the text, comprises 'Presidential Opinions'. Thus we have Washington on Jefferson: 'He will leave nothing unattempted to overturn the government of this country'; Truman on Pierce: '[He] didn't know what was going on and even if he had, he wouldn't have known what to do about it'; Theodore Roosevelt on McKinley: 'No more backbone than a chocolate eclair'; and LBJ on Gerald Ford: 'So dumb that he can't fart and chew gum at the same time'.

For the most part, though, the mood is up-beat. That, after all, is the spirit that built America, and why so many people responded to Barack Obama's oft-repeated affirmation, 'Yes we can'. As Bill Clinton said at his First Inauguration, 'There is nothing wrong with America that cannot be cured by what is right with America.' In war and peace, in recession and in the good times – and even though right, left and centre may have different plans as to how to build it – the American people still share Ronald Reagan's vision of America as 'that shining city on a hill.'

Ian Crofton
October 2009

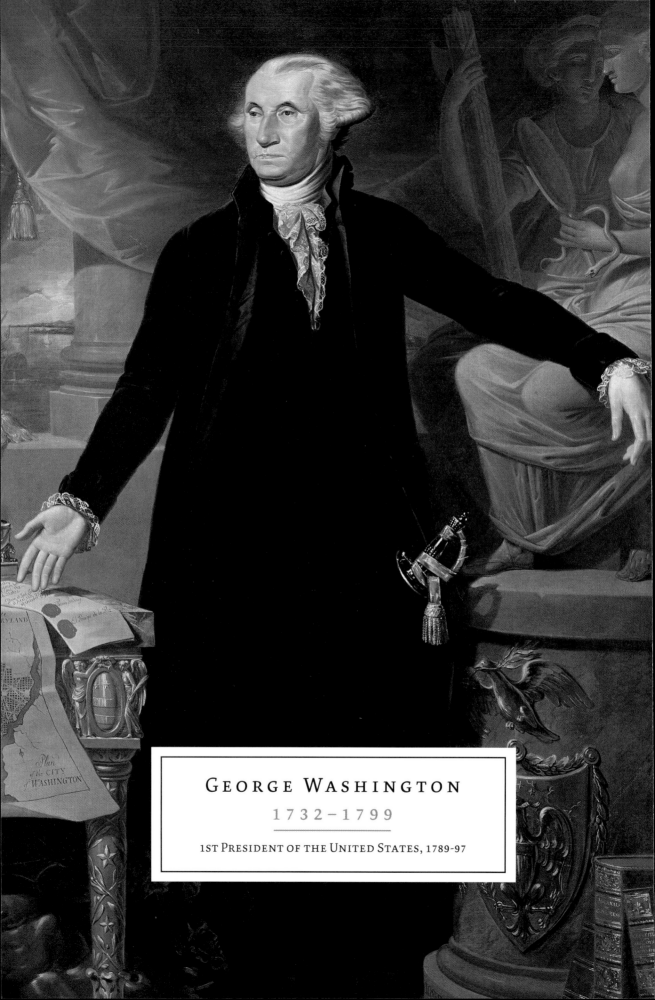

GEORGE WASHINGTON

1732–1799

1ST PRESIDENT OF THE UNITED STATES, 1789-97

GEORGE WASHINGTON

FULL NAME: George Washington
BORN: February 22, 1732 (Old Style February 11, 1731),
Westmoreland County, Virginia
DIED: December 14, 1799, Mount Vernon, Virginia
MARRIED: Martha Custis (née Dandridge;
she was the widow of Daniel Parke Custis)
CHILDREN: None (although Washington helped to raise
his stepchildren, John and Martha)
PARTY: Federalist (although he never officially joined the party)
PERIOD IN OFFICE: April 30, 1789–March 4, 1797
VICE-PRESIDENT: John Adams

* * *

GEORGE WASHINGTON was born into a well-off slave-owning planter family in Virginia. In 1749, at the age of only 17, he was appointed surveyor of the newly created Culpepper County, which inspired in him his lifelong interest in westward settlement. In 1752 he inherited his father's Mount Vernon estate, and in the same year became an officer in the Virginia militia, in which role he took part in operations during the French and Indian War. He was disappointed that he could not secure a commission in the British army, and thereafter felt a great resentment against the British officer class. In 1759 he married a wealthy widow, Martha Custis, thus enhancing his social standing and adding to his land holdings, which he continued to expand, by purchases and grants. By this time he was already involved in local politics, serving as a representative in Virginia's House of Burgesses, and he went on to become a member of the Virginian delegation at the first and second Continental Congresses. On June 15, 1775, following the outbreak of hostilities against the British that April, he was appointed commander-in-chief of the Continental Army. As a commander he kept himself above factional politics, and drew admiration for his generalship, which was characterized by courage, endurance and care for his troops. Although on occasion he showed a dashing streak in battle, he was by nature cautious.

With victory assured in 1783, Washington resigned his command and retired from public life, but in 1787 he attended the Constitutional Convention, of which he was elected president. The Convention, which went on to draft the Constitution, designed the US presidency with Washington in mind, and in 1789 the Electoral College unanimously elected Washington as 1st president of the United States; this unanimous vote was repeated in 1792, although Washington only reluctantly agreed to serve for a second term. As president, Washington's innate caution expressed itself as conservatism. Although not a member of any political party, he sided with the Federalists in his cabinet (especially Alexander Hamilton), and was accused by Jefferson and the Democratic-Republicans of monarchical tendencies. In his farewell address, Washington warned against the factionalism of party politics, and against the United States establishing permanent foreign alliances – the basis of American isolationism for the next century and a half. In 1797 he retired to Mount Vernon, although in 1798 he agreed to serve once more as commander-in-chief in the event of war with France. In December 1799 he caught a chill while inspecting his estates, and on the 14th of that month died of pneumonia. His last words were ''Tis well.'

In an account to his brother of a skirmish during the French and Indian War, Major Washington describes the thrill he found in battle:

> I fortunately escaped without a wound, though the right wing where I stood was exposed to & received all the enemy's fire ... I can with truth assure you, I heard the bullets whistle and believe me there was something charming in the sound.
>
> LETTER TO JOHN AUGUSTINE WASHINGTON, May 31, 1754. On reading this letter reprinted in the *Gentleman's Magazine*, George II, the last British monarch to lead his troops in battle, commented: 'He would not say so if he had been used to hear many.'

THE CHERRY TREE INCIDENT

* * *

In a famous, but almost certainly apocryphal, story, Washington's father is distressed to discover that his favourite cherry tree has been felled. Young Washington owns up:

> I can't tell a lie, Pa; you know I can't tell a lie. I did cut it with my hatchet.
>
> MASON LOCKE ('PARSON') WEEMS, *The Life of George Washington, with Curious Anecdotes Laudable to Himself and Exemplary to his Countrymen* (1806)

The words are often quoted as:

> Father, I cannot tell a lie. I did it with my little hatchet.

The story prompted Mark Twain to remark of Washington that:

> He was ignorant of the commonest accomplishments of youth. He could not even lie.

Many years later, when asked whether he really found the sound of bullets so charming, Washington replied:

> If I said so, it was when I was young.
>
> Quoted in William Gordon, *History of the Independence of the United States* (1788)

In the period of tension prior to the outbreak of the Revolution, Washington showed himself to be on the side of caution:

> I think I can announce it as a fact, that it is not the wish or interest of that government, or any other upon the continent, separately or collectively, to set up for independency. I am as well satisfied as I can be of my existence that no such thing is desired by any thinking man in all North America.
>
> LETTER TO CAPTAIN ROBERT MACKENZIE, October 9, 1774

But when it came to the crisis, Washington was not found wanting. Following his appointment on June 15, 1775 to command the new Continental Army, he remarked:

> I can answer but for three things: a firm belief in the justice of our cause, close attention in the prosecution of it, and the strictest integrity.

Privately, he was far from confident, telling Patrick Henry:

> This will be the commencement of the decline of my reputation.
>
> Quoted in W.E. Woodward, *George Washington: The Image and the Man* (1926)

Washington was to prove an inspirational commander. Before the Battle of Long Island, on August 27, 1776, he addressed his forces thus:

> The time is now near at hand which must probably determine whether Americans are to be freemen or slaves; whether they are to have any property they can call their own; whether their houses and farms are to be pillaged and destroyed, and themselves consigned to a state of wretchedness from which no human efforts will deliver them. The fate of unborn

millions will now depend, under God, on the courage and conduct of this army. Our cruel and unrelenting enemy leaves us only the choice of brave resistance, or the most abject submission. We have, therefore, to resolve to conquer or die.

In the midst of the fighting at the Battle of Princeton, on January 3, 1777, he rallied some fleeing troops with the following words:

Parade with us my brave fellows! There is but a handful of the enemy and we shall have them directly!

Despite his leadership qualities, Washington was gloomy about the prospects of a citizen militia defeating the regular forces of the Crown:

To place any dependence upon militia is, assuredly, resting upon a broken staff. Men just dragged from the tender scenes of domestic life, unaccustomed to the din of arms; totally unacquainted with every kind of military skill, which being followed by a want of confidence in themselves, when opposed to troops regularly trained, disciplined and appointed, superior in knowledge and superior in arms, makes them timid and ready to fly from their own shadows.

LETTER TO JOHN HANCOCK, president of the Continental Congress, September 24, 1776

By 1783, the year the war formally came to a conclusion, Washington could still not quite credit what he had achieved:

It will not be believed, that such a force as Great Britain has employed for eight years in this country could be baffled in their plan of subjugating it, by numbers infinitely less, composed of men oftentimes half starved, always in rags, without pay, and experiencing every species of distress, which human nature is capable of undergoing.

LETTER TO NATHANAEL GREENE, 1783

Rejecting suggestions by some of his officers that he should seize power:

You could not have found a person to whom your schemes were more disagreeable.

LETTER TO COLONEL LEWIS NICOLA, May 22, 1782

After he had resigned as commander-in-chief on December 23, 1783:

I feel myself eased of a load of public care. I hope to spend the remainder of my days in cultivating the affections of good men, and in the practise of the domestic virtues.

LETTER TO GEORGE CLINTON, governor of New York

With the war over, it was time to get down to the more difficult, less clear-cut business of politics:

I am lost in amazement when I behold what intrigue, the interested views of desperate characters, ignorance and jealousy of the minor part, are capable of effecting, as a scourge on the major part of our fellow citizens of the Union ... Let the reins of government then be braced and held with a steady hand, and every violation of the Constitution be reprehended. If defective, let it be amended, but not suffered to be trampled on whilst it has an existence. LETTER TO HENRY LEE, October 31, 1786

On liberty:

Liberty, when it begins to take root, is a plant of rapid growth.

LETTER TO JAMES MADISON, March 2, 1788

Reacting to the French Revolution:

> To forbear running from one extreme to another is no easy matter, and should this be the case, the rocks and shelves, not visible at present, may wreck the vessel, and give a higher-toned despotism than the one which already exists.
>
> LETTER TO GOUVERNEUR MORRIS, US envoy in Paris, October 13, 1789

Just after his first inauguration as president, on April 30, 1789, Washington wrote to his friends:

> I greatly fear that my countrymen will expect too much from me.

Washington was long a supporter of toleration, both before and during his term in office, and advocated the idea of America as a 'melting pot':

> The bosom of America is open to receive not only the opulent and respectable stranger, but the oppressed and persecuted of all nations and religions; whom we shall welcome to a participation of all our rights and privileges if, by decency and propriety of conduct, they appear to merit the enjoyment. December 1783

On his criteria for offering employment:

> If they are good workmen, they may be of Asia, Africa or Europe. They may be Mahometans [i.e. Muslims], Jews, or Christian or any sect – or they may be atheists.
>
> TO HIS AIDE, Tench Tilghman, March 24, 1784

All possess alike liberty of conscience and immunities of citizenship. It is now no more that toleration is spoken of, as if it was by the indulgence of one class of people that another enjoyed the exercise of their inherent natural rights. For happily the government of the United States, which gives to bigotry no sanction, to persecution no assistance, requires only that they who live under its protection should demean themselves as good citizens in giving it on all occasions their effectual support.

LETTER TO A JEWISH CONGREGATION in Newport, Rhode Island, August 18, 1790

In his farewell address, delivered on September 17, 1796, Washington outlined a number of principles. Uppermost in his mind was the importance of preserving the Union:

It is of infinite moment, that you should properly estimate the immense value of your national Union to your collective and individual happiness; that you should cherish a cordial, habitual and immovable attachment to it; accustoming yourselves to think and speak of it as of the Palladium of your political safety and prosperity; watching for its preservation with jealous anxiety; discountenancing whatever may suggest even a suspicion, that it can in any event be abandoned; and indignantly frowning upon the first dawning of every attempt to alienate any portion of our country from the rest, or to enfeeble the sacred ties which now link together the various parts.

The farewell address had in fact been drafted (by Alexander Hamilton and others) in 1792, when Washington did not intend to serve for a second term.

Washington also warned against foreign entanglements, and thus America …

… will avoid the necessity of those overgrown military establishments, which, under any form of government, are inauspicious to liberty, and which are to be regarded as particularly hostile to republican liberty.

As for the conduct of government within the Union, he deplored party politics:

The alternate domination of one faction over another, sharpened by the spirit of revenge, natural to party dissension, which in different ages and countries has perpetrated the most horrid enormities, is itself a frightful despotism. But this leads at length to a more formal and permanent despotism. The disorders and miseries which result gradually incline the minds of men to seek security and repose in the absolute power of an individual; and sooner or later the chief of some prevailing faction, more able or more fortunate than his competitors, turns this disposition to the purposes of his own elevation, on the ruins of public liberty … The common and continual mischiefs of the spirit of party are sufficient to make it the interest and duty of a wise people to discourage and restrain it.

Above all, the new commonwealth required two firm buttresses:

Of all the dispositions and habits, which lead to political prosperity, religion and morality are indispensable supports.

Later in the address Washington returned to the theme of avoiding foreign entanglements:

The great rule of conduct for us in regard to foreign nations is, in extending our commercial relations, to have with them as little *political* connection as possible … Why quit our own to stand upon foreign ground? Why, by intertwining our destiny with that of any part of Europe, entangle our peace and prosperity in the toils of European ambition, rivalship, interest, humor or caprice? ... Against the insidious wiles of foreign influence ... the jealousy of a free people ought to be constantly awake ... Taking care to keep ourselves by suitable establishments on a respectable defensive posture, we may safely trust to temporary alliances for extraordinary emergencies.

Towards the end of the address, Washington summarized what he wished to achieve:

In offering to you, my countrymen, these counsels of an old and affectionate friend, I dare not hope they will make the strong and lasting impression I could wish; that they will control the usual current of the passions, or prevent our nation from running the course, which has hitherto marked the destiny of nations. But, if I may even flatter myself, that they may be productive of some partial benefit, some occasional good; that they may now and then recur to moderate the fury of party spirit, to warn against the mischiefs of foreign intrigue, to guard against the impostures of pretended patriotism; this hope will be a full recompense for the solicitude for your welfare, by which they have been dictated.

What others said
★ ★ ★

One of the greatest captains of the age. Benjamin Franklin, letter, 1780

That dark designing sordid ambitious vain proud arrogant and vindictive knave.
General Charles Lee. As the most experienced candidate, Lee had expected to be appointed as commander-in-chief of the Continental Army rather than Washington.

He is polite with dignity, affable without formality, distant without haughtiness, grave without austerity; modest, wise and good. Abigail Adams, letter to John Adams, 1789

On hearing of Washington's intention to retire as commander-in- chief of the Continental Army in 1783, rather than holding onto power:

If he does that, he will be the greatest man in the world.
King George III of Great Britain and Ireland

On seeing a portrait of Washington hanging in an outhouse:

It is most appropriately hung. Nothing ever made the British shit like the sight of George Washington. Ethan Allen, commander of the Green Mountain Boys

You commenced your presidential career by encouraging and swallowing the greatest adulation, and you traveled America from one end to the other to put yourself in the way of receiving it ... As to what were your views, for, if you are not great enough to have ambition, you are little enough to have vanity, they cannot be directly inferred from expressions of your own ... As to you, sir ... a hypocrite in public life, the world will be puzzled to decide whether you are an apostate or an imposter, whether you have abandoned principles or whether you ever had any?
Thomas Paine, letter to George Washington, July 30, 1796

First in war, first in peace, and first in the hearts of his countrymen.
Henry Lee, eulogy for Washington, December 26, 1799

Posterity will talk of Washington as the founder of a great empire, when my name shall be lost in the vortex of revolution.   NAPOLEON BONAPARTE

Where may the wearied eye repose
When gazing on the Great;
Where neither guilty glory glows,
Nor despicable state?
Yes – one – the first – the last – the best –
The Cincinnatus of the West,
Whom envy dared not hate,
Bequeath'd the name of Washington,
To make man blush there was but one!

    LORD BYRON, 'Ode to Napoleon Bonaparte'

Washington's Republic lives on; Bonaparte's empire is destroyed. Washington and Bonaparte emerged from the womb of democracy: both of them born to liberty, the former remained faithful to her, the latter betrayed her. Washington acted as the representative of the needs, the ideas, the enlightened men, the opinions of his age; he supported, not thwarted, the stirrings of intellect; he desired only what he had to desire, the very thing to which he had been called: from which derives the coherence and longevity of his work. That man who struck few blows because he kept things in proportion has merged his existence with that of his country: his glory is the heritage of civilization; his fame has risen like one of those public sanctuaries where a fecund and inexhaustible spring flows.

    FRANÇOIS-RENÉ, VICOMTE DE CHATEAUBRIAND, *Mémoires d'outre tombe* (1848–50)

Nathaniel Hawthorne was amused by the fuss following the 1841 unveiling of Horatio Greenhough's statue of Washington as an antique Roman, stripped to the waist:

Did anyone see Washington nude? It is inconceivable. He had no nakedness, but I imagine he was born with his clothes on, and his hair powdered, and made a stately bow on his first appearance in the world.

Let him who looks for a monument to Washington look around the United States. Your freedom, your independence, your national power, your prosperity, and your prodigious growth are a monument to him.

    LAJOS KOSSUTH, leader of the 1848 revolution in Hungary

You have in American history one of the great captains of all times. It might be said of him, as it was of William the Silent [leader of the Dutch struggle for independence], that he seldom won a battle but he never lost a campaign.

    HELMUTH VON MOLTKE, Prussian field marshal and noted strategist, in 1874

I often say of George Washington that he was one of the few in the whole history of the world who was not carried away by power.   ROBERT FROST

I bet after seeing us, George Washington would sue us for calling him 'father'.   WILL ROGERS

JOHN ADAMS

1735 – 1826

2ND PRESIDENT OF THE UNITED STATES, 1797-1801

John Adams

Full name: John Adams
Born: October 30, 1735, Quincy, Massachusetts
Died: July 4, 1826, Quincy, Massachusetts
Married: Abigail Smith
Children: Abigail ('Nabby'), John Quincy (future 6th president of the US),
Susanna, Charles and Thomas, plus a still-born girl, Elizabeth
Party: Federalist
Period in office: March 4, 1797–March 4, 1801
Vice-president: Thomas Jefferson

* * *

Regarded as one of the most influential of the Founding Fathers, Adams was the scion of an old colonial family, and his second cousin, Samuel Adams, was another leading figure in the American Revolution. After studying at Harvard and working for a time as a schoolteacher, Adams entered the law. He became a prominent advocate of the rights of the American colonists, opposing the Stamp Act, writing extensively on government and liberty, and sitting in the Massachusetts legislature (1770–4) and the Continental Congress (1774–7). He also successfully defended the British soldiers brought to trial in 1770 for their part in the Boston Massacre. In Congress, Adams successfully pushed for the adoption of the resolution to declare independence. During the war with Britain Adams served as an effective US minister to France (1777–9) and to the Netherlands (1780–2), and played a key role in the negotiations culminating in the Treaty of Paris (1783), by which Great Britain recognized the independence of the USA. Adams subsequently served as minister to Great Britain (1785–8). On his return to the USA he was elected vice-president to the 1st president, George Washington, under whom he served two terms (1789–97). He defeated Thomas Jefferson in the presidential election of 1796, but his own presidency lasted only one term, and was marked by conflict with his fellow Federalists, such as Alexander Hamilton, whose calls for war with Revolutionary France he successfully resisted. There was also conflict with Jefferson, who had become his vice-president; Jefferson objected to the controversial Alien and Sedition Acts signed into law by Adams and aimed at Jefferson's fellow Democratic-Republicans. Adams was defeated by Jefferson in the presidential election of 1800, and thereafter retired to Massachusetts, where he and his wife Abigail raised a dynasty of politicians, diplomats and historians, including their son, John Quincy Adams, who was to become 6th president of the United States.

On the primacy of the law:

> The law, in all vicissitudes of government ... will preserve a steady undeviating course; it will not bend to the uncertain wishes, imaginations and wanton tempers of men ... On the one hand it is inexorable to the cries and lamentations of the prisoners; on the other it is deaf, deaf as an adder, to the clamors of the populace.
>
> Defending the British soldiers put on trial following the Boston Massacre, December 4, 1770

On government and liberty:

> The jaws of power are always opened to devour, and her arm is always stretched out, if possible, to destroy the freedom of thinking, speaking and writing.
>
> *A Dissertation on the Canon and Feudal Law* (1765)

Matrimonial Correspondence

***

Adams's wife Abigail was a spirited, witty, highly intelligent woman. On March 31, 1776, she wrote to her husband:

> In the new code of laws which I suppose it will be necessary for you to make I desire you would remember the ladies, and be more generous and favorable to them than your ancestors. Do not put such unlimited power into the hands of the husbands. Remember all men would be tyrants if they could. If particular care and attention is not paid to the ladies we are determined to foment a rebellion, and will not hold ourselves bound by any laws in which we have no voice, or representation. That your sex are naturally tyrannical is a truth so thoroughly established as to admit of no dispute, but such of you as wish to be happy willingly give up the harsh title of master for the more tender and endearing one of friend.

To this Adams replied:

> We are obliged to go fair and softly, and, in practise, you know we are the subjects. We have only the name of masters, and rather than give up this, which would completely subject us to the despotism of the petticoat, I hope General Washington and all our brave heroes would fight.

Shortly afterwards, on April 28, 1776, Adams wrote again:

> You bid me burn your letters. But I must forget you first.

Later in his career, Adams spent long periods in Europe on diplomatic duties, leading Abigail to reprimand him:

> No man, even if he is sixty years of age, ought to live more than three months at a time from his family.

To which Adams replied:

> How dare you hint or lisp a word about 'sixty years of age.' If I were near I would soon convince you that I am not above forty.
>
> Quoted in Page Smith, *John Adams* (1962)

There is danger from all men. The only maxim of a free government ought to be to trust no man living with power to endanger the public liberty.

NOTES FOR AN ORATION AT BRAINTREE, Spring 1772

Nip the shoots of arbitrary power in the bud, is the only maxim which can ever preserve the liberties of any people. THE 'NOVANGLIS' PAPERS, No. 3, in the *Boston Gazette*, 1774

A government of laws, and not of men.

THE 'NOVANGLIS' PAPERS, No. 7, in the *Boston Gazette*, 1774. The phrase was incorporated by Adams into article 30 of the Massachusetts Bill of Rights, 1780, which defined the principle of the separation of powers that was subsequently incorporated into the US Constitution. The phrase was later quoted by Gerald Ford, the 38th president (see p. 176).

Metaphysicians and politicians may dispute forever, but they will never find any other moral principle or foundation of rule or obedience, than the consent of governors and governed. THE 'NOVANGLIS' PAPERS, No. 7, in the *Boston Gazette*, 1774

The happiness of society is the end of government. *THOUGHTS ON GOVERNMENT* (1776)

Fear is the foundation of most governments.
THOUGHTS ON GOVERNMENT (1776)

Of the US Constitution, Adams remarked in 1789:

Every project has been found to be no better than committing the lamb to the custody of the wolf, except that one which is called balance of power.

On the Revolution:

I agree with you that in politics the middle way is none at all.
LETTER TO HORATIO GATES, March 23, 1776

The second day of July 1776 will be the most memorable epoch in the history of America … It ought to be solemnized with pomp and parade, with shows, games, sports, guns, bells, bonfires and illuminations from one end of this continent to the other, from this time forward, evermore.
LETTER TO HIS WIFE, Abigail Adams, July 3, 1776. The previous day, the Continental Congress had voted to accept Richard Henry Lee's resolution calling for independence from Britain. However, it was not until the 4th that Congress adopted the Declaration of Independence, and it was that date that has been commemorated ever since.

ADAMS THE AMERICAN
* * *

Adams fiercely maintained his American identity. When in 1785 a foreign ambassador in Paris asked him whether, being of English extraction, he had relatives in England (whither he was headed as US envoy), Adams indignantly retorted:

Neither my father or mother, grandfather or grandmother, great-grandfather or great-grandmother nor any other relation that I know or care a farthing for have been in England these 150 years. So that you see, I have not one drop of blood in my veins, but what is American.

The ambassador replied:

Ay, we have seen proofs enough of that!

Later in life Adams reflected on what the Revolution had meant:

What do we mean by the Revolution? The War? That was no part of the Revolution; it was only an effect and consequence of it. The Revolution was in the minds of the people, and this was effected from 1760 to 1775, before a drop of blood was shed at Lexington.
LETTER TO THOMAS JEFFERSON, August 24, 1815

During the Revolution, Adams served on numerous committees in the Continental Congress, but found the nitty-gritty quite wearing:

In Congress, nibbling and quibbling – as usual. There is no greater mortification than to sit with half a dozen wits, deliberating upon a petition, address or memorial. These great wits, these subtle critics, these refined geniuses, these learned lawyers, these wise statesman, are so fond of showing their parts and powers, as to make their consultations very tedious.
DIARY AND AUTOBIOGRAPHY OF JOHN ADAMS, ed. L.H. Butterfield (1962)

On holding the vice-presidency:

My country has in its wisdom contrived for me the most insignificant office that ever the invention of man contrived or his imagination conceived.
LETTER TO ABIGAIL ADAMS, December 19, 1793

At his own inauguration as president Adams believed that Washington appeared 'to enjoy a triumph over me'. After the ceremony he remarked to his wife:

Me-thought I heard him say, 'Ay, I am fairly out and you fairly in! See which of us will be happiest!'

Adams and Thomas Jefferson were always political rivals, but in old age they mellowed:

You and I ought not to die before we have explained ourselves to each other.
LETTER TO THOMAS JEFFERSON, July 15, 1813

Two years later, Adams tried to explain himself to Jefferson:

The fundamental article of my political creed is that despotism, or unlimited sovereignty, or absolute power, is the same in a majority of a popular assembly, an aristocratic council, an oligarchical junto and a single emperor. LETTER TO THOMAS JEFFERSON, November 13, 1815

To Jefferson, Adams also confided his view of the most radical, anti-monarchical pamphlet of the Revolution:

What a poor, ignorant, malicious, short-sighted, crapulous mass, is Tom Paine's *Common Sense*. LETTER TO THOMAS JEFFERSON, June 22, 1819. For Paine's views of Adams, see below.

Both Adams and Jefferson died on the 50th anniversary of the Declaration of Independence, Jefferson in the afternoon, and Adams around sunset. Adams's last words, uttered at about 1 p.m., were:

Jefferson survives!

What others said
* * *

It has been a political career of this man to begin with hypocrisy, proceed with arrogance, and to finish with contempt. THOMAS PAINE, 'To the Citizens of the United States' (1802–3)

Always an honest man, often a great one, but sometimes absolutely mad.
BENJAMIN FRANKLIN, quoted by Thomas Jefferson in a letter to James Madison, July 29, 1789. Adams had proposed that the president should be referred to as 'His Highness the President of the United States and protector of their liberties.'

An imagination sublimated and eccentric, propitious neither to the regular display of sound judgment nor to steady perseverance in a systematic plan of conduct.
ALEXANDER HAMILTON, quoted in Page Smith, *John Adams, 1784-1826* (1962)

THOMAS JEFFERSON

1743–1826

3RD PRESIDENT OF THE UNITED STATES, 1801–9

THOMAS JEFFERSON

FULL NAME: Thomas Jefferson
BORN: April 13, 1743, Shadwell, Virginia
DIED: July 4, 1826, Charlottesville, Virginia
MARRIED: Martha Skelton (née Wayles;
she was the widow of Bathurst Skelton)
CHILDREN: Martha Washington ('Patsy'), Jane Randolph,
Mary Wayles, Lucy Elizabeth I, Lucy Elizabeth II, plus a
stillborn son. It seems likely that Jefferson was also the
father of the six children of one of his household
slaves, Sally Hemings, who is thought to have become
his companion after his wife's death in 1782.
PARTY: Democratic-Republican
PERIOD IN OFFICE: March 4, 1801–March 4, 1809
VICE-PRESIDENTS: Aaron Burr (1801–5), George Clinton (1805–9)

* * *

JEFFERSON was born into one of the most prominent families of Virginia, and at the age of 14 inherited a considerable estate and many slaves. In 1762 he graduated from the College of William and Mary at Williamsburg, where he had studied mathematics and philosophy and become acquainted with the empirical thinking of Francis Bacon, Isaac Newton and John Locke – all highly influential thinkers in the development of Enlightenment thought. A noted polymath, Jefferson went on to study law, and was admitted to the bar in 1767. His marriage in 1772 to the wealthy widow Martha Wayles Skelton brought him more land and slaves. Meanwhile, Jefferson had been elected to the Virginia House of Burgesses, where he served from 1769 to 1775. He argued vociferously against the Coercive Acts imposed by Britain in 1774, on the grounds of the natural right of the American colonists to govern themselves. He became a member of the Continental Congress, and ensured enduring fame by drafting the Declaration of Independence in 1776. He served in the Virginia House of Delegates from 1776 to 1779, in the latter year drafting another momentous document, the Virginia Statute for Religious Freedom (adopted by Virginia in 1786), which established the separation of church and state, and became a model for the First Amendment. Jefferson served as governor of Virginia (1779–81), as a member of Confederation Congress (1783–4) and as US minister to France (1785–9).

In 1790 Washington made Jefferson his secretary of state, but the latter's Democratic-Republican sympathies brought him into conflict with Federalists in the government such as Alexander Hamilton, and he resigned in 1793. He was defeated by the Federalist John Adams in the presidential election of 1796, but, having come second, it was agreed that he should become Adams's vice-president. Jefferson defeated Adams in the presidential election of 1800, and his two terms in office are notable for the Louisiana Purchase of 1803, and for his success in keeping the USA neutral in the Napoleonic Wars. On his retirement he withdrew to Monticello, the house he had built on his Virginia estates, and helped to found the University of Virginia in 1819. He died on the same day as John Adams – the 50th anniversary of the Declaration of Independence.

THE DECLARATION OF INDEPENDENCE

* * *

Jefferson was given the task of drafting the Declaration by a subcommittee of Congress, although initially he tried to persuade John Adams to prepare a draft. However, Adams insisted that Jefferson take on the job, reasoning as follows:

> Reason first – you are a Virginian, and a Virginian ought to appear at the head of the business. Reason second – I am obnoxious, suspected and unpopular. You are very much otherwise. Reason third – you can write ten times better than I can.
>
> DIARY AND AUTOBIOGRAPHY OF JOHN ADAMS, ed. L.H. Butterfield (1962)

The result was subjected to scrutiny and revision by Congress, but the final version is still very much the work of Jefferson:

> When, in the course of human events, it becomes necessary for one people to dissolve the political bands which have connected them with another, and to assume among the powers of the earth the separate and equal station to which the laws of nature and of nature's God entitle them, a decent respect to the opinions of mankind requires that they should declare the causes which impel them to the separation.
>
> We hold these truths to be self-evident, that all men are created equal; that they are endowed by their Creator with inherent and inalienable rights; that among these, are life, liberty, and the pursuit of happiness; that to secure these rights, governments are instituted among men, deriving their just powers from the consent of the governed; that whenever any form of government becomes destructive of these ends, it is the right of the people to alter or abolish it, and to institute new government, laying its foundation on such principles, and organizing its powers in such form, as to them shall seem most likely to effect their safety and happiness. Prudence, indeed, will dictate that governments long established should not be changed for light and transient causes; and accordingly all experience hath shewn, that mankind are more disposed to suffer, while evils are sufferable, than to right themselves by abolishing the forms to which they are accustomed. But when a long train of abuses and usurpations, pursuing invariably the same object evinces a design to reduce them under absolute despotism, it is their right, it is their duty, to throw off such government, and to provide new guards for their future security. Such has been the patient sufferance of these colonies; and such is now the necessity which constrains them to alter their former systems of government.
>
> DECLARATION OF INDEPENDENCE, July 4, 1776

Jefferson's 'rough draft' of the opening of the second paragraph above had read:

> We hold these truths to be sacred and undeniable; that all men are created equal and independent, that from that equal creation they derive rights inherent and inalienable, among which are the preservation of life, and liberty, and the pursuit of happiness.

Of almost equal moment to the Declaration of Independence was the Virginia Statute for Religious Freedom, drafted by Jefferson in 1779. The statute established the separation of church and state and the principle of religious toleration:

> Almighty God hath created the mind free ... all attempts to influence it by temporal punishments or burthens, or by civil incapacitations, tend only to beget habits of hypocrisy and meanness, and are a departure from the plan of the Holy author of our religion, who being Lord both of body and mind, yet chose not to propagate it by coercions on either, as it was in his Almighty power to do ... the impious presumption of legislators and rulers, civil as well as ecclesiastical, who being themselves but fallible and uninspired men, have assumed dominion over the faith of others, setting up their own opinions and modes of thinking as the only true and infallible, and as such endeavoring to impose them on others, hath established and maintained false religions over the greatest part of the world, and through all time ...
>
> THE VIRGINIA STATUTE FOR RELIGIOUS FREEDOM, drafted by Jefferson in 1779 and passed by the Virginia state legislature in 1786

Jefferson also wrote extensively on oppression, liberty, revolution and the necessary limits of government:

> Every government degenerates when trusted to the rulers of the people alone. The people themselves therefore are its only safe depositories.
>
> NOTES ON THE STATE OF VIRGINIA (1785)

> The legitimate powers of government extend to such acts only as are injurious to others. But it does me no injury for my neighbor to say there are twenty gods, or no god. It neither picks my pocket nor breaks by leg. NOTES ON THE STATE OF VIRGINIA (1785)

> Experience declares that man is the only animal which devours his own kind; for I can apply no milder term to the governments of Europe, and to the general prey of the rich on the poor. LETTER TO COLONEL EDWARD CARRINGTON, January 16, 1787

> I hold it, that a little rebellion, now and then, is a good thing, and as necessary in the political world as storms in the physical.
>
> LETTER TO JAMES MADISON, January 30, 1787. He was referring to Shays's Rebellion in 1786 against high taxes.

> The tree of liberty must be refreshed from time to time with the blood of patriots and tyrants. It is its natural manure. LETTER TO W.S. SMITH, November 13, 1787

> A bill of rights is what the people are entitled to against every government on earth, general or particular, and what no just government should refuse to rest on inference.
>
> LETTER TO JAMES MADISON, December 20, 1787

But constitutions should not be immutable:

> Some men look at constitutions with sanctimonious reverence and deem them like the ark of the covenant, too sacred to be touched. LETTER TO SAMUEL KERCHEVAL, July 12, 1816

On the dangers of a single, all-powerful central government:

> If the principle were to prevail, of a common law being in force in the US ... it would become the most corrupt government on earth. LETTER TO GIDEON GRANGER, August 13, 1800

Jefferson saw virtue in the common man, especially if, after the Roman model, he was to follow the vocation of yeoman farmer:

> I think our governments will remain virtuous for many centuries; as long as they are chiefly agricultural; and this will be as long as there shall be vacant lands in any part of America. When they get piled upon one another in large cities, as in Europe, they will become corrupt as in Europe. LETTER TO JAMES MADISON, December 20, 1787

> State a moral case to a ploughman and a professor. The former will decide it as well, and often better than the latter, because he has not been led astray by artificial rules.
> LETTER TO PETER CARR, August 10, 1787

> There is not a single crowned head in Europe whose talents or merits would entitle him to be elected a vestryman by the people of any parish in America.
> LETTER FROM PARIS, May 2, 1788

> I agree with you that there is a natural aristocracy among men. The grounds of this are virtue and talents. LETTER TO JOHN ADAMS, October 28, 1813

Although he lived off the proceeds of slave labor, Jefferson was only too aware of the moral contradictions of his position:

> I tremble for my country, when I reflect that God is just; and that his justice cannot sleep forever ... NOTES ON THE STATE OF VIRGINIA (1785)

On slavery:

> We have the wolf by the ears, and we can neither hold him nor safely let him go. Justice is in one scale, self-preservation in the other. LETTER TO JOHN HOLMES, April 22, 1820

On public office:

> When a man assumes a public trust, he should consider himself as public property.
> LETTER TO BARON VON HUMBOLDT, 1807

Jefferson used his First Inaugural Address to outline a number of guiding principles:

> Though the will of the majority is in all cases to prevail, that will to be rightful must be reasonable ... the minority possess their equal rights, which equal law must protect, and to violate would be oppression. FIRST INAUGURAL ADDRESS, March 4, 1801

> Every difference of opinion is not a difference of principle. We have called by different names brethren of the same principle. We are all Republicans, we are all Federalists.
> FIRST INAUGURAL ADDRESS, March 4, 1801

Would the honest patriot, in the full tide of successful experiment, abandon a government which has so far kept us free and firm? FIRST INAUGURAL ADDRESS, March 4, 1801

A wise and frugal government, which shall restrain men from injuring one another, shall leave them otherwise free to regulate their own pursuits of industry and improvement, and shall not take from the mouth of labor the bread it has earned.
FIRST INAUGURAL ADDRESS, March 4, 1801

Equal and exact justice to all men, of whatever state or persuasion, religious or political; peace, commerce and honest friendship with all nations, entangling alliances with none; the support of the state governments in all their rights, as the most competent administrations for our domestic concerns and the surest bulwarks against anti-republican tendencies; the preservation of the general government in its whole constitutional vigor, as the sheet anchor of our peace at home and safety abroad; a jealous care of the right of election by the people ... freedom of religion; freedom of the press, and freedom of person under the protection of the *habeas corpus*, and trial by juries impartially selected. These principles form the bright constellation which has gone before us, and guided our steps through an age of revolution and reformation.
FIRST INAUGURAL ADDRESS, March 4, 1801

I have learnt to expect that it will rarely fall to the lot of imperfect man to retire from this station with the reputation and the favor which bring him into it.

FIRST INAUGURAL ADDRESS, March 4, 1801

On the importance of education in a democracy:

If a nation expects to be ignorant and free, in a state of civilization, it expects what never was and never will be. LETTER TO COLONEL CHARLES YANCEY, January 6, 1816

I know no safe depository of the ultimate powers of the society but the people themselves; and if we think them not enlightened enough to exercise their control with a wholesome discretion, the remedy is not to take it from them, but to inform their discretion by education. LETTER TO WILLIAM CHARLES JARVIS, September 28, 1820

On the Missouri Compromise, by which Missouri was admitted to the Union as a slave state, and Maine as a free state:

This momentous question, like a fireball in the night, awakened and filled me with terror. I considered it at once as the knell of the Union. It is hushed, indeed, for the moment. But this is a reprieve only, not a final sentence. A geographical line, coinciding with a marked principle, moral and political, once conceded and held up to the angry passions of men, will never be obliterated, and every new irritation will mark it deeper and deeper.

LETTER TO JOHN HOLMES, April 22, 1820

Even in old age, Jefferson kept alive his hopes for the future:

And even should the cloud of barbarism and despotism again obscure the science and libraries of Europe, this country remains to preserve and restore light and liberty to them. In short, the flames kindled on the fourth of July, 1776, have spread over too much of the globe to be extinguished by the feeble engines of despotism; on the contrary, they will consume these engines and all who work them. LETTER TO JOHN ADAMS, September 12, 1821

Jefferson still saw struggle ahead in the achievement of universal republicanism:

To attain all this ... rivers of blood must yet flow, and years of desolation pass over; yet the object is worth rivers of blood, and years of desolation.

LETTER TO JOHN ADAMS, September 4, 1823

All eyes are opened, or opening, to the rights of man. The general spread of the light of science has already laid open to every view the palpable truth, that the mass of mankind has not been born with saddles on their backs, nor a favored few booted and spurred, ready to ride them legitimately, by the grace of God.

LETTER TO ROGER C. WEIGHTMAN, June 24, 1826, declining an invitation to attend the celebrations in Washington on the 50th anniversary of the Declaration of Independence.

This is the Fourth?

LAST WORDS, spoken at 11 o'clock in the evening of July 3, 1826. Nicholas P. Trist, a young friend at his bedside, at first said nothing, but when Jefferson asked again, Trist nodded. Apparently content, Jefferson fell into a sleep from which he did not wake.

In his life, Jefferson was capable of great graciousness. On his arrival as US minister in Paris, the French minister in charge of foreign affairs asked him if he replaced Benjamin Franklin, to which Jefferson replied:

I succeed him. No one can replace him.

Quoted in Henry S. Randall, *The Life of Thomas Jefferson* (1858)

On another occasion, Jefferson was out riding with his grandson near Monticello, when a slave bowed and doffed his hat. Jefferson reciprocated the gesture, but seeing that his grandson did not, reprimanded him in the following terms:

Thomas, do you permit a slave to be more of a gentleman than you are?

Quoted in Henry S. Randall, *The Life of Thomas Jefferson* (1858)

What others said

* * *

Murder, robbery, rape, adultery and incest will be openly taught and practiced, the air will be rent with the cries of distress, the soil soaked with blood, and the nation black with crimes. Where is the heart that can contemplate such a scene without shivering with horror? THE NEW ENGLAND COURANT on Jefferson's election to the presidency, 1800

Oh Lord! wilt Thou bestow upon him a double portion of Thy grace, *for Thou knowest he needs it.*

UNNAMED FEDERALIST MINISTER IN CONNECTICUT, quoted in Dixon Wecter, *The Hero in America* (1941)

The moral character of Jefferson was repulsive. Continually puling about liberty, equality and the degrading curse of slavery, he brought his own children to the hammer, and made money of his debaucheries. ALEXANDER HAMILTON

I cannot live in this miserable, undone country, where, as the Turks follow their sacred standard, which is a pair of Mahomet's breeches, we are governed by the old red breeches of that prince of projectors, St Thomas of Cantingbury; and surely, Becket himself never had more pilgrims at his shrine than the Saint of Monticello.

JOHN RANDOLPH OF ROANOKE (1773–1833), leader of the 'Old Republican' faction in the Democratic-Republican Party

His hot-headed democracy has done a fearful injury to his country. Hollow and unsound as his doctrines are, they are but too palatable to a people, each individual of whom would rather derive his importance from believing that none are above him, than from the consciousness that in his station he makes part of a noble whole. The social system of Mr Jefferson, if carried into effect, would make of mankind an unamalgamated mass of grating atoms, where the darling 'I'm as good as you,' would soon take place of the law and the Gospel. As it is, his principles, though happily not fully put in action, have yet produced most lamentable results ... FRANCES TROLLOPE, *Domestic Manners of the Americans* (1832)

A gentleman of thirty-two who could calculate an eclipse, survey an estate, tie an artery, plan an edifice, try a cause, break a horse, dance a minuet, and play the violin.

JAMES PARTON, *Life of Thomas Jefferson, Third President of the United States* (1874)

James Madison

1751–1836

4TH PRESIDENT OF THE UNITED STATES, 1809–17

JAMES MADISON

FULL NAME: James Madison
BORN: March 16, 1751, Port Conway, Virginia
DIED: June 28, 1836, Montpelier, Virginia
MARRIED: Dolley Todd (née Payne; she was the widow of John Todd)
CHILDREN: none (though he had a stepson, John Payne Todd)
PARTY: Democratic-Republican
PERIOD IN OFFICE: March 4, 1809–March 4, 1817
VICE-PRESIDENTS: George Clinton (1809–12), Elbridge Gerry (1813–14)
There was no vice-president in 1812–13 or 1814–17.

* * *

MADISON inherited a plantation from his father in Orange County, Virginia, and later expanded his landholdings to become the biggest estate owner in the county. Hard work saw him through a degree course at Princeton (then the College of New Jersey) in two years, and thereafter he studied law, though he was never admitted to the bar. A protégé of Thomas Jefferson, he served in the Virginia legislature from 1776 till 1779, and helped to draft the state constitution and Jefferson's Virginia Statute for Religious Freedom (see p. 24). In 1780, at the age of only 29, he became a delegate to the Continental Congress, and after the end of the Revolutionary War he returned to the Virginia state legislature. Concerned that the Articles of Confederation were insufficient to hold the United States together, he pressed for a new constitution that would establish a strong central government. At the Constitutional Convention of 1787 he put forward detailed suggestions that ensured that the proposed federal government would be harnessed by various checks and balances, such as a separation of powers between the executive, the legislature and the judiciary, and a subjection to the popular will via regular elections. All these contributions earned him the title of 'Father of the Constitution'.

Initially Madison aligned himself with Federalists such as Alexander Hamilton in opposing a Bill of Rights and increased states' rights, but later backtracked on both points, and in 1789, as a member of the US House of Representatives, he proposed 12 amendments to the Constitution, 10 of which were ratified by the end of 1791, becoming the Bill of Rights. Madison served as President Jefferson's secretary of state (1801–9), and his own presidency was dominated by the War of 1812 with Great Britain, which reinforced the USA's sense of national identity. Madison himself came to accept Federalist calls for a central bank and a standing army and navy, but at the end of his term of office vetoed a bill for central government to fund domestic improvement on the grounds that it breached states' rights. On his retirement in 1817 he returned to his Montpelier estate in Virginia, and in 1826 succeeded Jefferson as rector of the University of Virginia. He died ten years later, the last survivor of the Founding Fathers.

On liberty:

> Liberty is to faction what air is to fire, an ailment without which it instantly expires. But it could not be less folly to abolish liberty, which is essential to political life, because it nourishes faction than it would be to wish the annihilation of air, which is essential to animal life, because it imparts to fire its destructive agency.
>
> THE FEDERALIST, No. 10, November 22, 1787

On property:

The most common and durable source of factions has been the various and unequal distribution of property. THE FEDERALIST, No. 10, November 22, 1787

On framing the Constitution:

If men were angels, no government would be necessary. If angels were to govern men, neither external nor internal controls on government would be necessary. In framing a government which is to be administered by men over men, the great difficulty lies in this: you must first enable the government to control the governed; and in the next place oblige it to control itself. THE FEDERALIST, No. 51, February 6, 1788

On the dangers to minorities in a democracy:

On a candid examination of history, we shall find that turbulence, violence and abuse of power by the majority trampling on the rights of the minority have produced factions and commotions, which, in republics, have, more frequently than any other cause, produced despotism. SPEECH AT THE VIRGINIA CONVENTION to ratify the US Constitution, June 6, 1788

Wherever the real power in a government lies, there is the danger of oppression. In our governments, the real power lies in the majority of the community, and the invasion of private rights is chiefly to be apprehended, not from the acts of government contrary to the sense of its constituents, but from acts in which the government is the mere instrument of the major number of the constituents. LETTER TO THOMAS JEFFERSON, October 17, 1788

On the limitations of the powers of the federal government:

The government of the United States is a definite government, confined to specified objects. It is not like the state governments, whose powers are more general. Charity is no part of the legislative duty of the government.

SPEECH IN THE HOUSE OF REPRESENTATIVES, January 10, 1794. The debate concerned a proposal to provide federal relief to French refugees from the revolution in Haiti.

On the separation of church and state:

Who does not see that the same authority which can establish Christianity, in exclusion of all other religions, may establish with the same ease any particular sect of Christians, in exclusion of all other sects? that the same authority which can force a citizen to contribute three pence only of his property for the support of any one establishment, may force him to conform to any other establishment in all cases whatsoever?

MEMORIAL AND REMONSTRANCE AGAINST RELIGIOUS ASSESSMENTS (1785)

His aim as president:

To avoid the slightest interference with the right of conscience or the functions of religion, so wisely exempted from civil jurisdiction.

FIRST INAUGURAL ADDRESS, March 4, 1809

Religion and government will both exist in greater purity, the less they are mixed together.

LETTER TO EDWARD LIVINGSTON, July 10, 1822

On States' Rights

***

Madison held that the states had the right to strike down federal legislation judged unconstitutional:

This Assembly doth explicitly and peremptorily declare, that it views the powers of the federal government, as resulting from the compact, to which the states are parties, as limited by the plain sense and intention of the instrument constituting the compact; as no further valid than they are authorized by the grants enumerated in that compact; and that in case of deliberate, palpable, and dangerous exercise of other powers, not granted by the said compact, the states who are parties thereto, have the right, and are in duty bound, to interpose, for arresting the progress of the evil, and for maintaining within their respective limits, the authorities, rights and liberties appertaining to them.

THE VIRGINIA RESOLUTIONS, drafted by Madison and passed by the Virginia legislature on December 24, 1798

On the dangers of maintaining a standing army:

A standing military force, with an overgrown executive, will not long be safe companions to liberty. The means of defense against foreign danger, have been always the instruments of tyranny at home.

SPEECH AT THE CONSTITUTIONAL CONVENTION, June 29, 1787

Perhaps it is a universal truth that the loss of liberty at home is to be charged against provisions against danger, real or pretended from abroad.

LETTER TO THOMAS JEFFERSON, May 13, 1798

On the press:

It is better to leave a few of its noxious branches to their luxuriant growth, than, by pruning them away, to injure the vigor of those yielding the proper fruits. And can the wisdom of this policy be doubted by anyone who reflects that to the press alone, checkered as it is with abuses, the world is indebted for all the triumphs which have been gained by reason and humanity over error and oppression?

REPORT OF THE HOUSE OF REPRESENTATIVES on the Virginia Resolutions regarding the Alien and Sedition Laws, January 20, 1800

On his plans for the Native Americans:

To carry on the benevolent plans which have been so meritoriously applied to the conversion of our aboriginal neighbors from the degradation and wretchedness of savage life to a participation of the improvements of which the human mind and manners are susceptible in a civilized state.

FIRST INAUGURAL ADDRESS, March 4, 1809

Never one for show, or showy occasions, at the 1809 Inaugural Ball Madison told a friend:

I would much rather be in bed.

When late in his life a correspondent referred to Madison as 'the writer of the Constitution of the US,' Madison replied:

You give me credit to which I have no claim ... This was not, like the fabled Goddess of Wisdom, the offspring of a single brain. It ought to be regarded as the work of many heads and many hands. LETTER TO WILLIAM COGSWELL, March 10, 1834

Madison kept his dry wit about him into old age:

> Having outlived so many of my contemporaries, I ought not to forget that I may be thought to have outlived myself. Quoted in Paul Wilstach, *Patriots Off Their Pedestals* (1927)

During his last illness, a visitor pleaded with him not to talk while lying in bed. To which he answered:

> I always talk most easily when I lie. Quoted in Maude Gilder Godwin, *Dolly Madison* (1896)

Madison left some posthumous advice to his country:

> The advice nearest to my heart and deepest in my convictions is that the Union of the States be cherished and perpetuated. Let the open enemy to it be regarded as a Pandora with her box opened; and the disguised one, as the Serpent creeping with his deadly wiles into Paradise. 'ADVICE TO MY COUNTRY', found among his papers after his death

What others said
* * *

Madison had as much to do as any man in framing the Constitution, and as much to do as any man in administering it.
> DANIEL WEBSTER, quoted in *Register of Debates in Congress* (1837)

As to Jemmy Madison – ah! poor Jemmy! he is but a withered Apple-John.
> WASHINGTON IRVING, remark after the 1809 Inaugural Ball, quoted in Gaillard Hunt, *The Life of James Madison* (1902)

One Washington barber was not impressed with the soberly dressed President Madison's lack of flair in the hair department, and to a senator whom he was shaving held forth as follows:

> What presidents we might have had, sir! Look at Daggett, of Connecticut, and Stockton, of New Jersey, with queues as big as your wrist, and powdered every day, like real gentlemen they are! But this little Jim Madison with a queue no bigger than a pipe-stem! Sir, it is enough to make a man forswear his country!
> Quoted in Mrs E.F. Ellet, *The Court Circles of the Republic* (1869)

But his conversation could dazzle, one lady who visited him in 1828 reporting that it was:

> ... so rich in sentiments and facts, so enlivened by anecdotes and epigrammatic remarks, so frank and confidential as to opinions on men and measures, that it had an interest and charm, which the conversation of few men now living, could have ... His little blue eyes sparkled like stars from under his bushy grey eyebrows and amidst the deep wrinkles of his poor thin face.
> MARGARET BAYARD SMITH, *The First Forty Years in Washington Society* (1906)

JAMES MONROE

1758–1831

5TH PRESIDENT OF THE UNITED STATES, 1817–25

James Monroe

FULL NAME: James Monroe
BORN: April 28, 1758, Westmoreland County, Virginia
DIED: July 4, 1831, Albany, New York
MARRIED: Elizabeth Kortright
CHILDREN: Eliza and Maria (a son died in infancy)
PARTY: Democratic-Republican
PERIOD IN OFFICE: March 4, 1817–March 4, 1825
VICE-PRESIDENT: Daniel D. Tompkins

* * *

BORN INTO A LANDED, slave-owning Virginia family, Monroe graduated from the College of William and Mary in 1776, and then joined the Continental Army. He was wounded at the Battle of Trenton, fought at Brandywine and Germantown, and endured the winter at Valley Forge. He resigned his commission in 1780 to study law with Thomas Jefferson, and after his marriage he purchased a farm near Charlottesville, Virginia. Monroe served in the Continental Congress (1783–6) and in 1790 was elected to the US Senate. Between 1794 and 1796 he was minister to Paris, where he expressed sympathy for the French Revolution, so antagonizing the pro-British Federalists. Monroe was twice governor of Virginia (1799–1802, 1811), and helped to negotiate the Louisiana Purchase of 1803. He was secretary of state and secretary of war under James Madison, before assuming the presidency. This was dubbed 'the era of good feelings', as it witnessed the eclipse of the Federalist party and the decline of partisan politics. Monroe's presidency was marked by the First Seminole War, acquisition of the Floridas from Spain, the Missouri Compromise, which deflected a showdown over slavery, and the enunciation of what became known as the Monroe Doctrine (see below), suggested to him by his secretary of state, John Quincy Adams. Monroe's part in founding Liberia in 1822 as a colony for freed slaves is commemorated in the name of that country's capital: Monrovia.

Responding to his daughter, who had declared that America did not have roads like those in France:

That's true. Our country may be likened to a new house. We lack many things, but we possess the most precious of all – liberty!

Quoted in Freeman Hunt, *American Anecdotes* (1830)

He subsequently observed to Lord Henry Holland, the British diplomat:

I find your monarchy more republican than monarchical, and the French republic more monarchical than your monarchy. Quoted in George Morgan, *The Life of James Monroe* (1921)

On democracy:

It is only when the people become ignorant and corrupt, when they degenerate into a populace, that they are incapable of exercising their sovereignty. Usurpation is then an easy attainment, and an usurper soon found. The people themselves become the willing instruments of their own debasement and ruin. FIRST INAUGURAL ADDRESS, March 4 1817

THE MONROE DOCTRINE

* * *

The Monroe Doctrine, which effectively claimed US hegemony over the whole of the Americas, was drafted by Secretary of State John Quincy Adams and announced by Monroe in 1823. However, it did not become known as the Monroe Doctrine until the 1850s.

The American continents, by the free and independent condition which they have assumed and maintain, are henceforth not to be considered as subjects for future colonization by any European powers ... We owe it, therefore, to candor and to the amicable relations existing between the United States and those powers to declare that we should consider any attempt on their part to extend their system to any portion of this hemisphere as dangerous to our peace and safety.

ANNUAL MESSAGE TO CONGRESS, December 2, 1823

On the importance of national defense:

We must support our rights or lose our character, and with it, perhaps, our liberties. A people who fail to do it can scarcely be said to hold a place among independent nations. National honor is national property of the highest value.

FIRST INAUGURAL ADDRESS, March 4, 1817

On America's unique destiny:

If we look to the history of other nations, ancient or modern, we find no example of a growth so rapid, so gigantic, of a people so prosperous and happy ... If we persevere in the career in which we have advanced so far and in the path already traced, we cannot fail, under the favor of a gracious Providence, to attain the high destiny which seems to await us.

FIRST INAUGURAL ADDRESS, March 4, 1817

On the spread of European settlement into Native American territories:

It is our duty to make new efforts for the preservation, improvement and civilization of the native inhabitants. The hunter state can exist only in the vast uncultivated desert. It yields to the more dense and compact form and greater force of civilized population; and of right it ought to yield, for the earth was given to mankind to support the greatest number of which it is capable, and no tribe or people have a right to withhold from the wants of others more than is necessary for their own support and comfort. ANNUAL MESSAGE TO CONGRESS, December 2, 1817

Some things never change. In his 1819 address to Congress Monroe observed:

A derangement has been felt in some of our moneyed institutions which has proportionably affected their credit. ANNUAL MESSAGE TO CONGRESS, December 7, 1819

On being asked by a friend at an official reception whether he was not 'completely worn out', he replied:

Oh no. A little flattery will support a man through great fatigue.

Quoted in Mary Clemmer Ames, *Ten Years in Washington* (1880)

PRESIDENTIAL OPINIONS: THE 3RD ON THE 5TH

* * *

A man whose soul might be turned wrong side outward, without discovering a blemish to the world.

THOMAS JEFFERSON, quoted in Daniel C. Gilman, *James Monroe* (1883)

JOHN QUINCY ADAMS

1767–1848

6TH PRESIDENT OF THE UNITED STATES, 1825–9

JOHN QUINCY ADAMS

FULL NAME: John Quincy Adams
BORN: July 11, 1767, Braintree, Massachusetts
DIED: February 23, 1848, Washington DC
MARRIED: Louise Catherine Johnson
CHILDREN: Louisa, George Washington, John, Charles Francis
PARTY: National Republican
PERIOD IN OFFICE: March 4, 1825–March 4, 1829
VICE-PRESIDENT: John C. Calhoun

* * *

ADAMS WAS THE SON of the 2nd US president, John Adams, and until the election of George W. Bush in 2000, he was the only son of a president to follow in his father's footsteps. As a youth, Adams accompanied his father on his diplomatic missions to Europe. This was followed by study at Harvard, from where he graduated in 1788. He then trained as a lawyer, and was admitted to the bar in 1791. In 1794 he began his own diplomatic career, as ambassador to the Netherlands, and subsequently served as ambassador to Prussia, Russia and the United Kingdom. In 1803 he was elected to the US Senate as a Federalist, but fell out with his fellow-Federalists over his support for President Jefferson's Embargo Act and the Louisiana Purchase. He resigned from the Senate in 1808 to resume his legal and diplomatic careers, and negotiated the Treaty of Ghent ending the War of 1812. As President Monroe's secretary of state from 1817 to 1825, he was involved in the acquisition of Florida, and it was he who formulated the Monroe Doctrine (see p. 36).

In 1824 Adams ran for the presidency against Andrew Jackson as a conservative Democrat, and his faction of the party coalesced into the anti-Jacksonian National Republicans. Although Jackson won the popular vote, there was no majority for any candidate in the electoral college, and the House of Representatives voted for Adams. As president, Adams attempted to implement a program of domestic improvement, but his plans were thwarted by Congress. Adams refused to bestow patronage on the Jacksonian Democrats, who in turn sniped at him throughout his term in office, calling his assumption of the presidency (with the support of Henry Clay) a 'corrupt bargain'. In the 1828 presidential election Jackson, nominated by the Democrats, defeated Adams. In a highly unusual step for a former president, Adams returned to Congress, and served as a representative for Massachusetts right up until his death, most notably campaigning against the 'gag rule' that prohibited the discussion of petitions regarding slavery.

On himself:

> I am a man of reserved, cold, austere and forbidding manners: my political adversaries say, a gloomy misanthropist, and my personal enemies, an unsocial savage. DIARY, June 4, 1819

On others:

> All men profess honesty as long as they can. To believe all men honest would be folly. To believe none so is something worse. LETTER TO WILLIAM EUSTIS, June 22, 1809

Adams had a strong sense of American national destiny:

> Think of your forefathers! Think of your posterity!
>
> ORATION AT PLYMOUTH, Massachusetts, December 22, 1802

On westward expansion:

> Westward the star of empire takes its way.
>
> ORATION AT PLYMOUTH, December 22, 1802, misquoting Bishop George Berkeley's line 'Westward the course of empire takes its way' (*On the Prospect of Planting Arts and Learning in America*, 1729)

A decade later he elaborated on this imperialist theme:

> The whole continent of North America appears to be destined by Divine Providence to be peopled by one nation, speaking one language, professing one general system of religious and political principles, and accustomed to one general tenor of social usages and customs.
>
> LETTER TO JOHN ADAMS, August 31, 1811

On America's moral duties:

> *Fiat justitia, pereat coelum* [Let justice be done, though heaven fall]. My toast would be, may our country always be successful, but whether successful or otherwise, always right.
>
> LETTER TO JOHN ADAMS, August 1, 1816, referring to Stephen Decatur's famous toast at Norfolk, Virginia, April 1816: 'Our Country! In her intercourse with foreign nations may she always be in the right, but our country, right or wrong.'

On the need for European (specifically German) immigrants to assimilate:

> If they cannot accommodate themselves to the character, moral, political and physical, of this country, the Atlantic is always open to them to return to the land of their nativity and their fathers. To one thing they must make up their minds; or, they be disappointed in every expectation of happiness as Americans. They must cast off the European skin, never to resume it. They must look forward to their posterity rather than backward to their ancestors. June 4, 1819

On the Missouri Compromise regarding slavery in the new territories (see p. 27):

> I take it for granted that the present question is a mere preamble – a title-page to a great tragic volume. REMARK, 1820

PRESIDENTIAL OPINIONS:
THE 9TH AND THE 15TH ON THE 6TH
★ ★ ★

Coarse, dirty, clownish in his address and stiff and abstracted in his opinions, which are drawn from books exclusively. WILLIAM HENRY HARRISON

His disposition is as perverse and mulish as that of his father. JAMES BUCHANAN

On slavery:

The conflict between the principle of liberty and the fact of slavery is coming gradually to an issue. Slavery has now the power, and falls into convulsions at the approach of freedom. That the fall of slavery is predetermined in the counsels of Omnipotence I cannot doubt; it is a part of the great moral improvement in the condition of man, attested by all the records of history. But the conflict will be terrible … JOURNAL, December 11, 1838

On America's foreign policy:

She goes not abroad, in search of monsters to destroy.

ADDRESS TO THE HOUSE OF REPRESENTATIVES while Secretary of State, July 4, 1821. He went on to warn that America should not 'become the dictatress of the world'.

On history:

The public history of all countries, and all ages, is but a sort of mask, richly colored. The interior working of the machinery must be foul. DIARY, November 9, 1822

On liberty and power:

Individual liberty is individual power, and as the power of a community is a mass compounded of individual powers, the nation which enjoys the most freedom must necessarily be in proportion to its numbers the most powerful nation.

LETTER TO JAMES LLOYD, October 1, 1822

During his Inaugural Address, Adams admitted to the American people that his support in the preceding election had been far from overwhelming:

Less possessed of your confidence in advance than any of my predecessors, I am deeply conscious of the prospect that I shall stand more and oftener in need of your indulgence.

INAUGURAL ADDRESS, March 4, 1825

After his defeat in the 1828 presidential election, Adams was deeply despondent:

The sun of my political life sets in deepest gloom.

Quoted in John T. Morse, *John Quincy Adams* (1882)

However, when in 1830 his neighbors asked whether he would be prepared to stand as their representative, even though he had held the highest office in the land, he replied:

No person could be degraded by serving the people as a representative to Congress. Nor in my opinion would an ex-president of the United States be degraded by serving as a selectman of his town, if elected thereto by the people.

MEMOIRS OF JOHN QUINCY ADAMS, ed. Charles Francis Adams (1874–7)

He went on to tell Henry Clay of his determination to continue in public service:

Labor I shall not refuse, so long as my hands, my eyes and my brain do not desert me.

Quoted in Josiah Quincy, *Memoir of the Life of John Quincy Adams* (1858)

He was as good as his word, and was still serving as a congressman at the time of his death:

This is the last of Earth! I am content. LAST WORDS, February 21, 1848. He died two days later.

ANDREW JACKSON

1767–1845

7TH PRESIDENT OF THE UNITED STATES, 1829–37

ANDREW JACKSON

FULL NAME: Andrew Jackson
BORN: March 15, 1767, the Waxhaws area on the borders
of North and South Carolina
DIED: June 8, 1845, Nashville, Tennessee
MARRIED: Rachel Robards (née Donelson; she had previously
been married to Colonel Lewis Robards)
CHILDREN: Jackson adopted ten children: Andrew Jackson Jr,
Lyncoya Jackson, John Samuel Donelson, Daniel Smith Donelson,
Andrew Jackson Donelson, Andrew Jackson Hutchings,
Carolina Butler, Eliza Butler, Edward Butler, Anthony Butler
PARTY: Democratic
PERIOD IN OFFICE: March 4, 1829–March 4, 1837
VICE-PRESIDENT: John C. Calhoun (1829–32), Martin Van Buren (1833–7)
There was no vice-president in 1832–3.

* * *

JACKSON WAS THE youngest son of Presbyterian Scots-Irish immigrants, and was born in a backwoods area of the Carolinas three weeks after his father's death. His education was rough and ready, and at the age of 13, during the Revolutionary War, he joined up as a courier. Captured by the British, he was subjected to brutal treatment, and most of his family, including his mother, died during the hostilities. He went on to study law, and was admitted to the bar in 1787. The following year he moved to Tennessee, and represented the state in the US House of Representatives (1796–7) and Senate (1797–8) as a Democratic-Republican. At the same time, he began to acquire land and slaves. In 1801 he became colonel of the Tennessee militia, which he commanded in the Creek War. In the War of 1812 he was commissioned into the US army, and at the Battle of New Orleans led his force to victory over a larger British force. He went on to lead an aggressive campaign in Florida in the First Seminole War (1817–18).

Despite his fame as a war hero, he controversially lost the 1824 presidential election to John Quincy Adams. His supporters, blaming the result on the corruption of an elite political clique, coalesced into the new Democratic Party, and Jackson's popular nationalism helped him to victory in the 1828 presidential election. During his two terms as president, Jackson insisted that the federal government's powers were limited to those specifically assigned to it in the Constitution, and opposed the renewal of the charter of the Bank of the United States. However, he stood firm against the rights claimed by some states, especially in the South, to nullify federal legislation on the grounds of unconstitutionality. This came to a head over federal import tariffs in the Nullification Crisis of 1832–3, which resulted in the resignation of Jackson's vice-president, John C. Calhoun, who had championed states' rights in the matter. Perhaps the bitterest legacy of Jackson's presidency, however, was his implementation of the Indian Removal Act, by which the 'Five Civilized Tribes' were evicted from their lands in the southeast and transplanted, via the 'Trail of Tears', to lands west of the Mississippi.

Jackson made his name as a vociferously patriotic soldier during the War of 1812:

The individual who refuses to defend his rights when called by his government, deserves to be a slave, and must be punished as an enemy of his country and friend to her foe.

PROCLAMATION TO THE PEOPLE OF LOUISIANA, September 21, 1814

The brave man inattentive to his duty is worth little more to his country than the coward who deserts her in the hour of danger.

REMARK during the Battle of New Orleans, January 8, 1815, to troops who had abandoned their positions

Elevate them guns a little lower.

ORDER TO HIS ARTILLERY at the Battle of New Orleans

Jackson cultivated the image of a straight-talking frontiersman all his life, contrasting himself with the educated sophisticates of the northeast. In 1833 he told an audience at Harvard, where he had just received an honorary doctorate and been subjected to a laudatory speech in Latin:

I shall have to speak in English, not being able to return your compliment in what appears to be the language of Harvard. All the Latin I know is *E pluribus unum*.

On the Union:

Our Federal Union! It must and shall be preserved!

TOAST ON THE OCCASION OF JEFFERSON'S BIRTHDAY, April 13, 1830. In response, Vice-President Calhoun, champion of states' rights, proposed: 'The Union, next to our liberty, most dear.'

On the claim by certain states that they had the right to nullify federal legislation that they regarded as unconstitutional:

The claim was asserted of a right by a state to annul the laws of the Union, and even to secede from it at pleasure ... If it be the will of Heaven that the recurrence of its primeval curse for the shedding of a brother's blood should fall upon our land, that it be not called down by any offensive act on the part of the United States.

PROCLAMATION TO THE PEOPLE OF SOUTH CAROLINA, December 10, 1832

Prior to his formal pronouncement on the issue, Jackson asked a Congressman from South Carolina to give the nullificationists in his state a message:

JACKSON THE DUELLER

★ ★ ★

Jackson had something of a reputation as a brawler and dueller, perhaps following his mother's advice:

Never sue for assault or slander, settle them cases yourself.

Quoted in W.H. Sparks, *The Memories of Fifty Years* (1870)

Many of his fights were over the honor of his wife Rachel, whom he had 'married' in Natchez, Mississippi prior to her divorce from her first husband. One of the men who had slurred her 'sacred name', Charles Dickinson, succeeded in wounding Jackson in the rib in the ensuing duel. When it came to Jackson's turn to fire, the result was fatal to Dickinson. Jackson remarked:

I intended to kill him. I would have stood up long enough to kill him if he had put a bullet in my brain.

Quoted in James Parton, *Life of Andrew Jackson* (1861)

In 1803 Jackson challenged John 'Nolichucky Jack' Sevier, governor of Tennessee, to a duel after the latter had told him:

I know of no services you have rendered to this country other than taking a trip to Natchez with another man's wife!

One man who wounded Jackson in a duel, Thomas Hart Benton, later became one of Jackson's strongest supporters in the Senate. In later life he was fond of telling people:

General Jackson was a very great man. I shot him, sir. Yes, I had a fight with Jackson. A fellow was hardly in the fashion who didn't.

Tell them that they can talk and write resolutions to their hearts' content. But if one drop of blood be shed there in defiance of the laws of the United States, I will hang the first man of them I can get my hands on to the first tree I can find.

Quoted in August C. Buell, *History of Andrew Jackson* (1904)

Jackson never forgave Calhoun, telling a Presbyterian minister towards the end of his life of his greatest regret:

Posterity will condemn me more because I was persuaded not to hang John C. Calhoun as a traitor than for any other act in my life!

Quoted in James Parton, *Life of Andrew Jackson* (1861)

On government:

There are no necessary evils in government. Its evils exist only in its abuses.

Vetoing the Bank Bill, July 10, 1832

PRESIDENTIAL OPINIONS: THE 3RD AND 6TH ON THE 7TH

* * *

I feel much alarmed at the prospect of seeing General Jackson president. He is the most unfit man I know for such a place.

Thomas Jefferson, during the 1824 presidential campaign

A barbarian who could scarcely spell his own name.

John Quincy Adams, quoted in John T. Morse, *John Quincy Adams* (1882)

Jackson was nothing if not a populist in his attacks on the Bank of the United States:

It is to be regretted that the rich and powerful too often bend the acts of government to their selfish purposes ... but when the laws undertake ... to make the rich and powerful more potent, the humble members of society – the farmers, mechanics and laborers – who have neither the time nor the means of securing like favors to themselves, have a right to complain of the injustice of their government. Vetoing the Bank Bill, July 10, 1832

Addressing the Native Americans of the southeast, Jackson assumed the role of Father of the Nation:

You and my white children are too near to each other to live in harmony and peace ... Beyond the great river Mississippi, where a part of your nation has gone, your father has provided a country large enough for all of you, and he advises you to remove to it. There your white brothers will not trouble you; they will have no claim to the land, and you can live upon it, you and all your children, as long as the grass grows or the water runs, in peace and plenty. It will be yours forever. Address to the Creek Nation, March 23, 1829

In 1833 Jackson consulted a doctor after coughing up blood and experiencing pains in his side:

Now Doctor, I can do anything you think proper to order, and bear as much as most men. There are only two things I can't give up; one is coffee, and the other is tobacco.

Quoted in James Parton, *Life of Andrew Jackson* (1861)

What others said

＊＊＊

Tough as old hickory.

> DESCRIPTION OF JACKSON on the battlefield by the men he commanded – hence his nickname, Old Hickory

One of his boyhood friends remembered his determination as a wrestler:

> I could throw him three times out of four, but he would never stay throwed. He was dead game and never would give up.
>
> Quoted in James Parton, *Life of Andrew Jackson* (1861)

In the 1780s Jackson taught school and studied law at Salisbury, North Carolina. Years later, a resident of the town remembered the young hell-raiser:

> Andrew Jackson was the most roaring, rollicking, game-cocking, horse-racing, card-playing, mischievous fellow that ever lived in Salisbury.
>
> Quoted in James Parton, *Life of Andrew Jackson* (1861)

> I cannot believe that the killing of two thousand Englishmen at New Orleans qualifies a person for the various difficult and complicated duties of the presidency.
>
> HENRY CLAY, letter, 1825

Thousands of Jackson's supporters flocked to Washington to witness his inauguration:

> It was a proud day for the people. General Jackson is their own president.
>
> AMOS KENDALL, editorial in the *Argus of Western America* (Frankfort, Kentucky), March 18, 1829

> Persons have come five hundred miles to see General Jackson, and they really seem to think that the country is rescued from some awful danger!
>
> DANIEL WEBSTER, quoted in James Parton, *Life of Andrew Jackson* (1861)

Regarding Jackson's attack on the Bank of the United States (see above), the head of the bank had this to say:

> It has all the fury of a chained panther biting the bars of his cage. It really is a manifesto of anarchy – such as Marat or Robespierre might have issued to the Faubourg St Antoine, and my hope is that it will contribute to relieve the country of the dominion of these miserable people.
>
> NICHOLAS BIDDLE, letter to Senator Henry Clay, August 1, 1832

In 1833 Josiah Quincy, president of Harvard, proposed that Jackson be awarded an honorary doctorate of laws. When one of the Board of Overseers, Jackson's old political rival John Quincy Adams, objected, President Quincy replied:

> As the people have twice decided that this man knows enough law to be their ruler, it is not for Harvard College to maintain that they are mistaken.
>
> Quoted in Edwin P. Hoyt, *John Quincy Adams* (1963)

MARTIN VAN BUREN

1782–1862

8TH PRESIDENT OF THE UNITED STATES, 1837–41

Martin Van Buren

FULL NAME: Martin Van Buren
BORN: December 5, 1782, Kinderhook, New York
DIED: July 24, 1862, Kinderhook, New York
MARRIED: Hannah Hoes
CHILDREN: Abraham, John, Martin, Smith Thompson
PARTY: Democratic
PERIOD IN OFFICE: March 4, 1837–March 4, 1841
VICE-PRESIDENT: Richard Mentor Johnson

* * *

VAN BUREN'S parents were both of Dutch descent, and his father was a farmer and tavern-keeper in Kinderhook, New York. After a basic schooling, Van Buren became apprenticed to a local lawyer, and started his own practise in Kinderhook in 1803. A follower of Thomas Jefferson, he espoused states' rights and opposed strong federal government and federally funded improvement schemes. He was a state senator in New York from 1812 to 1820, and served as state attorney general. Elected to the US Senate in 1821, he helped set up the party machine known as the Albany Regency, and during the presidency of John Quincy Adams he was instrumental in forming a coalition including the supporters of Andrew Jackson and John C. Calhoun to form what became the Democratic Party. He served as Jackson's secretary of state (1829–31) and then as his vice-president (1833–7). With Jackson's backing, he was selected unanimously as the Democratic candidate in the 1836 presidential election, in which he defeated the Whig candidate, William Henry Harrison. He began his term as president during a financial crisis and economic depression, and his Independent Treasury Act of 1840, by which federal funds were redistributed to state banks, caused many Democrats to desert to the Whig Party. His conduct of the Second Seminole War also proved unpopular, as did his refusal to support the annexation of Texas, and he was defeated by Harrison in the 1840 presidential election. He sought the Democratic candidacy again in 1844, but was defeated by James K. Polk, who favored the annexation of Texas. In the 1848 presidential election he stood for the anti-slavery Free Soil Party, but only won 10 per cent of the popular vote. He spent his last years in retirement at his home in Kinderhook.

At the famous celebration of Jefferson's birthday on April 13, 1830, when President Jackson toasted the Union and Vice-President Calhoun toasted states' rights (see p. 43), Van Buren proposed a compromise, raising his glass to:

Mutual forbearance and reciprocal concessions.

Van Buren's reputation as a man who would not commit himself is reflected in the following reported (though probably apocryphal) exchange:

SENATOR: Matt, it's been rumored that the sun rises in the east. Do you believe it?
VAN BUREN: Well, senator, I understand that's the common acceptance, but as I never get up till after dawn, I can't really say.

Quoted by Van Buren himself in his *Autobiography* (not published until 1918)

The clever, manipulative, behind-the-scenes party-machine manager Van Buren was aware that he lacked the glamor and fire of his predecessor, Andrew Jackson:

> I tread in the footsteps of illustrious men ... In receiving from the people the sacred trust twice confided to my illustrious predecessor, and which he has discharged so faithfully and so well, I know that I cannot expect to perform the arduous task with equal ability and success. INAUGURAL ADDRESS, March 4, 1837

> All the lessons of history and experience must be lost upon us if we are content to trust alone to the peculiar advantages we happen to possess. INAUGURAL ADDRESS, March 4, 1837

On the subject of slavery, he was typically evasive:

> The last, perhaps the greatest, of the prominent sources of discord and disaster supposed to lurk in our political condition was the institution of domestic slavery. Our forefathers were deeply impressed with the delicacy of this subject, and they treated it with a forbearance so evidently wise that in spite of every sinister foreboding it never until the present period disturbed the tranquility of our common country. Such a result is sufficient evidence of the justice and the patriotism of their course ...
> INAUGURAL ADDRESS, March 4, 1837

His presidency saw many attacks on him in the press, which baffled Van Buren:

> Why the deuce is it that they have such an itching for abusing me? I try to be harmless, and positively good natured, and a most decided friend of peace.
> Quoted in Charles R. King, ed., *The Life and Correspondence of Rufus King* (1898)

PRESIDENTIAL OPINIONS:
THE 6TH AND 7TH ON THE 8TH
* * *

His principles are all subordinate to his ambitions.
JOHN QUINCY ADAMS

One of the most frank men I ever knew ... a true man with no guile.
ANDREW JACKSON, quoted in Edward M. Shepard, *Martin van Buren* (1888)

That man loves me; he tries to conceal it, but there is always some fixed way by which I can tell my friends from my enemies.
ANDREW JACKSON, remark to Peggy Eaton, quoted in Benjamin Perley Poore, *Perley's Reminiscences of Sixty Years* (1886)

What others said
* * *

On the great ovation given to Andrew Jackson at Van Buren's inauguration:

> For once the rising sun was eclipsed by the setting sun.
> SENATOR THOMAS HART BENTON, *Thirty Years View* (1866)

> He rode to his object with muffled oars. JOHN RANDOLPH OF ROANOKE (1773–1833)

WILLIAM HENRY HARRISON

1 7 7 3 – 1 8 4 1

9TH PRESIDENT OF THE UNITED STATES, 1841

WILLIAM HENRY HARRISON

FULL NAME: William Henry Harrison
BORN: February 9, 1773, Charles City County, Virginia
DIED: April 4, 1841, Washington DC
MARRIED: Anna Tuthill Symmes
CHILDREN: Elizabeth Bassett, John Cleves Symmes, Lucy Singleton,
William Henry, John Scott, Mary Symmes, Benjamin,
Carter Bassett, Anna Tuthill, James Findlay
PARTY: Whig
PERIOD IN OFFICE: March 4, 1841–April 4, 1841
VICE-PRESIDENT: John Tyler

* * *

HARRISON was descended on both sides from wealthy and influential Virginian planter families, and his father, Benjamin Harrison, had been a signatory of the Declaration of Independence. Harrison studied medicine in Richmond, Virginia, before taking a commission in the army. He served in the campaign against the Northwest Indian Confederation that culminated in the Battle of Fallen Timbers (1794), and in 1800 was made governor of the new Indiana Territory, in which role he oversaw a number of treaties that deprived the local Native American tribes of vast tracts of land. This led to considerable resentments culminating in an uprising led by Tecumseh, which was defeated by Harrison at the Battle of Tippecanoe (1811). During the War of 1812 he defeated the British and their Native American allies in Ontario at the Battle of the Thames (1813), in which Tecumseh was killed. Entering politics as a war hero, Harrison served in the US House of Representatives (1816–19), the Ohio Senate (1819–21), the US Senate (1825–8) and as US minister to Colombia (1828–9). He stood as a Whig in the 1836 presidential election, but was defeated by Martin Van Buren. He was successful in the 1840 election, exploiting his image as a cider-drinking, Indian-fighting frontiersman. Up to that date he was the oldest person to take up the office of president, and within a month he was dead of pneumonia, supposedly contracted while delivering the longest inaugural address ever given. His grandson, Benjamin Harrison, was to become 23rd president.

On liberty and power:

The strongest of all governments is that which is most free.
LETTER TO SIMÓN BOLÍVAR, September 29, 1829

On government:

We admit of no government by divine right ... The only legitimate right to govern is an express grant of power from the governed. INAUGURAL ADDRESS, March 4, 1841

Shortly after Harrison's inauguration, one of his servants made a farmer, who had come to see the president, wait in a bare room, telling his master that he was worried that the man would make the carpet in the drawing room dirty. Harrison upbraided his servant, telling him:

Never mind the carpet another time. The man is of the people, and the carpet and the house, too, belong to the people.
Quoted in Mrs E.F. Ellet, *The Court Circles of the Republic* (1869)

His last words, apparently intended for Vice-President Tyler, were:

> Sir, I wish you to understand the principles of the government. I wish them carried out. I ask nothing more.
>
> Quoted in Charles S. Todd and Benjamin Drake, *Sketches of the Civil and Military Services of William Henry Harrison* (1847)

PRESIDENTIAL OPINIONS: THE 6TH, 7TH AND 8TH ON THE 9TH

* * *

Harrison comes in upon a hurricane. God grant he may not go out upon a wreck!

JOHN QUINCY ADAMS, responding to Harrison's election, quoted in the *Cincinnati Daily Gazette*, April 13, 1841

[An] active but shallow mind, a political adventurer not without talents, but self-sufficient, vain and indiscreet.

JOHN QUINCY ADAMS, quoted in Alfred Steinberg, *The First Ten* (1967)

Our present imbecile chief. ANDREW JACKSON

He is as tickled with the presidency as a young woman is with a new bonnet.

MARTIN VAN BUREN, quoted in Mrs E.F. Ellet, *The Court Circles of the Republic* (1869)

What others said

* * *

Give him a barrel of hard cider and a pension of two thousand a year and, our word for it, he will sit the remainder of his days in a log cabin by the side of a 'sea coal' fire and study moral philosophy.

THE *BALTIMORE REPUBLICAN*, December 11, 1839. Harrison's supporters turned this intended slur to their advantage, depicting their man (in fact the son of a wealthy Virginia planter) as a down-to-earth frontiersman, with cider and log cabins featuring prominently in Harrison's successful 1840 'Log Cabin and Hard Cider' presidential campaign.

Tippecanoe and Tyler too!

ELECTION SLOGAN during the 1840 'Log Cabin and Hard Cider' campaign, referring to Harrison's 1811 victory and to his vice-presidential running-mate. Harrison was nicknamed 'Old Tippecanoe' or 'Old Tip' – transformed into 'Old Tippler' by his political opponents.

Among the many campaign songs sung by Harrison's supporters was this, contrasting their man's modest style with the supposedly high-falutin' ways of his opponent, Martin Van Buren:

> Old Tip he wears a homespun coat
> He has no ruffled shirt-wirt-wirt
> But Mat he has the golden plate
> And he's a little squirt-wirt-wirt.

JOHN TYLER

1790–1862

10TH PRESIDENT OF THE UNITED STATES, 1841–5

JOHN TYLER

FULL NAME: John Tyler, Jr
BORN: March 29, 1790, Charles City County, Virginia
DIED: January 18, 1862, Richmond, Virginia
MARRIED: (1) Letitia Christian, (2) Julia Gardiner
CHILDREN: Mary, Robert, John, Letitia, Elizabeth, Anne Contesse,
Alice, Tazewell (by his first wife); David Gardiner, John Alexander,
Julia Gardiner, Lachlan, Lyon Gardiner, Robert Fitzwalter,
Pearl (by his second wife)
PARTY: independent (through his presidency)
PERIOD IN OFFICE: April 4, 1841–March 4, 1845
(He actually took the oath of office on April 6, 1841.)
VICE-PRESIDENT: none

* * *

TYLER'S FATHER was a Virginia planter and circuit judge who became governor of Virginia and who imbued in his son a belief in states' rights and a strict interpretation of the Constitution. Tyler graduated from the College of King William and Mary in 1807, then studied law with his father and was admitted to the bar in 1809. He went on to sit in the Virginia House of Delegates (1811–16, 1823–5, 1838–40), and followed in his father's footsteps as governor of Virginia (1825–7). In 1816 he was elected as a Democratic-Republican to the US House of Representatives, in which he served till 1821. He was a US senator from 1827 to 1836, initially supporting Andrew Jackson, but later moving towards the Whigs. He was the sole senator to vote against Jackson's proposed use of force during the Nullification Crisis. Tyler ran unsuccessfully as William Henry Harrison's running mate in the 1836 presidential election, but their joint ticket, running under the slogan 'Tippecanoe and Tyler too', won the 1840 election. With Harrison's death just a month after his inauguration, Vice-President Tyler assumed the presidency, and demonstrated his independence by vetoing many Whig proposals in Congress, notably the bill to re-charter the Bank of the United States. On September 11, 1841, after Tyler's second veto of the bank bill, all of his cabinet except Daniel Webster resigned. Despite his lack of support, Tyler went on to achieve a number of successes, including a settlement of the border between Maine and Canada, the ending of the Second Seminole War, and the securing of Congressional approval for the annexation of Texas. In 1843 an impeachment attempt against Tyler failed, and in the 1844 presidential race he put his support behind the successful candidate, James Polk. Tyler then withdrew from politics until the Civil War, when he was elected to the Confederate Congress, although he died before taking his seat.

On popularity:

> Popularity, I have always thought, may aptly be compared to a coquette – the more you woo her, the more apt is she to elude your embrace. December 18, 1816

On religious freedom:

> Let it, then, be henceforth proclaimed to the world, that man's conscience was created free; that he is no longer accountable to his fellow man for his religious opinions, being responsible therefore only to his God. FUNERAL ORATION FOR THOMAS JEFFERSON, July 11, 1826

Tyler opposed Andrew Jackson's system of political patronage:

Patronage is the sword and cannon by which war may be made on the liberty of the human race. SPEECH IN CONGRESS, February 24, 1834

On becoming president following the death of William Henry Harrison, Tyler found many of the latter's cabinet ranged against him:

I can never consent to being dictated to as to what I shall or shall not do. I, as president, shall be responsible for my administration. I hope to have your hearty cooperation in carrying out its measures. So long as you see fit to do this, I shall be glad to have you with me. When you think otherwise, your resignations will be accepted.

TO HIS CABINET, as recorded by John Alexander Tyler. On September 11, 1841, all but one of Tyler's cabinet resigned.

As he looked forward to leaving office in March 1845, Tyler remarked:

In 1840 I was called from my farm to undertake the administration of public affairs, and I foresaw that I was called to a bed of thorns. I now leave that bed, which has afforded me little rest, and eagerly seek repose in the quiet enjoyments of rural life.

Late in life Tyler wrote the following epitaph for his favourite horse, 'The General':

Here lies the body of my good horse 'The General'. For twenty years he bore me around the circuit of my practise and in all that time he never made me blunder. Would that his master could say the same.

What others said

* * *

I could not believe that a man so commonplace, so absolutely inferior to many 15-shilling lawyers with whom you may meet at every county court in Virginia, would seriously aspire to the first station among mankind.

JOHN H. PLEASANTS, editor of the *Richmond Whig*

His Accidency.

Nickname awarded to Tyler following the circumstances of his succession to the presidency

The accident of an accident.

How irate Whig politicians dubbed Tyler after he had twice vetoed the bill to re-charter the Bank of the United States in 1841

A president without a party.

HENRY CLAY, Tyler's leading opponent, after the resignation of the president's cabinet in September 1841

He looked somewhat worn and anxious, and well he might; being at war with everybody – but the expression of his face was mild and pleasant, and his manner was remarkably unaffected, gentlemanly and agreeable. I thought that in his whole carriage and demeanor, he became his station singularly well.

CHARLES DICKENS, who visited Tyler in 1842

James K. Polk

1795–1849

11th President of the United States, 1845–9

JAMES K. POLK

FULL NAME: James Knox Polk
BORN: November 2, 1795, Pineville, North Carolina
DIED: June 15, 1849, Nashville, Tennessee
MARRIED: Sarah Childress
CHILDREN: none (though he and his wife raised a nephew,
Marshall Tate Polk)
PARTY: Democratic
PERIOD IN OFFICE: March 4, 1845–March 4, 1849
VICE-PRESIDENT: George M. Dallas

* * *

POLK, who was of Scots-Irish descent, was born in rural North Carolina, where his father was a prosperous farmer and slave-owner. At the age of 11 he moved with his family to Tennessee. After graduating from the University of North Carolina in 1818 he studied law, and was admitted to the bar two years later. A supporter of Andrew Jackson, Polk sat in the US House of Representatives from 1825 to 1839, latterly as speaker. At the 1844 Democratic convention Polk emerged as the compromise candidate to run in that year's presidential election, which he duly won. His presidency is best remembered for his policy of territorial expansionism, which he

---

MANIFEST DESTINY
* * *

Tyler believed that the USA had a 'manifest destiny' to spread across the North American continent – specifically, in this instance, Texas, which a decade earlier had achieved its independence from Mexico:

> Our Union is a confederation of independent states, whose policy is peace with each other and all the world. To enlarge its limits is to extend the dominions of peace over additional territories and increasing millions ... Foreign powers should therefore look on the annexation of Texas to the United States not as the conquest of a nation seeking to extend her dominions by arms and violence, but as the peaceful acquisition of a territory once her own, by adding another member to our confederation, with the consent of that member. INAUGURAL ADDRESS, March 4, 1845

The phrase 'manifest destiny' was actually coined later the same year by the journalist and diplomat John L. O'Sullivan. Attacking those opposed to the annexation of Texas, O'Sullivan wrote of:

> A spirit of hostile interference towards us ... checking the fulfillment of our manifest destiny to overspread the continent allotted by Providence for the free development of our yearly multiplying millions. UNITED STATES MAGAZINE AND DEMOCRATIC REVIEW (1845), vol. 17

At the end of the same year, Tyler stated:

> The people of this continent alone have the right to decide their own destiny. ANNUAL ADDRESS TO CONGRESS, December 2, 1845

---

justified by his doctrine of 'manifest destiny' (see box opposite). His pursuit of the annexation of Texas led to the Mexican War (1846–8), which in turn resulted in the acquisition not only of Texas, but also of California and much of the modern states of New Mexico, Arizona, Utah, Nevada, Colorado and Wyoming. Polk also resolved territorial disputes over the border with British Canada, as a result of which the USA acquired Washington, Oregon and Idaho. Although he achieved many of his stated policy objectives, Polk alienated many of his subordinates, including General Zachary Taylor, who was to succeed him as president. Polk died within a short time of leaving office.

On his strict interpretation of the Constitution:

The Constitution itself ... binding together in the bonds of peace and union this great and increasing family of free and independent states, will be the chart by which I shall be directed. It will be my first care to administer the government in the true spirit of that instrument, and to assume no powers not expressly granted or clearly implied in its terms.
    INAUGURAL ADDRESS, March 4, 1845

On equality:

All distinctions of birth or of rank have been abolished. All citizens, whether native or adopted, are placed upon terms of precise equality. All are entitled to equal rights and equal protection. INAUGURAL ADDRESS, March 4, 1845

On Congressmen:

There is more selfishness and less principle among members of Congress, as well as others, than I had any conception, before I became president of the US. DIARY, December 16, 1846

Polk was a poor delegator:

No president who performs his duties faithfully and conscientiously can have any leisure. If he entrusts the details and smaller matters to subordinates constant errors will occur. I prefer to supervise the whole operations of the government myself ...
    DIARY, December 29, 1848

I am heartily rejoiced that my term is so near its close. I will soon cease to be a servant and will become a sovereign. DIARY, February 13, 1849. Within three months of leaving office he was dead.

PRESIDENTIAL OPINIONS:
THE 7TH, 16TH AND 32ND ON THE 11TH
* * *

I never betrayed a friend or was guilty of the black sin of ingratitude. I fear Mr Polk cannot say as much.
    ANDREW JACKSON, quoted in Eric L. McKitrick, *Andrew Johnson: A Profile* (1960)

He is a bewildered, confounded and miserably perplexed man.
    ABRAHAM LINCOLN, who opposed the Mexican War

James K. Polk, a great president. Said what he intended to do, and did it.
    HARRY S. TRUMAN

ZACHARY TAYLOR

1784–1850

12TH PRESIDENT OF THE UNITED STATES, 1849–50

ZACHARY TAYLOR

FULL NAME: Zachary Taylor
BORN: November 24, 1784, Barboursville, Virginia
DIED: July 9, 1850, Washington DC
MARRIED: Margaret ('Peggy') Mackall Smith
CHILDREN: Ann Mackall, Sarah Knox (future wife of Jefferson Davis,
the Confederate president), Octavia Pannill, Mary Smith, Mary Elizabeth, Richard
PARTY: Whig
PERIOD IN OFFICE: March 4, 1849–July 9, 1850
VICE-PRESIDENT: Millard Fillmore

* * *

ALTHOUGH BORN IN VIRGINIA, Taylor spent much of his boyhood in a cabin in the woods on the Kentucky frontier, where there was little in the way of formal schooling. However, Taylor's father grew prosperous enough to acquire 10,000 acres and two dozen slaves. Taylor joined the army in 1808, and served for 40 years, seeing action in the War of 1812, the Black Hawk War, the Second Seminole War and the Mexican War, by which time he had achieved the rank of major general. Taylor – nicknamed 'Old Rough and Ready' by his men – became a national hero during the Mexican campaign, capturing Monterey in 1846 and defeating a force three or four times the size of his own at Buena Vista in 1847. His military success led various Whig politicians to consider him as a potential presidential candidate – a notion that he at first rejected out of hand. But in due course Taylor came round to the idea, and went on to win the Whig nomination and defeat Lewis Cass, the Democratic candidate, in the presidential election of 1848. The Whigs had thought that Taylor, as a slaveholder, would support the extension of slavery into the new territories, but he refused to do so, and threatened vigorous action against the South should it secede. He opposed the Compromise of 1850, but did not live to see its adoption. On Independence Day 1850 he fell ill with gastroenteritis, and died five days later.

On being asked to surrender by Mexican General Santa Anna prior to the Battle of Buena Vista, February 22, 1847:

Tell him to go to hell!

On war:

My life has been devoted to arms, yet I look upon war at all times, and under all circumstances, as a national calamity, to be avoided if compatible with national honor.

Quoted in Maxim E. Armbruster, *The Presidents of the United States* (1960)

It eminently becomes a government like our own, founded on the morality and intelligence of its citizens and upheld by their affections, to exhaust every resort of honorable diplomacy before appealing to arms.

INAUGURAL ADDRESS, March 5, 1849. (Taylor's inauguration was delayed by a day, as March 4 was a Sunday.)

To a Whig who was urging him to stand for president:

Shut up and drink your whiskey!

On another occasion he remarked:

The idea that I should become president seems to me too visionary to require a serious answer. It has never entered my head, nor is it likely to enter the head of any other person.

Once he had decided to run for president, Taylor was careful not to appear too committed to a single party:

I have no private purpose to accomplish, no party objectives to build up, no enemies to punish – nothing to serve but my country.

He cautiously described himself as:

A Whig, but not an ultra-Whig. Quoted in Brainerd Dyer, *Zachary Taylor* (1946)

PRESIDENTIAL OPINIONS:
THE 11TH AND 16TH ON THE 12TH
* * *

General Taylor is, I have no doubt, a well-meaning old man. He is, however, uneducated, exceedingly ignorant of public affairs, and I should judge, of very ordinary capacity. JAMES POLK

Taylor was known for his vagueness as to policy:

The people say to General Taylor: 'If you are elected, shall we have a national bank?' He answers, 'Your will, gentlemen, not mine.' 'What about the tariff ?' 'Say yourselves.' 'Shall our rivers and harbors be improved?' 'Just as you please. If you desire a bank, an alteration of the tariff, internal improvements, any or all, I will not hinder you. If you do not desire them, I will not attempt to force them on you.' ABRAHAM LINCOLN

To three Southern Whig Congressmen who talked of secession:

If it becomes necessary, in executing the laws, I will take command of the army myself, and, if you are taken in rebellion against the Union, I will hang you with less reluctance than I hanged deserters and spies in Mexico!

Quoted as reported speech in Charles E. Hamlin, *The Life and Times of Hannibal Hamlin* (1899)

A week later he told Congressman Horace Mann that he could end any secession in the South by means of naval blockades and tariffs:

I can save the Union without shedding a drop of blood. It is not true, as reported in the North, that I said I would march an army and subdue them: there would be no need of any.

Quoted in Mary Mann, *Life of Horace Mann* (1888)

I have always done my duty. I am ready to die. My only regret is for the friends I leave behind me. LAST WORDS

MILLARD FILLMORE

1800–1874

13TH PRESIDENT OF THE UNITED STATES, 1850–3

MILLARD FILLMORE

FULL NAME: Millard Fillmore
BORN: January 7, 1800, Summerhill, New York
DIED: March 8, 1874, Buffalo, New York
MARRIED: (1) Abigail Powers, (2) Caroline McIntosh (née Carmichael;
she was the widow of Ezekiel C. McIntosh)
CHILDREN: Millard Powers, Mary Abigail (both by his first wife)
PARTY: Whig
PERIOD IN OFFICE: July 9, 1850–March 4, 1853
VICE-PRESIDENT: none

* * *

FILLMORE was born of poor parents in a log cabin in upstate New York. He had little formal schooling, and was apprenticed to a wool-carder at the age of 15. In 1819 he began work as a legal clerk in Montville, New York, and was admitted to the bar in 1823. He entered politics in 1828 as a member of the Anti-Masonic Party, serving a term in the New York State Assembly. In 1834 he joined the Whigs, and sat in the US House of Representatives in 1833–5 and 1837–43, becoming a staunch supporter of Henry Clay. He stood unsuccessfully for governor of New York in 1844, but served as state comptroller in 1848–9. With Clay's backing, he became Zachary Taylor's running mate in the 1848 presidential election, and took over the presidency on Taylor's sudden death in 1850. His attitude to slavery was appeasing: he supported the Compromise of 1850 (which Taylor had opposed), and alienated many in the North through his strict enforcement of the Fugitive Slave Act, which obliged the federal government to forcibly return runaway slaves who had taken refuge in free states. Beyond the borders of the USA, Fillmore looked towards the Pacific, negotiating a convention with Great Britain over the construction of a canal between the Atlantic and the Pacific (which did not come to fruition until the following century), and sent Commodore Perry of the US Navy to open up trade with Japan. Fillmore failed to get the divided Whig Party's nomination in the 1852 presidential election, but ran for the anti-immigrant Know-Nothing Party in 1856, coming third. He then retired to Buffalo.

On losing the Whig nomination to run as governor of New York:

> An honorable defeat is better than a dishonorable victory. SPEECH, September 13, 1844

On states' rights:

> Every citizen who truly loves the Constitution and desires the continuance of its existence and its blessings will resolutely and firmly resist any interference in those domestic affairs which the Constitution has clearly and unequivocally left to the exclusive authority of the states. ANNUAL MESSAGE TO CONGRESS, December 2, 1850

On slavery:

> God knows that I detest slavery, but it is an existing evil, for which we are not responsible, and we must endure it, and give it such protection as is guaranteed by the Constitution, till we can get rid of it without destroying the last hope of free government in the world.
> Quoted in Frank H. Severance, ed., *Millard Fillmore Papers* (1959)

On relations with other nations:

Among the acknowledged rights of nations is that which each possesses of establishing that form of government which it may deem most conducive to the happiness and prosperity of its own citizens, of changing that form as circumstances may require, and of managing its internal affairs according to its own will. The people of the United States claim this right for themselves, and they readily concede it to others. Hence it becomes an imperative duty not to interfere in the government or internal policy of other nations; and although we may sympathize with the unfortunate or the oppressed everywhere in their struggles for freedom, our principles forbid us from taking any part in such foreign contests. ANNUAL MESSAGE TO CONGRESS, December 2, 1850

A SECOND-HAND PRESIDENT
* * *

On one occasion, Fillmore was considering buying a carriage from its previous owner, and asked 'Old Edward' Moran, a White House servant:

How would it do for the president of the United States to ride around in a second-hand carriage?

Moran replied:

But sure, your excellency is only a second-hand president!

On refusing an honorary degree from Oxford University on a visit to England in 1855:

I have not the advantage of a classical education, and no man should, in my judgment, accept a degree he cannot read.

Quoted in Frank H. Severance, ed., *Millard Fillmore Papers* (1959)

May God save the country, for it is evident that the people will not. ATTRIBUTED

It is not strange … to mistake change for progress. ATTRIBUTED

It is a national disgrace that our presidents, after having occupied the highest position in the country, should be cast adrift, and, perhaps, be compelled to keep a corner grocery for subsistence. ATTRIBUTED

PRESIDENTIAL OPINIONS: THE 33RD ON THE 13TH
* * *

At a time we needed a strong man, what we got was a man that swayed with the slightest breeze. HARRY S. TRUMAN

What others said
* * *

Fillmore is a great man; but it takes pressure to make him show his highest powers.
ALBANY EVENING JOURNAL, January 26, 1843

He had the peculiar faculty of adapting himself to every position in which he served.
UNNAMED CONTEMPORARY, quoted in Robert J. Rayback, *Millard Fillmore* (1959)

FRANKLIN PIERCE

1804–1869

14TH PRESIDENT OF THE UNITED STATES, 1853–7

FRANKLIN PIERCE

FULL NAME: Franklin Pierce
BORN: November 23, 1804, Hillsborough, New Hampshire
DIED: October 8, 1869, Concord, New Hampshire
MARRIED: Jane Means Appleton
CHILDREN: Franklin Jr, Frank Robert, Benjamin
PARTY: Democratic
PERIOD IN OFFICE: March 4, 1853–March 4, 1857
VICE-PRESIDENT: William R. King (1853). There was no vice-president
after King's death on April 18, 1853.

* * *

BORN IN A LOG CABIN in New Hampshire, Pierce was the son of a frontier farmer who had fought in the Revolutionary War, and who went on to serve twice as state governor. After attending a number of schools, in 1820 Pierce commenced his studies at Bowdoin College in Brunswick, Maine. After graduation he studied law, and was admitted to the bar in 1827. Shortly afterwards he entered politics as a Democrat, and sat in the New Hampshire Assembly (1829–33), becoming speaker at the age of just 27. He went on to serve in the US House of Representatives from 1833 to 1837, when he became a US senator, aged 32. In 1842 he left the US Senate to resume his law career, but with the outbreak of the Mexican War in 1846 he joined the army, enlisting as a private and ending up as a brigadier general. He was selected as a compromise candidate at the 1852 Democratic convention, and went on to beat the Whig candidate, General Winfield Scott, in that year's presidential election. A 'sourdough' (a Northerner with Southern sympathies), Pierce defended the constitutional right of the Southern states to maintain slavery. He supported the Compromise of 1850, the acquisition of Cuba as a slave state, and the Kansas–Nebraska Act. This last measure opened these formerly free territories to slavery, resulting in violent turmoil between pro- and anti-slavery factions. Pierce's inept handling of these issues lost him the support of the Democratic Party, which refused to reselect him as its candidate in the 1856 presidential election. After leaving office, Pierce declined into alcoholism, and during the Civil War attracted accusations of treason to the Union when he criticized the conflict as aimless, unnecessary and unconstitutional.

On becoming president:

You have summoned me in my weakness. You must sustain me by your strength.
INAUGURAL ADDRESS, March 4, 1853

On the Union and the danger of secession:

From that radiant constellation which both illumines our own way and points out to struggling nations their course, let but a single star be lost, and, if these be not utter darkness, the luster of the whole is dimmed. INAUGURAL ADDRESS, March 4, 1853

On slavery:

I believe that involuntary servitude, as it exists in different states of this Confederacy, is recognized by the Constitution. I believe that it stands like any other admitted right, and that the states where it exists are entitled to efficient remedies to enforce the constitutional provisions. INAUGURAL ADDRESS, March 4, 1853

On leaving office:

There's nothing left but to get drunk.

> He was as good as his word, dying of cirrhosis in 1869. Quoted in Harry Barnard, *Rutherford B. Hayes and His America* (1954).

PRESIDENTIAL OPINIONS:
THE 26TH AND 33RD ON THE 14TH
* * *

A small politician, of low capacity and mean surroundings, proud to act as the servile tool of men worse than himself but also stronger and abler. He was ever ready to do any work the slavery leaders set him, and to act as their attorney in arguing in its favor, – to quote [Thomas Hart] Benton's phrase, with 'undaunted mendacity, moral callosity [and] mental obliquity.' THEODORE ROOSEVELT, *Life of Thomas Hart Benton* (1886)

He was another one that was a complete fizzle ... Pierce didn't know what was going on and even if he had, he wouldn't have known what to do about it. HARRY S. TRUMAN

Pierce continued to blame Northern abolitionists for the threat to the Union:

I have never believed that actual disruption of the Union can occur without blood; and if, through the madness of Northern abolitionists, that dire calamity must come, the fighting will not be along Mason's and Dixon's line merely. It [will] be within our own borders, in our own streets, between the two classes of citizens to whom I have referred [namely 'those who respect their political obligations' and those who have 'a fanatical position on the subject of domestic slavery']. LETTER TO JEFFERSON DAVIS, January 6, 1860

When it came, Pierce was vociferous in his opposition to the Civil War:

I never justify, sustain, or in any way or to any extent uphold this cruel, heartless, aimless, unnecessary war. LETTER TO HIS WIFE, March 3, 1863

The mailed hand of military usurpation strikes down the liberties of the people, and its foot tramples on a desecrated Constitution.

> SPEECH TO THE CITIZENS OF CONCORD, New Hampshire, July 4, 1863

What others said
* * *

Deep, deep, deep ... has in him many of the elements of the great ruler.

> NATHANIEL HAWTHORNE, former classmate of Pierce at Bowdoin College, quoted in Horatio Bridge, *Personal Reminiscences of Hawthorne* (1893)

Many persons have difficulty remembering what President Franklin Pierce is best remembered for, and he is therefore probably best forgotten.

> RICHARD ARMOUR, poet and humorist

JAMES BUCHANAN

1791–1868

15TH PRESIDENT OF THE UNITED STATES, 1857–61

JAMES BUCHANAN

FULL NAME: James Buchanan
BORN: April 23, 1791, near Mercersburg, Pennsylvania
DIED: June 1, 1868, Lancaster, Pennsylvania
MARRIED: never married
CHILDREN: none
PARTY: Democratic
PERIOD IN OFFICE: March 4, 1857–March 4, 1861
VICE-PRESIDENT: John C. Breckinridge

* * *

BUCHANAN'S FATHER, a Scottish-Irish Presbyterian storekeeper, had immigrated from Ulster in 1783, and his mother came from a similar background. Buchanan himself was born in a log cabin in rural Pennsylvania, and attended the village academy. He went on to study at Dickinson College, Carlisle, Pennsylvania, graduating in 1809, then studied law in Lancaster, being admitted to the bar in 1812. He started his political career as a Federalist, sitting in the Pennsylvania assembly (1814–16) and later in the US House of Representatives (1821–31), identifying himself with the Jacksonian wing of the emerging Democratic Party. He was the US minister to Russia (1831–3) during the presidency of Andrew Jackson, and a US senator (1834–45). As secretary of state (1845–9) under President Polk he was involved in the resolution of the border dispute with Great Britain that resulted in the acquisition of Washington, Oregon and Idaho. He was US minister to Britain from 1853 to 1856.

On three occasions (1844, 1848 and 1852) Buchanan failed to secure the nomination as the Democrats' presidential candidate, but was selected in 1856 because it was thought that as a 'sourdough' (a Northerner with Southern sympathies) he would prevent the secession of the Southern states. He went on to win that year's presidential election. Buchanan held that slavery was wrong, but believed the alternative was worse. He also believed that secession was illegal, but that the forcible prevention of secession on the part of the federal government was also illegal. Thus his presidency was marked by paralysis in the face of the mounting crisis, his actions being restricted to the enforcement of the Fugitive Slave Act and the suppression of Northern abolitionist agitation. By February 1861, following the victory of the Republican Abraham Lincoln in the 1860 presidential election, seven Southern states had seceded, and war seemed inevitable. Buchanan famously expressed his relief as he handed over the reins of power to his successor on March 4, 1861, and died in the mistaken belief that posterity would justify his actions.

As a young man, Buchanan had been engaged to Ann Coleman, who died (possibly by her own hand) in 1819 shortly after the engagement was broken off. Buchanan wrote to her father:

> You have lost a child, a dear, dear child. I have lost the only earthly object of my affection ... I have now one request to make ... deny me not. Afford me the melancholy pleasure of seeing her body before interment.
>
> The letter was returned unopened, and Buchanan vowed never to marry.

Buchanan is the only US president never to have married, a circumstance that led to the following exchange:

LADY VISITING THE WHITE HOUSE: Mr Buchanan, we have looked all through this house – it is very elegant and well kept but we have noted one deficiency.

BUCHANAN: What is that, madam?

LADY: That you have no lady of the house.

BUCHANAN: That, madam, is my misfortune, not my fault.

> Quoted in L.A. Gobright, *Recollections of Men and Things at Washington* (1869). In fact, Buchanan's niece, Harriet Lane, acted as his hostess in the White House.

On America's 'manifest destiny':

It is, beyond question, the destiny of our race to spread themselves over the continent of North America, and this at no distant day. LETTER TO CONGRESS, 1858

Buchanan's presidency was, of course, dominated by a single issue:

All agree that under the Constitution slavery in the states is beyond the reach of any human power except that of the respective states themselves wherein it exists. May we not, then, hope that the long agitation on this subject is approaching its end, and that the geographical parties to which it has given birth, so much dreaded by the Father of his Country, will speedily become extinct? Most happy will it be for the country when the public mind shall be diverted from this question to others of more pressing and practical importance. INAUGURAL ADDRESS, March 4, 1857

Buchanan found himself in a constitutional quandary over how to deal with states that sought to secede from the Union:

Has the Constitution delegated to Congress the power to coerce a state into submission which is attempting to withdraw or has actually withdrawn from the confederacy? If answered in the affirmative, it must be on the principle that the power has been conferred upon Congress to declare and to make war against a state. After much serious reflection I have arrived at the conclusion that no such power has been delegated to Congress or to any other department of the federal government.

ANNUAL MESSAGE TO CONGRESS, December 3, 1860

PRESIDENTIAL OPINIONS:
THE 7TH AND 11TH ON THE 15TH
★ ★ ★

On appointing Buchanan his minister to Russia:

It was as far as I could send him out of my sight, and where he could do the least harm. I would have sent him to the North Pole if we had kept a minister there.

ANDREW JACKSON, quoted in Augustus C. Buell, *History of Andrew Jackson* (1904)

Mr Buchanan is an able man, but in small matters without judgment and sometimes acts like an old maid. JAMES POLK, diary entry

Much earlier, in 1826, Buchanan had enunciated his views on slavery:

> I believe it to be a great political and a great moral evil. I thank God, my lot has been cast in a state where it does not exist. But while I entertain these opinions, I know it as an evil at present without remedy ... It is, however, one of those moral evils from which it is impossible to escape, without the introduction of evils infinitely greater. There are portions of this Union, in which, if you emancipate your slaves, they will become masters ... Is there a man in this Union who could for a moment indulge in the horrible idea of abolishing slavery by the massacre of the high-minded, and the chivalrous race of men in the South? I trust there is not one ... For my own part I would, without hesitation, buckle on my knapsack, and march ... in defense of their cause.
>
> SPEECH IN THE HOUSE OF REPRESENTATIVES, 1826

Buchanan was at a Washington ball when he was told that South Carolina had voted to secede (on December 20, 1860):

> Please, someone, won't someone call a carriage. I must go.

As one by one the Southern states fell away from the Union, Buchanan would tell people:

> I am the last president of the United States.
>
> Quoted in Horace Greeley, *Recollections of a Busy Life* (1868)

As the end of his presidency – and perhaps the Union itself – approached, Buchanan told Congress:

> I feel that my duty has been faithfully, though it may be imperfectly, performed, and, whatever the result may be, I shall carry to my grave the consciousness that I at least meant well for my country. SPEECH TO CONGRESS, January 8, 1861

On leaving the White House:

> If you are as happy, my dear sir, on entering this house as I am in leaving it and returning home, you are the happiest man in the country.
>
> REMARK TO HIS SUCCESSOR, ABRAHAM LINCOLN, March 4, 1861

Justifying his presidency shortly before his death:

> I have always felt and still feel that I discharged every public duty imposed upon me constitutionally. I have no regret for any public act of my life, and history will vindicate my memory. Quoted in Philip S. Klein, *President James Buchanan* (1962)

What others said

* * *

There is no such person running as James Buchanan. He is dead of lockjaw. Nothing remains but a platform and a bloated mass of political putridity.

> THADDEUS STEVENS, leader of the Radical Republicans, quoted in Fawn M. Brodie, *Thaddeus Stevens, Scourge of the South* (1959)

The Constitution provides for every accidental contingency in the executive, except for a vacancy in the mind of the president.

> JOHN SHERMAN, Republican member of the House of Representatives

ABRAHAM LINCOLN

1809–1865

16TH PRESIDENT OF THE UNITED STATES, 1861–5

ABRAHAM LINCOLN

FULL NAME: Abraham Lincoln
BORN: February 12, 1809, near Hodgenville, Kentucky
DIED: April 15, 1865, Washington DC
MARRIED: Mary Todd
CHILDREN: Robert Todd, Edward, Willie, Tad
PARTY: Republican
PERIOD IN OFFICE: March 4, 1861–April 15, 1865
VICE-PRESIDENT: Hannibal Hamlin (1861–5), Andrew Johnson (1865)

* * *

LINCOLN was born in a log cabin in the backwoods of Kentucky, the son of a modest farmer. When he was seven, the family moved to Indiana, where they set up a new farm on virgin land. Lincoln's mother died two years later, but his father remarried, and his second wife proved a loving stepmother. Young Lincoln had very little formal education, but (unlike his parents) he learnt to read and write. In 1830 the family moved again, to Illinois, but Lincoln had no desire to be a farmer, and tried a number of occupations, including storekeeper, postmaster, blacksmith and surveyor. In 1832 he volunteered for the militia in the Black Hawk War, and – always liked for his humor and his story-telling abilities – was elected captain of his unit. Two years later he entered politics as a Whig in the Illinois state legislature, where he served until 1842. During this time, he taught himself law, and was admitted to the bar in 1836, opening his own practise in Springfield, Illinois, the following year. Lincoln served in the US House of Representatives in 1847–9, but lost his seat over his criticisms of the Mexican War. His opposition to slavery, and in particular its spread to the new territories, prompted Lincoln to leave the Whigs for the Republicans in 1856.

Two years later Lincoln stood against the up-and-coming Democratic politician, Stephen A. Douglas, in the race to secure Illinois's seat in the US Senate, a contest marked by the nationally reported Lincoln–Douglas debates on slavery. In 1860 Lincoln again faced Douglas, this time in the presidential election, in which Lincoln emerged the winner. Although he believed that slavery, where it already existed in the United States, enjoyed protection under the Constitution, and although he asserted the moral and intellectual superiority of the white man, Lincoln was vehemently denounced in the Southern slave-holding states, which began to secede even before his inauguration. Lincoln's principal aim when the Civil War broke out was not to abolish slavery, but to preserve the Union, and he defended the Emancipation Proclamation of 1863 as a means to that end. Lincoln scored a narrow victory over his Democratic rival, General George McClellan, in the presidential election of 1864. With the defeat of the Confederacy, Lincoln intended a reconciliatory approach to the restoration of the Union. However, before he could put his intentions into action, he was shot by an actor, John Wilkes Booth, while attending a performance at Ford's Theatre, Washington DC.

On the Declaration of Independence:

> [It] gave liberty alone to the people of this country, but hope to all the world, for all future time ... I would rather be assassinated on the spot than surrender it.
>
> SPEECH, February 22, 1861

As a nation we began by declaring that 'all men are created equal.' We now practically read it 'all men are created equal except negroes.' When the [anti-immigration] Know-Nothings get control, it will read 'all men are created equal, except negroes, and foreigners, and Catholics.' When it comes to this I should prefer emigrating to some country where they make no pretense of loving liberty – to Russia, for instance, where despotism can be taken pure, and without the base alloy of hypocrisy. SPEECH, August 24, 1855

Asked how he felt when in 1858 he lost the Illinois senatorial race to Stephen A. Douglas:

I feel like the boy who stubbed his toe; I am too big to cry and too badly hurt to laugh.

On government and democracy:

No man is good enough to govern another man without that man's consent.
SPEECH at Peoria, Illinois, October 16, 1858

It is not our frowning battlements ... or the strength of our gallant and disciplined army. These are not our reliance against a resumption of tyranny ... Our defense is in the preservation of the spirit which prizes liberty as the heritage of all men, in all lands, everywhere. SPEECH, September 11, 1858

To give victory to the right, not bloody bullets, but peaceful ballots only, are necessary.
SPEECH, May 18, 1858. Popularly recorded as 'The ballot is stronger than the bullet.'

This country, with its institutions, belongs to the people who inhabit it. Whenever they shall grow weary of the existing government, they can exercise their constitutional right of amending it, or their revolutionary right to dismember or overthrow it.
FIRST INAUGURAL ADDRESS, March 4, 1861

On right and might:

Let us have faith that right makes might, and in that faith, let us, to the end, dare to do our duty as we understand it.
SPEECH, February 27, 1860

> ## ONE OF THE COMMON PEOPLE
> ***
> The President tonight has a dream:– He was in a party of plain people, and, as it became known who he was, they began to comment on his appearance. One of them said:– 'He is a very common-looking man.' The President replied:– 'The Lord prefers common-looking people. That is the reason he makes so many of them.'
> As reported by John Hay in his diary, December 23, 1863
>
> *On another occasion, during a discussion of ancestry, Lincoln is said to have declared:*
> I don't care who my grandfather was. I am much more concerned to know what his grandson will be.

On conservatism:

What is conservatism? Is it not adherence to the old and tried, against the new and untried?
SPEECH, February 27, 1860

On slavery:

'A house divided against itself cannot stand.' I believe this government cannot endure permanently, half slave and half free; I do not expect the Union to be dissolved; I do not expect the house to fall; but I do expect it will cease to be divided. It will become all one thing, or all the other.

SPEECH AT THE REPUBLICAN STATE CONVENTION, Springfield, Illinois, June 16, 1858. The opening quotation is from Mark 3:25: 'And if a house be divided against itself, that house cannot stand.'

Those who deny freedom to others, deserve it not for themselves.

LETTER TO H.L. PIERCE AND OTHERS, April 6, 1859

But Lincoln had in mind only very limited rights for African Americans – this at least was his public position prior to his election and the Civil War:

I am not, nor ever have been, in favor of bringing about in any way the social and political equality of the white and black races – I am not … in favor of making voters or jurors of Negroes, nor of qualifying them to hold office.

THE FIRST LINCOLN–DOUGLAS DEBATE, August 21, 1858

On becoming president, Lincoln sought to reassure the Southern states over the issue of slavery:

I have no purpose, directly or indirectly, to interfere with the institution of slavery in the States where it exists. I believe I have no lawful right to do so, and I have no inclination to do so. FIRST INAUGURAL ADDRESS, March 4, 1861

Lincoln ended his First Inaugural Address with an appeal to the Southern secessionists:

In your hands, my dissatisfied fellow-countrymen, and not in mine, is the momentous issue of civil war. The government will not assail you. You can have no conflict without being yourselves the aggressors … I am loath to close. We are not enemies, but friends. We must not be enemies. Though passion may have strained, it must not break our bonds of affection. The mystic chords of memory, stretching from every battlefield and patriot grave to every living heart and hearthstone, all over this broad land, will yet swell the chorus of the Union, when again touched, as surely they will be, by the better angels of our nature.

FIRST INAUGURAL ADDRESS, March 4, 1861

With war seemingly imminent, Lincoln penned a short letter to the governor of Pennsylvania:

I think the necessity of being ready increases. Look to it.

LETTER TO GOVERNOR ANDREW CURTIN, April 8, 1861

Saving the Union was always Lincoln's top priority as president, but once the war was well underway he was prepared – publicly if equivocally – to hold out the possibility of emancipation as a means of achieving this:

My paramount object in this struggle is to save the Union … If I could save the Union without freeing any slave, I would do it; and if I could save it by freeing all the slaves, I would do it; and if I could save it by freeing some and leaving others alone, I would also do that … I have here stated my purpose according to my views of official duty and I intend no modification of my oft-expressed personal wish that all men everywhere could be free.

LETTER TO HORACE GREELEY, editor of the *New York Tribune*, August 22, 1862

In giving freedom to the slave, we assure freedom to the free – honorable alike in what we give and what we preserve. We shall nobly save, or meanly lose, the last, best hope of earth.

ANNUAL MESSAGE TO CONGRESS, December 1, 1862

LINCOLN AND THE GENERALS

* * *

In the early years of the Civil War, Lincoln was impatient with the apparent lack of action on the part of his generals, notably George B. McClellan:

> If you don't want to use the army, I should like to borrow it for a while. Yours respectfully, A. Lincoln.
>
> UNSENT LETTER TO GENERAL GEORGE B. MCCLELLAN, who was relieved of his commands in 1862

For his part, in late 1861 McClellan wrote to his wife to complain about Lincoln:

> The president is nothing more than a well-meaning baboon ... I went to the White House directly after tea where I found 'the original Gorilla' about as intelligent as ever. What a specimen to be at the head of our affairs now!

When calls were made for the dismissal of the most effective Union commander, Ulysses S. Grant, Lincoln retorted:

> I can't spare this man. He fights.

In 1863 a number of Congressmen suggested that Grant's heavy drinking made him unsuitable to high command. Lincoln responded:

> Let me know what brand of whiskey Grant uses. For if it makes fighting generals like Grant, I should like to get some of it for distribution.
>
> Reported in the *New York Herald*, November 26, 1863. Lincoln denied he'd said any such thing, but said he enjoyed the story.

When running again for president in 1864, Lincoln was told by his friends that his only chance of being beaten was if General Grant took Richmond and then decided to run against him. To this, Lincoln replied:

> Well, I feel very much like the man who said he didn't want to die particularly, but if he had to die that was precisely the disease he would like to die of.

Lincoln was all too aware of the importance of delegation:

> I could as easily bail out the Potomac River with a teaspoon as attend to all the details of the army.
>
> Quoted in Allen Thorndike Rice, *Reminiscences of Abraham Lincoln* (1886)

However, his demand for detailed reports from his generals infuriated McClellan, who sent a message to the White House saying:

> We have just captured six cows. What shall we do with them?

To which Lincoln replied:

> Milk them.

Exactly a month later, on January 1, 1863, Lincoln issued the Emancipation Proclamation, freeing all slaves in the Confederate states. But, for fear of further secessions, the Proclamation did not apply to slaves in non-rebel Union territories where slavery was still legal.

I do order and declare that all persons held as slaves within said designated states, and parts of states, are, and henceforward shall be free; and that the executive government of the United States, including the military and naval authorities thereof, will recognize and maintain the freedom of said persons.

And I hereby enjoin upon the people so declared to be free to abstain from all violence, unless in necessary self-defense; and I recommend to them that, in all cases when allowed, they labor faithfully for reasonable wages.

And I further declare and make known, that such persons of suitable condition, will be received into the armed service of the United States to garrison forts, positions, stations, and other places, and to man vessels of all sorts in said service.

And upon this act, sincerely believed to be an act of justice, warranted by the Constitution, upon military necessity, I invoke the considerate judgment of mankind, and the gracious favor of Almighty God. EMANCIPATION PROCLAMATION, January 1, 1863

When Lincoln was introduced to Harriet Beecher Stowe, whose 1852 novel Uncle Tom's Cabin *had done so much to fire the abolitionist cause, he reputedly said to her:*

So you're the little woman who wrote the book that made this great war!
Quoted in Carl Sandburg, *Abraham Lincoln: The War Years* (1936)

The capture of Vicksburg in July 1863 meant that the entire Mississippi was now under Union control, leading Lincoln to comment:

The Father of Waters again goes unvexed to the sea.

Lincoln was realistic about the power that could be wielded by a single man in time of war:

I claim not to have controlled events, but confess plainly that events have controlled me.
LETTER TO A.G. HODGES, April 4, 1864

When asked how it felt to be president:

You have heard about the man tarred and feathered and ridden out of town on a rail? A man in the crowd asked how he liked it, and his reply was that if it wasn't for the honor of the thing, he would much rather walk. Quoted in Brant House, *Lincoln's Wit* (1958)

Yet he was sure he was the right man for the job:

It is best not to swap horses when crossing streams.
REPLY TO THE NATIONAL UNION LEAGUE, June 9, 1864

Lincoln was duly re-elected, and in his Second Inaugural Address he looked forward to the imminent conclusion of the Civil War:

Fondly do we hope, fervently do we pray, that this mighty scourge of war may speedily pass away ... With malice toward none, with charity for all, with firmness in the fight as God gives us to see the right, let us strive on to finish the work we are in, to bind up the nation's

The Gettysburg Address

***

Gettysburg – fought over three days in July 1863 – was the decisive battle of the Civil War, and Lincoln's short address at the dedication of the battlefield cemetery on November 19, 1863, has become the most famous speech in American history.

Four score and seven years ago our fathers brought forth on this continent, a new nation, conceived in liberty, and dedicated to the proposition that all men are created equal. Now we are engaged in a great civil war, testing whether that nation or any nation so conceived and so dedicated, can long endure. We are met on a great battlefield of that war. We have come to dedicate a portion of that field, as a final resting place for those who here gave their lives that that nation might live. It is altogether fitting and proper that we should do this. But, in a larger sense, we cannot dedicate, we cannot consecrate, we cannot hallow, this ground. The brave men, living and dead, who struggled here, have consecrated it, far above our poor power to add or detract. The world will little note, nor long remember what we say here, but it can never forget what they did here. It is for us the living, rather, to be dedicated here to the unfinished work which they who fought here have thus far so nobly advanced. It is rather for us to be here dedicated to the great task remaining before us – that from these honored dead we take increased devotion to that cause for which they gave the last full measure of devotion – that we here highly resolve that these dead shall not have died in vain – that this nation, under God, shall have a new birth of freedom – and that government of the people, by the people, for the people, shall not perish from the earth.

It has often been said that Lincoln jotted down these words – which he spoke from memory – on the back of an envelope on the train to Gettysburg. However, it is thought likely that there were in fact a number of drafts of the speech. Not all the phrasing is entirely original. In 1830 Daniel Webster had spoken of:

The people's government, made for the people, made by the people, and answerable to the people.

SECOND SPEECH IN THE US SENATE ON FOOTE'S RESOLUTION, *January 26, 1830*

Lincoln also possessed a copy of the Rev. Theodore Parker's anti-slavery orations, in which the president had marked the following words from an 1858 speech:

… democracy is direct self-government, over all the people, by all of the people, for all of the people.

At the time many newspapers either ignored the Gettysburg Address altogether, or disparaged it. For example, the Chicago Times *opined:*

An offensive exhibition of boorishness and vulgarity … We did not conceive it possible that even Mr Lincoln would produce a paper so slipshod, so loose-jointed, so puerile, not alone in its literary construction, but in its ideas, its sentiments, its grasp. He has outdone himself … The cheek of every American must tingle with shame as he reads the silly, flat and dishwatery utterances of the man who has to be pointed out to intelligent foreigners as the president of the United States.

wounds, to care for him who shall have borne the battle and for his widow and his orphan, to do all which may achieve and cherish a just and lasting peace among ourselves and with all nations. SECOND INAUGURAL ADDRESS, March 4, 1865

In victory, Lincoln was conciliatory:

They will never shoulder a musket in anger again. And if Grant is wise he will leave them their guns to shoot crows with, and their horses to plow with. It would do no harm.

April 5, 1865. Four days later the Confederate commander General Robert E. Lee surrendered to Grant at Appomattox Court House.

With victory achieved, the day before his assassination Lincoln declared:

Enough lives have been sacrificed. We must extinguish our resentments if we expect harmony and union.

ADDRESS TO HIS CABINET, April 14, 1865

On an earlier occasion he had said:

Die when I may, I want it said of me by those who know me best, that I have always plucked a thistle and planted a flower where I thought a flower would grow.

Various other often-quoted remarks have been attributed to Lincoln:

People who like this sort of thing will find this is the sort of thing they like.

Attributed in G.W.E. Russell, *Collections and Recollections* (1898)

To the South Carolina commissioners in 1865:

As president, I have no eyes but constitutional eyes; I cannot see you.

You may fool all the people some of the time; you can even fool some of the people all of the time; but you can't fool all the people all the time.

Attributed in Alexander K. McClure, *Lincoln's Yarns and Stories* (1904). Also attributed to the American showman Phineas T. Barnum (1810–91).

His definition of a hypocrite:

The man who murdered his parents, then pleaded for mercy on the grounds that he was an orphan. Attributed in Anthony Gross, ed., *Lincoln's Own Stories* (1912)

Some felt that the president was sometimes unduly frivolous, for example when he summoned a special cabinet meeting on September 21, 1862, and proceeded to read them a humorous story by Artemus Ward. They remained silent.

Gentlemen, why don't you laugh? With the fearful strain that is upon me night and day, if I did not laugh I should die, and you need this medicine as much as I do.

He then proceeded to read them a draft of the Emancipation Proclamation, saying first:

I have made a promise to myself – and to my Maker. I am now going to fulfil that promise.

What others said

* * *

He could make a cat laugh.

> BILL GREEN, a friend from Lincoln's younger years, quoted in Carl Sandburg, *Abraham Lincoln: The Prairie Years* (1926)

One advantage the Americans have is the possession of a president who is not only the first magistrate, but the chief joker in the land.

> *SATURDAY REVIEW* (London), quoted in Carl Sandburg, *Abraham Lincoln: The War Years* (1939)

Not all were so indulgent. Edwin Stanton, Lincoln's secretary of war, described the president as:

> A damned fool.

When told of this, Lincoln replied:

> If Stanton said I was a damned fool, then I must be one, for he is nearly always right and generally says what he means.

> God damn your god damn old hellfired god damned soul to hell god damn you and god damn your god damned family's god damned hellfired god damned soul to hell and good damnation god damn them and god damn your god damned friends to hell.

> PETER MUGGINS, a US citizen, in a letter to the president

Mr Lincoln is like a waiter in a large eating house where all the bells are ringing at once; he cannot serve them all at once and so some grumblers are to be expected.

> JOHN BRIGHT, the British radical politician, in the *Cincinnati Gazette*, 1864

PRESS NOTICES

* * *

The newspapers were not universally kind to Lincoln during his presidency. Here are just a few judgments:

> The small intellect ... growing smaller ... a fourth-rate lecturer who cannot speak good grammar and who ... delivers hackneyed, illiterate compositions.
>
> *NEW YORK HERALD*

> A horrid wretch he is, sooty and scoundrelly in aspect, a cross between a nutmeg dealer, the horse swapper, the night man, a creature fit evidently for petty treason, small stratagems and all sorts of spoils. *CHARLESTON MERCURY*

> Lincoln is the leanest, lankest, most ungainly mass of legs and arms and hatchet face ever strung on a single frame. He has most unwarrantably abused the privilege, which all politicians have, of being ugly.
>
> *HOUSTON TELEGRAPH*

> The craftiest and most dishonest politician that ever disgraced an office in America. *ILLINOIS STATE REGISTER*

> His soul seems made of leather, and incapable of any grand or noble emotion. Compared with the mass of men, he is a line of flat prose in a beautiful and spirited lyric. He lowers, he never elevates you ... Even wisdom from him seems but folly.
>
> *NEW YORK POST*

This man's appearance, his pedigree, his coarse low jokes and anecdotes, his vulgar similes and his frivolity, are a disgrace to the seat he holds.

> JOHN WILKES BOOTH, Lincoln's assassin, quoted in Lord Longford, *Abraham Lincoln* (1974)

After the deed, Booth declared:

> Our country owes all our troubles to him, and God simply made me an instrument of his punishment.

After Lincoln's assassination:

> Now he belongs to the ages ... There lies the most perfect ruler of men the world has ever seen. EDWIN STANTON, Lincoln's secretary of war, remark, April 15, 1863

> My heart burned within me with indignation and grief; we could think of nothing else. All night long we had but little sleep, waking up perpetually to the sense of a great shock and grief. Everyone is feeling the same. I never knew such a universal feeling.
> ELIZABETH GASKELL, the English novelist, letter to C.E. Norton, April 28, 1865

> The catastrophe of Lincoln, though it was a great shock, does not cloud the prospect. How could one have wished him a happier death? He died almost unconsciously in the fullness of success, and martyrdom in so great a cause consecrates his name through all history. Such a death is the crown of a noble life.
> JOHN STUART MILL, letter to Max Kyllman, May 30, 1865

Lincoln's death prompted one of the greatest elegies in American poetry:

> When lilacs last in the dooryard bloomed,
> And the great star early dropped in the western sky in the night,
> I mourned, and yet shall mourn with ever-returning spring.
> WALT WHITMAN, 'When Lilacs Last in the Dooryard Bloomed' (1865), published in *Sequel to Drum-Taps* (1866)

> Lincoln was not a type. He stands alone – no ancestors, no fellows, no successors.
> ROBERT G. INGERSOLL, *Reminiscences of Abraham Lincoln* (1886)

> The color of the ground was in him, the red earth,
> The smack and tang of elemental things.
> EDWIN MARKHAM, 'Lincoln, the Man of the People' (1901)

PRESIDENTIAL OPINIONS:
THE 23RD AND 44TH ON THE 16TH
★ ★ ★

Lincoln had faith in time, and time has justified his faith.
BENJAMIN HARRISON, Lincoln Day Address, 1898

I cannot swallow whole the view of Lincoln as the Great Emancipator.
BARACK OBAMA, 'Uncovering the Real Abe Lincoln: What I See in Lincoln's Eyes', in *Time*, June 26, 2005

ANDREW JOHNSON

1808–1875

17TH PRESIDENT OF THE UNITED STATES, 1865–9

ANDREW JOHNSON

FULL NAME: Andrew Johnson
BORN: December 29, 1808, Raleigh, North Carolina
DIED: July 31, 1875, near Carter Station, Tennessee
MARRIED: Eliza McCardle
CHILDREN: Martha, Charles, Mary, Robert, Andrew Jr
PARTY: Democratic
PERIOD IN OFFICE: April 15, 1865–March 4, 1869
VICE-PRESIDENT: none

* * *

JOHNSON WAS RAISED IN POVERTY. His father, a porter in an inn, died when Johnson was three. At the age of 14 Johnson was apprenticed to a tailor, and in 1826 moved to Greeneville, Tennessee, where he set up his own tailoring shop. He never attended school, but taught himself to read and write, acquiring a knowledge of history, oratory and the US Constitution. He formed a workingman's party, and by the age of 24 was mayor of Greeneville. In 1835, as a Jacksonian Democrat, he was elected for a term in the Tennessee House of Representatives, and went on to serve in the state Senate (1839–43), in the US House of Representatives (1843–53), as governor of Tennessee (1853–7), and in the US Senate (1857–62). Although owning a few slaves himself, Johnson had no sympathies for the wealthy planters of the South, and was the only senator from a seceded state to support the Union and continue to sit in Congress. In 1862 Lincoln appointed Johnson as military governor of Tennessee, and his vigor in combating the Confederates there, together with his status as a pro-Union Southern Democrat, prompted Lincoln to select him as his running-mate on the National Union ticket in the 1864 presidential election.

Within a few weeks of being inaugurated Lincoln was assassinated, and Johnson succeeded to the presidency. In office Johnson continued Lincoln's policy of conciliation, offering the seceded states rapid readmission to the Union. His refusal to secure the civil rights of freed slaves and his reluctance to implement Reconstruction alienated the Republicans in Congress and led to Johnson's impeachment on charges of breaching the Tenure of Office Act. When it came to the vote in the Senate in May 1868, Johnson avoided conviction by only one vote short of the necessary two-thirds majority. Although acquitted, Johnson sat out the remainder of his presidency as a lame duck. Out of office, he ran twice for Congress before finally being elected a US senator again in 1875, shortly before his death.

Johnson, a tailor, was a proud member of the artisanal class:

> Adam, the father of the race, was a tailor by trade, for he sewed fig-leaves together for aprons. Tubal Cain was an artificer of brass and iron; Joseph, the husband of Mary, the mother of Jesus, was a carpenter by trade, and the probability is strong that our Savior himself followed the same.
>
> SPEECH TO A MEETING OF MECHANICS in his hometown of Greeneville, Tennessee, May 1843

> I am a mechanic, and when a blow is struck on that class I will resent it. I know we have an illegitimate, swaggering, bastard, scrub aristocracy which assumes to know a great deal,

but which, when the flowing veil of pretension is torn off, is seen to possess neither talents nor information on which one can rear a useful superstructure.

SPEECH IN CONGRESS, quoted in Robert R. Winston, *Andrew Johnson: Plebeian and Patriot* (1928).

On Jefferson Davis, after he had become president of the Confederacy:

I cannot understand how he can be willing to hail another banner, and turn from that of his country ... If I could not unsheathe my sword in vindication of the flag of my country, its glorious stars and stripes, I would return the sword to its scabbard; I would never sheathe it in the bosom of my mother; never! never! never!

SENATE SPEECH, quoted in Jon L. Wakelyn, *Southern Pamphlets on Secession, November 1860–April 1861* (1996)

Of Southern secession:

Hell-born and hell-bound.

Quoted in Lloyd Paul Stryker, *Andrew Johnson: A Study in Courage* (1936)

It was the preservation of the Union, not the emancipation of the slaves, that motivated Johnson during the Civil War:

Damn the negroes, I am fighting those traitorous aristocrats, their masters.

Quoted in Clifton Hall, *Andrew Johnson, Military Governor of Tennessee* (1916)

On the prospects of racial harmony:

We must ... avoid hasty assumptions of any natural impossibility for the two races to live side by side in a state of mutual benefit and good will.

ANNUAL MESSAGE TO CONGRESS, December 4, 1865

On the recently freed slaves:

The career of free industry must be fairly opened to them, and then their future prosperity and condition must, after all, rest mainly on themselves . If they fail, and so perish away, let us be careful that the failure shall not be attributable to any denial of justice.

ANNUAL MESSAGE TO CONGRESS, December 4, 1865

I AM A PLEBIAN!

* * *

Johnson was widely thought to be intoxicated during his first address as vice-president, on March 5, 1865:

I am a-goin' for to tell you here today; yes, I'm a-goin for to tell you all, that I'm a plebian! I glory in it; I am a plebian! The people – yes, the people of the United States have made me what I am; and I am a-goin' for to tell you here today – yes, today, in this place – that the people are everything.

Subsequently, Senator Zachariah T. Chandler wrote to his wife:

The inauguration went off very well except that the Vice-President Elect was too drunk to perform his duties and disgraced himself and the Senate by making a drunken foolish speech. I was never so mortified in my life, had I been able to find a hole I would have dropped through it out of sight.

For his part, Lincoln remarked:

I have known Andy for many years ... he made a bad slip the other day, but you need not be scared. Andy ain't a drunkard.

However, Johnson proved unwilling to safeguard the civil rights of freedmen:

This is a country for white men, and by God, as long as I am president, it shall be a government for white men. Remark to Thomas C. Fletcher, governor of Missouri, 1866

On succeeding to the presidency, Johnson had given hope to the Radical Republicans that he would deal harshly with the defeated South:

Robbery is a crime; rape is a crime; murder is a crime; *treason* is a *crime* and *crime* must be punished. The law provides for it and the courts are open. Treason must be made infamous and traitors must be impoverished.

Reply to Senator Ben Wade of Ohio, quoted in George W. Julian, *Recollections, 1840 to 1872* (1884)

On hearing that he was to be impeached, in February 1868:

Impeach me for violating the Constitution! Damn them! Haven't I been struggling ever since I have been in this chair to uphold the Constitution they trample under foot!

Quoted in Lately Thomas, *The First President Johnson* (1968)

PRESIDENTIAL OPINIONS:
THE 16TH AND 18TH ON THE 17TH

* * *

This Johnson is a queer man.

Abraham Lincoln, remark to Shelby M. Cullom, after Johnson had inquired whether his presence was necessary at the 1865 inauguration

He is such an infernal liar.

Ulysses S. Grant

What others said

* * *

The age of statesmen is gone; the age of rail-splitters and tailors, of buffoons, boors and fanatics has succeeded ... In a crisis of the most appalling magnitude requiring statesmanship of the highest order, the country is asked to consider the claims of two ignorant, boorish, third-rate backwoods lawyers for the highest stations in the government. Such nominations, in such a conjuncture, are an insult to the common sense of the people. God save the Republic!

The *New York World*, June 1864, on Johnson's selection as Lincoln's running-mate in that year's presidential election

On this inauguration day ... I was standing in the crowd by the side of Mrs Thomas J. Dorsey, when Mr Lincoln touched Mr Johnson, and pointed me out to him. The first expression which came to his face, and which I think was the true index of his heart, was one of bitter contempt and aversion. Seeing that I observed him, he tried to assume a more friendly appearance; but it was too late; it was useless to close the door when all within had been seen. His first glance was the frown of the man, the second was the bland and sickly smile of the demagogue. I turned to Mrs Dorsey and said, 'Whatever Andrew Johnson may be, he certainly is no friend of our race.'

Frederick Douglass, *The Life and Times of Frederick Douglass* (1881)

Ulysses S. Grant

1822–1885

18TH PRESIDENT OF THE UNITED STATES, 1869–77

Ulysses S. Grant

FULL NAME: Ulysses Simpson Grant (born Hiram Ulysses Grant)
BORN: April 27, 1822, Point Pleasant, Ohio
DIED: July 23, 1885, Mount McGregor, New York
MARRIED: Julia Boggs Dent
CHILDREN: Jesse, Ulysses Jr, Nellie, Frederick
PARTY: Republican
PERIOD IN OFFICE: March 4, 1869–March 4, 1877
VICE-PRESIDENT: Schuyler Colfax (1869–73), Henry Wilson (1873–5)
There was no vice-president in the period 1875–7.

* * *

GRANT'S FATHER WAS A TANNER, who put his son's name down for West Point without consulting the boy. Grant was reluctant to go, and did not enjoy the experience. Commissioned into the army, he demonstrated considerable gallantry in the Mexican War, even though he came to regard that conflict as unjustified. He resigned his commission in 1854 to be with his wife and children in St Louis, where he tried his hand as a farmer, debt collector, firewood salesman and clerk. With the outbreak of the Civil War he raised a volunteer infantry regiment, and in August 1861 was promoted to brigadier general. He first came to national attention with his capture of Fort Henry and Fort Donnelson in February 1862, and success the following year in the siege of Vicksburg secured his reputation. On March 9, 1864 he was appointed commander-in-chief of all the Union armies, and went on to pursue a single-minded war of attrition on all the resources of the South, leading to ultimate victory. In 1868 Grant was an obvious choice to run as the Republican candidate, and won that year's presidential election, and was re-elected in 1872. Grant's presidency was marred by a number of scandals, although he was not personally involved in any of them. In the era of Reconstruction, he sought reconciliation with the South at the same time as suppressing the Ku Klux Klan and supporting civil rights for freed slaves – although he achieved little in this latter respect. After leaving office, he spent his last years writing his best-selling memoirs, which recouped some of the losses he had incurred in an ill-judged investment.

Grant first saw action in the Mexican War, which he later described as:

> One of the most unjust wars ever waged by a stronger against a weaker nation.
>
> PERSONAL MEMOIRS OF ULYSSES S. GRANT (1885–6)

He went on to make a connection between that war and the US Civil War:

> The Southern rebellion was largely the outgrowth of the Mexican War. Nations, like individuals, are punished for their transgressions. We got our punishment in the most sanguinary and expensive war of modern times.
>
> PERSONAL MEMOIRS OF ULYSSES S. GRANT (1885–6)

Grant summed up his military philosophy thus:

> The art of war is simple enough. Find out where your enemy is. Get at him as soon as you can. Strike him as hard as you can, as often as you can, and keep moving on.
>
> REMARK TO JOHN HILL BRINTON, early in 1862, at the start of the Tennessee River campaign, quoted in *Personal Memoirs of John H. Brinton, Major and Surgeon USV, 1861–1865* (1914)

I don't underrate the value of military knowledge, but if men make war in slavish obedience to rules, they will fail.

Quoted in Alfred Vagts, A History of Militarism: Romance and Realities of a Profession (1937)

While besieging Fort Donelson, Tennessee, Grant issued a famous ultimatum:

No terms except unconditional and immediate surrender can be accepted. I propose to move immediately upon your works.

MESSAGE TO SIMON BOLIVAR BUCKNER, the Confederate commander, February 16, 1862

Two years later he was displaying the same determination:

I purpose to fight it out on this line, if it takes all summer.

DISPATCH TO WASHINGTON, May 11, 1864

He was clear what, and whom, he was fighting for:

God gave us Lincoln and Liberty, let us fight for both.

TOAST AT THE BEGINNING OF THE VICKSBURG CAMPAIGN, February 22, 1863

Ordering the Army of the Shenandoah to lay waste the Shenandoah Valley:

Eat out Virginia clear and clean, so far as they go crows flying over it will have to carry their provender with them. ORDER TO GENERAL HENRY W. HALLECK, August 1864

When Confederate commander Robert E. Lee eventually surrendered at Appomattox, Grant forbade his men to cheer:

The war is over – the rebels are our countrymen again. April 9, 1865

PRESIDENTIAL OPINIONS: THE 16TH ON THE 18TH
★ ★ ★

For more of Lincoln on Grant, see 'Lincoln and the Generals', p. 75.

If Grant only does this thing right down there – I don't care how, so long as he does it *right* – why, Grant is my man and I am his the rest of the war!

ABRAHAM LINCOLN, remark on the Vicksburg campaign, July 5, 1863. In fact, Grant had taken Vicksburg the day before.

When Grant once gets possession of a place, he holds on to it as if he had inherited it.

ABRAHAM LINCOLN, letter, June 22, 1864

Late in life Grant reflected upon the cost of rebellion:

The right of revolution is an inherent one. When people are oppressed by their government, it is a natural right they enjoy to relieve themselves of the oppression, if they are strong enough, either by withdrawal from it, or by overthrowing it and substituting a government more acceptable. But any people or part of a people who resort to this remedy, stake their lives, their property, and every claim for protection given by citizenship – on the issue. Victory, or the conditions imposed by the conqueror – must be the result.

PERSONAL MEMOIRS OF ULYSSES S. GRANT (1885–6)

After the war, Grant somewhat disingenuously claimed:

I am more of a farmer than a soldier. I take little or no interest in military affairs.

> REMARK TO THE PRUSSIAN CHANCELLOR, Count Otto von Bismarck, at a military review in his honor at Potsdam, quoted in J.T. Headley, *The Life and Travels of General Grant* (1880)

To the 2nd Duke of Wellington, son of the victor of Waterloo:

My lord, I have heard that your father was a military man. Was that the case?

> Quoted in William Shepard Walsh, *Handy-book of Literary Curiosities* (1892)

Grant had a notoriously tin ear for music:

I know only two tunes. One of them is 'Yankee Doodle' and the other isn't.

> ATTRIBUTED

Accepting the Republican nomination to run for president:

Let us have peace.

> LETTER TO GENERAL JOSEPH R. HAWKEY, May 29, 1868. The words are inscribed on Grant's mausoleum in Manhattan.

On becoming president, he famously stated:

I know of no method to secure the repeal of bad or obnoxious laws so effective as their stringent execution. FIRST INAUGURAL ADDRESS, March 4, 1869

Departing from the conventional pieties spouted by many another president, Grant did not regard the Constitution as drafted by the Founding Fathers as perfect and immutable:

It is preposterous to suppose that the people of one generation can lay down the best and only rules of government for all who are to come after them, and under unforeseen contingencies. PERSONAL MEMOIRS OF ULYSSES S. GRANT (1885–6)

On the Whiskey Ring tax scandal, in which his personal secretary, Orville Babcock, was involved:

Let no guilty man escape, if it can be avoided ... No personal considerations should stand in the way of performing a public duty.

> ENDORSEMENT OF A LETTER received July 29, 1875. In fact, Grant's intervention ensured that Babcock was not among those convicted.

In the end, Grant conceded that his presidency had not been the greatest of successes:

Failures have been errors of judgment, not of intent.

> ANNUAL MESSAGE TO CONGRESS, December 5, 1876

I never wanted to get out of a place as much as I did to get out of the presidency.

> Quoted in John Russell Young, *Around the World with General Grant*, Vol. 2 (1879)

RUTHERFORD B. HAYES

1822–1893

19TH PRESIDENT OF THE UNITED STATES, 1877–81

RUTHERFORD B. HAYES

FULL NAME: Rutherford Birchard Hayes
BORN: October 4, 1822, Delaware, Ohio
DIED: January 17, 1893, Fremont, Ohio
MARRIED: Lucy Ware Webb
CHILDREN: Birchard Austin, James Webb Cook, Rutherford Platt,
Joseph Thompson, George Crook, Fanny, Scott Russell, Manning Force
PARTY: Republican
PERIOD IN OFFICE: March 4, 1877–March 4, 1881
VICE-PRESIDENT: William A. Wheeler

* * *

HAYES'S FATHER, a farmer, died before he was born, but his mother's brother, Sardis Birchard, helped to raise him. Hayes came top of his class at Kenyon College, Ohio, in 1842, studied law at Harvard, and was admitted to the bar in 1845. He went on to set up a successful legal practise in Cincinnati, and defended a number of fugitive slaves. He started his political life as a Whig, then, opposing the expansion of slavery following the Compromise of 1850, joined the Free Soil Party, and then the Republicans. Hayes fought with distinction during the Civil War, was wounded several times, and ended up a general. He served in the US House of Representatives (1865–7), and as governor of Ohio (1868–72, 1876–7), before emerging as a dark-horse candidate at the 1876 Republican convention. There followed one of the most controversial elections in US history, in which the Democrat Samuel J. Tilden secured the popular vote, but suggestions of voting irregularities left Tilden one vote short in the Electoral College. Congress set up an electoral commission to adjudicate, which voted along party lines, just coming out in favor of Hayes. The Southern Democrats only agreed to accept the outcome in return for a promise from Hayes to end Reconstruction. Hayes, a man of considerable moral rectitude, managed to recover his reputation during his presidency, which marked a contrast to the scandals that dogged the previous administration of Ulysses S. Grant. Hayes moved to reform the civil service, which was rotten with political patronage (the so-called 'spoils system'), earning the enmity of corrupt Republican party bosses, the so-called Stalwarts, who were also antagonized by Hayes's conciliatory policies towards the South and his lack of sympathy for big business. Hayes had pledged not to stand for a second term, and in his retirement devoted himself to good causes.

As a young man, Hayes determined to succeed on his own merits:

> For honest merit to succeed amid the tricks and intrigues which are now so lamentably common, I know is difficult; but the honor of success is increased by the obstacles which are to be surmounted. Let me triumph as a man or not at all. DIARY, November 7, 1841

Hayes believed in minimal government:

> Is there anything in which the people of this age and country differ more from those of other lands and former times than in this – their ability to preserve order and protect rights without the aid of government? … We are realizing the paradox, 'that country is governed best which is governed least.' DIARY, July 23, 1851

On the imminence of civil war:

Disunion and civil war are at hand; and yet I fear disunion and war less than compromise. We can recover from them. The free states alone, if we must go on alone, will make a glorious nation. Diary, January 4, 1861

On slavery and the Union:

The man who thinks that the perpetuity of slavery is essential to the existence of the Union is unfit to be trusted. The deadliest enemy the Union has is slavery – in fact, its only enemy.
Diary, June 5, 1862, reflecting on those Union generals ('semi-traitors') who did not condemn slavery

On war:

War is a cruel business and there is brutality in it on all sides.
Letter to his wife, July 2, 1864, rejecting her use of the phrase 'brutal Rebels'. Her brother had just died, a prisoner of the Confederates in the notorious Andersonville Prison.

Wars will remain while human nature remains. I believe in my soul in cooperation, in arbitration; but the soldier's occupation we cannot say is gone until human nature is gone.
Diary, August 11, 1890

On his personal style:

I have a talent for silence and brevity. I can keep silent when it seems best to do so, and when I speak I can, and do usually, quit when I am done. Diary, November 20, 1872

As president, he declared a higher loyalty than to party:

The president of the United States of necessity owes his election to office to the suffrage and zealous labors of a political party, the members of which cherish with ardor and regard as of essential importance the principles of their party organization; but he should strive to be always mindful of the fact that he serves his party best who serves the country best.
Inaugural Address, March 5, 1877

HAYES THE SOLDIER

* * *

In 1864, General Hayes was persuaded to stand for Congress, but refused to campaign in person:

Any man who would leave the army at this time to electioneer for Congress ought to be scalped.

Quoted in Russell H. Conwell, *Life and Services of Gov. Rutherford B. Hayes* (1876)

Once elected, he refused to take his seat until the Southern capital was retaken by the Union:

I shall never come to Washington until I can come by way of Richmond.

Quoted in Russell H. Conwell, *Life and Services of Gov. Rutherford B. Hayes* (1876)

Of the Native Americans:

Many, if not most, of our Indian wars have had their origin in broken promises and acts of injustice upon our part. Annual Message to Congress, December 3, 1877

On the spoils system:

All appointments hurt. Five friends are made cold or hostile for every appointment; no new friends are made. All patronage is perilous to men of real ability or merit. It aids only those who lack other claims to public support.
Letter to William McKinley, December 27, 1892

Even after little more than two years in the White House, Hayes had had quite enough:

I am heartily tired of this life of bondage, responsibility and toil. I wish it was at an end … It is one of our greatest comforts that the pledge not to take a second term relieves us from considering it. DIARY, June 6, 1879

However, he felt he left office with his reputation restored:

Coming in, I was denounced as a fraud by all the extreme men of the opposing party, and as an ingrate and a traitor by the same class of men in my own party. Going out, I have the good will, blessings and approval of the best people of all parties and sections.

DIARY, January 23, 1881

Towards the end of his life, Hayes regretted that he had been quite so upstanding:

In avoiding the appearance of evil, I am not sure but I have sometimes unnecessarily deprived myself and others of innocent enjoyments.

Quoted in Harry Barnard, *Rutherford B. Hayes and his America* (1954)

On the telephone:

That's an amazing invention, but who would ever want to use one of them?

REMARK TO ALEXANDER GRAHAM BELL, 1876. Hayes later had a telephone installed, and the first call he made was to Bell. He went on to hail the telephone as 'the greatest invention since creation.'

What others said

* * *

It may be asked whether this man of destiny had any marked peculiarities. I answer none whatever. Neither his body nor his mind runs into rickety proportions.

UNNAMED FRIEND, quoted in H.J. Eckenrode, *Rutherford B. Hayes: Statesman of Reunion* (1930)

A third rate nonentity, whose only recommendation is that he is obnoxious to no one.

HENRY C. ADAMS, quoted in Brooks D. Simpson, *The Political Education of Henry Adams* (1996)

No liquor was served in the Hayes White House, leading Secretary of State William M. Evarts to recall, after yet another dry official dinner:

It was a brilliant affair; the water flowed like champagne.

James A. Garfield

1831–1881

20th President of the United States, 1881

JAMES A. GARFIELD

FULL NAME: James Abram Garfield
BORN: November 19, 1831, Moreland Hills (then part of Orange Township), Ohio
DIED: September 19, 1881, Elberon (now in Long Branch), New Jersey
MARRIED: Lucretia Rudolph
CHILDREN: Eliza Arabella, Harold (Harry) Augustus, James Rudolph,
Mary, Irvin McDowell, Abram, Edward
PARTY: Republican
PERIOD IN OFFICE: March 4, 1881–September 19, 1881
VICE-PRESIDENT: Chester A. Arthur

* * *

GARFIELD, the last president to be born in a log cabin, was the son of a poor Ohio farmer who died when Garfield was less than two years old. As a youth Garfield found employment as a canal boatman, and studied at Western Reserve Eclectic Institute, Hiram, Ohio, and Williams College, Massachusetts, graduating in 1856. He then returned as a teacher to the Eclectic Institute. He was ordained as a minister, and taught himself law, being admitted to the bar in 1860. He opposed the extension of slavery, joined the Republican Party, and in 1859 was elected to the Ohio legislature. In the Civil War he helped to form a volunteer regiment and became its colonel, fighting with distinction at Shiloh and Chickamauga. In December 1863, by now a major general, he resigned his commission to take up a seat in the US House of Representatives. He continued to sit in the House until 1880. He became a dark-horse candidate at that year's Republican convention, opposing the corrupt, conservative 'Stalwarts' who supported the candidacy of Ulysses S. Grant (although Garfield himself had been touched by one of the scandals that had rocked Grant's administration). Garfield won the nomination, and the following election. In office, he struggled to come to grips with the 'spoils system' of political patronage, and on July 2, 1881, just four months after his inauguration, he was shot by a disappointed, half-crazed office-seeker, Charles J. Guiteau, and died two months later.

On himself:

I am a poor hater. DIARY, April 26, 1876

I love to deal with doctrines and events. The contests of men about men I greatly dislike.
DIARY, March 14, 1881

On the assassination of Abraham Lincoln:

Fellow citizens: God reigns, and the government at Washington lives!
ADDRESSING A CROWD IN NEW YORK, April 16, 1865, the day after the assassination. In fact, this
'speech' appears to have been retrospectively credited to Garfield by his campaign managers.

Garfield was a supporter of 'hard money':

I am an advocate of paper money, but that paper money must represent what it professes to represent on its face. I do not wish to hold in my hands the printed lies of government.
SPEECH TO CONGRESS, 1866

He did not believe in 'big government':

> The chief duty of government is to keep the peace and stand out of the sunshine of the people. LETTER TO H.N. ELDRIDGE, December 14, 1869

On slavery:

> The sin of slavery is one of which it may be said that without the shedding of blood there is no remission. DIARY, June 8, 1881

> Then, after the storms of battle, were heard the calm words of peace spoken by the conquering nation, saying to the foe that lay prostrate at its feet: 'This is our only revenge – that you join us in lifting into the serene firmament of the Constitution, to shine like stars for ever and ever, the immortal principles of truth and justice: that all men, white or black, shall be free, and shall stand equal before the law.'
>
> SPEECH AT THE REPUBLICAN CONVENTION, June 5, 1880, nominating John Sherman. However, his oratory inspired many to vote for Garfield himself.

One of his finest passages comes from the same speech:

> I have seen the sea lashed into fury and tossed into spray, and its grandeur moves the soul of the dullest man; but I remember that it is not the billows, but the calm level of the sea, from which all heights and depths are measured.

On radicalism:

> I am trying to do two things: dare to be a radical and not a fool, which is a matter of no small difficulty. ATTRIBUTED

On the presidency:

> My God! What is there in this place that a man should ever want to get into it?
>
> DIARY, June 8, 1881

His last written words:

> *Strangulatus pro republica* [Tortured for the Republic]. September 17, 1881

His last spoken words:

> My work is done.
>
> REMARK TO COLONEL ROCKWELL, his personal secretary, September 18, 1881, the day before his death

---

PRESIDENTIAL OPINIONS:
THE 18TH AND THE 19TH ON THE 20TH

* * *

No man ever started so low that accomplished so much, in all our history.
RUTHERFORD B. HAYES

Garfield has shown that he is not possessed of the backbone of an angle-worm.
ULYSSES S. GRANT

CHESTER A. ARTHUR

1829–1886

21ST PRESIDENT OF THE UNITED STATES, 1881–5

CHESTER A. ARTHUR

FULL NAME: Chester Alan Arthur
BORN: October 5, 1829, North Fairfield, Vermont
DIED: November 18, 1886, New York, New York
MARRIED: Ellen ('Nell') Lewis Herndon
CHILDREN: William Lewis Herndon, Chester Alan II,
Ellen Hansbrough Herndon
PARTY: Republican
PERIOD IN OFFICE: September 19, 1881–March 4, 1885
VICE-PRESIDENT: none

* * *

RAISED IN VERMONT, Arthur was the son of an Irish-born preacher of Scottish descent. He graduated from Union College, Schenectady, New York, in 1848, went on to study law, and was admitted to the bar in 1854. Practicing in New York, he became involved in various cases relating to the rights of both slaves and free African Americans. His abolitionist beliefs led him to join the Republican Party in the 1850s, and he served as a quartermaster general during the Civil War, after which he emerged as a powerful party-machine operator in New York. With the backing of Senator Roscoe Conkling, 'Stalwart' Republican boss in New York and prime manipulator of the 'spoils system' of political patronage, he was appointed customs collector for the port of New York under President Grant, and in this role gave jobs to many Conkling supporters – earning a reputation as 'the spoilsman's spoilsman.' Wishing to reform the civil service and reduce Conkling's influence, President Hayes suspended Arthur in 1878, even though Arthur had been influential in Hayes's election. At the 1880 Republican convention Arthur was selected as James Garfield's running-mate to placate Conkling and the other Stalwarts, and when Arthur duly became vice-president, it was the first elected office he ever held. Succeeding to the presidency after Garfield's death after only a few months in office, Arthur disappointed his Stalwart supporters by coming out in favor of civil service reform. Arthur also began the build-up of the US navy into a world-class fleet, and ended his presidency held in much higher public esteem than he had begun it. The alienated Stalwarts blocked his re-adoption as the Republican candidate for the presidency in 1884, and Arthur, now in poor health, retired from public life, dying in November 1886.

On the death of President Garfield:

Men may die, but the fabric of our free institutions remains unshaken.
STATEMENT, September 19, 1881

On competitive examinations for civil-service applicants:

There are very many characteristics which go to make a model civil servant. Prominent among them are probity, industry, good sense, good habits, good temper, patience, order, courtesy, tact, self-reliance, manly deference to superior officers, and manly consideration for inferiors. The absence of these traits is not supplied by wide knowledge of books, or by promptitude in answering questions, or by any other quality likely to be brought to light by competitive examination. To make success in such a contest, therefore, an indispensable condition of public employment would very likely result in the practical exclusion of the older applicants, even though they might possess qualifications far superior to their younger and more brilliant competitors.

> ANNUAL MESSAGE TO CONGRESS, December 6, 1881. Just over a year later, however, he signed the Pendleton Act, which introduced such examinations.

To a temperance campaigner:

Madam, I may be president of the United States, but my private life is nobody's damn business. Quoted in Thomas C. Reeves, *Gentleman Boss: The Life of Chester A. Arthur* (1975)

On refusing a favor to a New York Republican:

Since I came here I have learned that Chester A. Arthur is one man and the president of the United States is another. Quoted in James Morgan, *Our Presidents* (1958)

Asked his plans on leaving office:

Well, there doesn't seem anything else for an ex-president to do but to go to the country and raise big pumpkins.

> Quoted in the *New York Herald*, November 19, 1886, the day after Arthur's death. In fact, Arthur retired to New York City.

What others said
★ ★ ★

First in ability on the list of second-rate men. THE *NEW YORK TIMES*, February 20, 1872

Chet Arthur president of the United States? Good God!

> UNNAMED REPUBLICAN POLITICIAN, quoted in David C. Whitney, *The American Presidents* (1967)

In contrast to the austere tenure of President Hayes, when temperance ruled in the White House, President Arthur was a lavish entertainer, leading one Washington socialite to proclaim:

It is not that he is handsome and agreeable – for he was both long ago, but it is his ease, polish and perfect manner that make him the greatest society lion we have had in many years. Quoted in Thomas C. Reeves, *Gentleman Boss: The Life of Chester A. Arthur* (1975)

By the end of his tenure, Arthur had earned the respect of many:

I am but one in 55,000,000; still, in the opinion of this one-fifty-five millionth of the country's population, it would be hard to better President Arthur's administration.

> MARK TWAIN, quoted in George Frederick Howe, *Chester A. Arthur: A Quarter Century of Machine Politics* (1934)

PRESIDENTIAL OPINIONS: THE 28TH ON THE 21ST
★ ★ ★

A nonentity with side whiskers.
WOODROW WILSON

GROVER CLEVELAND

1837–1908

22ND AND 24TH PRESIDENT OF THE UNITED STATES
1885–9, 1893–7

GROVER CLEVELAND

FULL NAME: Stephen Grover Cleveland
BORN: March 18, 1837, Caldwell, New Jersey
DIED: June 24, 1908, Princeton, New Jersey
MARRIED: Frances Clara Folsom
CHILDREN: Ruth, Esther, Marion, Richard Folsom, Francis Grover
PARTY: Democratic
PERIOD IN OFFICE: March 4, 1885–March 4, 1889; March 4, 1893–March 4, 1897
VICE-PRESIDENT: Thomas A. Hendricks (1885), Adlai E. Stevenson (1893–7)
There was no vice-president from 1885 to 1889.

* * *

CLEVELAND WAS THE SON of a Presbyterian minister, and spent much of his childhood in various localities in New York state. He abandoned his schooling on his father's death in 1853 and worked in various jobs to help to support the family (he was one of nine children). He later moved to Buffalo, where he clerked in a law office, and was admitted to the bar in 1859. He started his own practise in 1862, and avoided conscription in the Civil War by the legal device of hiring another man to serve in his stead. He gained a reputation as a hard-working, dedicated lawyer, living modestly while supporting his mother and sisters (he did not marry until after he had entered the White House). In 1863 he became an assistant district attorney, and in 1870–3 a county sheriff. Standing against corruption in public life, he was elected mayor of Buffalo in 1881 and governor of New York in 1882, and in 1884 received the Democratic nomination to run for president. In the next three presidential elections his honesty and integrity helped him to win the popular vote, but in 1888 he lost in the Electoral College to Benjamin Harrison. He is thus the only president to have served two discontinuous terms. Cleveland opposed taxes and protectionist import tariffs, and vetoed more bills than any previous president. However, his belief in minimal government intervention proved inadequate to deal with the disastrous economic depression that marked his second term, and the belief that he favored big business over the working man was strengthened when he sent federal troops to break the Pullman strike of 1894. A divided Democratic Party refused to renominate him in 1896, and Cleveland retired to New Jersey, becoming a trustee of Princeton University.

Cleveland prided himself on his integrity and probity:

Public office is a public trust.

> CAMPAIGN SLOGAN repeated many times by Cleveland during the 1884 presidential election. The phrase was actually devised by the journalist William C. Hudson.

On how his campaign managers should deal with the revelation that as a young bachelor he had fathered an illegitimate child:

Whatever you do, tell the truth. TELEGRAM TO CHARLES W. GOODYEAR, July 23, 1884

Later he was famously to state:

Party honesty is party expediency.

> INTERVIEW in The *New York Commercial Advertiser*, September 19, 1889

On the duties of office holders:

Office holders are the agents of the people, not their masters.

MESSAGE TO DEPARTMENT HEADS in the federal civil service, July 14, 1886

On taxation:

When more of the people's sustenance is exacted through the form of taxation than is necessary to meet the just obligations of government and expenses of its economical administration, such exaction becomes ruthless extortion and a violation of the fundamental principles of free government.

ANNUAL MESSAGE TO CONGRESS, December 1886

Over his career, Cleveland offered different views on the duties of government vis à vis working men and women:

The laboring classes constitute the main part of our population. They should be protected in their efforts peaceably to assert their rights when endangered by aggregated capital, and all statutes on this subject should recognize the care of the state for honest toil, and be framed with a view of improving the condition of the working man.

LETTER ACCEPTING THE NOMINATION TO RUN FOR GOVERNOR OF NEW YORK, October 1882

PRESIDENT VETO

★ ★ ★

Cleveland vetoed more bills (413) than any previous president, hence the popular ditty:

A fat man once sat in a president's chair,
Singing Ve-to, Ve-to,
With never a thought of trouble or care,
Singing Ve-to, Ve-to.

Cleveland himself, late in life, confided to a friend:

If you knew the absurd things proposed to me at various times while I have been in public life, and which I sat down – and sat down hard – upon …!

Quoted in John S. Wise, *Recollections of Thirteen Presidents* (1960)

I do not believe that the power and duty of the general government ought to be extended to the relief of individual suffering which is in no manner properly related to the public service or benefit … The lesson should be constantly enforced that though the people support the government, the government should not support the people.

VETOING A BILL IN THE HOUSE OF REPRESENTATIVES, February 16, 1887

I have considered the pension list of the republic a roll of honor.

VETOING THE DEPENDENT PENSION BILL, July 5, 1888

Communism is a hateful thing and a menace to peace and organized government; but the communism of combined wealth and capital, the outgrowth of overweening cupidity and selfishness, which insidiously undermines the justice and integrity of free institutions, is not less dangerous than the communism of oppressed poverty and toil, which, exasperated by injustice and discontent, attacks with wild disorder the citadel of rule. He mocks the people who proposes that the government shall protect the rich and that they in turn will care for the laboring poor.

ANNUAL MESSAGE TO CONGRESS, December 3, 1888

The lessons of paternalism ought to be unlearned and the better lesson taught that while the people should patriotically and cheerfully support their government, its functions do not include the support of the people.

> SECOND INAUGURAL ADDRESS, March 4, 1893, rejecting the Populists' call for federal intervention in the economic crisis

After leaving office:

A sensitive man is not happy as president.

It is fight, fight, fight all the time. I looked forward to the close of my term as a happy release from care. But I am not sure I wasn't more unhappy out of office than in … After the long exercise of power, the ordinary affairs of life seem petty and commonplace. An ex-president practicing law or going into business is like a locomotive hauling a delivery wagon …

> Quoted in *American Magazine*, September 1908, three months after Cleveland's death

DEDICATING THE STATUE OF LIBERTY

* * *

It was Cleveland who dedicated the Statue of Liberty, presented to the USA by the people of France to celebrate the centenary of the Declaration of Independence:

We are not here today to bow before the representation of a fierce warlike god, filled with wrath and vengeance, but we joyously contemplate instead our own deity keeping watch and ward before the open gates of America and greater than all that have been celebrated in ancient song. Instead of grasping in her hand thunderbolts of terror and of death, she holds aloft the light which illumines the way to man's enfranchisement. We will not forget that Liberty has here made her home, nor shall her chosen altar be neglected. Willing votaries will constantly keep alive its fires and these shall gleam upon the shores of our sister Republic thence, and joined with answering rays a stream of light shall pierce the darkness of ignorance and man's oppression, until Liberty enlightens the world.

> SPEECH IN NEW YORK, October 28, 1886

His last words:

I have tried so hard to do right.

What others said

* * *

The Republicans greeted the revelation that Cleveland had fathered an illegitimate child with the chant:

Ma, Ma, where's my Pa?

When Cleveland was elected president anyway, the Democrats added the line:

Gone to the White House! Ha, ha, ha!

Cleveland had alienated many corrupt politicians:

They love Cleveland for his character, but they love him also for the enemies he has made!

> GENERAL EDWARD S. BRAGG, seconding Cleveland's nomination at the June 1884 Democratic convention

To nominate Grover Cleveland would be to march through a slaughterhouse into an open grave.

> HENRY WATTERSON, Democratic politician and journalist

He sailed through American history like a steel ship loaded with monoliths of granite.

> H.L. MENCKEN, in 1933

BENJAMIN HARRISON

1833–1901

23RD PRESIDENT OF THE UNITED STATES, 1889–93

BENJAMIN HARRISON

FULL NAME: Benjamin Harrison
BORN: August 20, 1833, North Bend, Ohio
DIED: March 13, 1901, Indianapolis, Indiana
MARRIED: (1) Caroline ('Carrie') Lavinia Scott, (2) Mary Dimmick
(née Mary Scott Lord; she was the niece of Harrison's first wife,
and the widow of Walter Erskine Dimmick)
CHILDREN: Russell Benjamin, Mary Scott (by his first wife);
Elizabeth (by his second wife)
PARTY: Republican
PERIOD IN OFFICE: March 4, 1889–March 4, 1893
VICE-PRESIDENT: Levi P. Morton

* * *

HARRISON WAS THE SCION of a distinguished old planter family in Virginia; his grandfather, William Henry Harrison, had been 9th president of the United States, and his great-grandfather had signed the Declaration of Independence. The young Harrison graduated from Miami University, Oxford, Ohio, in 1852, then studied law, establishing his own practise in Indianapolis in 1854. He served in the Union army during the Civil War, rising to the rank of brigadier-general. After the war he returned to his law practise, supported Radical Reconstruction, and stood unsuccessfully for the governorship of Indiana in 1876. Later, as a US senator (1881–7), he became known as 'the soldier's legislator' for his campaign to secure pensions for Union veterans. He also campaigned for the rights of homesteaders and Native American tribes against the incursions of the railroads, for civil service reform, and for protectionist tariffs. In 1888 he was selected as the Republican presidential candidate, and went on to defeat Grover Cleveland in the subsequent election. As president, he supported the Sherman Anti-Trust Act (1890), aimed at preventing monopolistic practises, but after the Democrats won back a large majority in the House of Representatives in 1890, Harrison was left as something of a lame duck. Although reselected by the Republicans in 1892, his appetite for campaigning disappeared following the illness and death of his first wife. He lost many votes to the Populist candidate James Weaver, giving Cleveland the presidency once more. On leaving office, Harrison remarried and returned to the law.

Young Benjamin Harrison did not welcome references to his being the grandson of President William Henry Harrison, declaring in 1856:

> I want it understood that I am the grandson of nobody. I believe that every man should stand on his own merits.
>
> Quoted in Harry J. Sievers, *Benjamin Harrison, Hoosier Warrior: 1833–1865* (1952)

On losing his Senate seat to a Democrat in 1887:

> I am a dead statesman but a living and rejuvenated Republican.
>
> Harrison went on to win the 1888 presidential nomination under the banner of 'Rejuvenated Republicanism'.

On the need to control big business:

If our great corporations would more scrupulously observe their legal limitations and duties, they would have less cause to complain of the unlawful limitations of their rights or of violent interference with their operations. INAUGURAL ADDRESS, March 4, 1889

On the real cost of cheap goods:

I pity the man who wants a coat so cheap that the man or woman who produces the cloth will starve in the process. ATTRIBUTED

On class relations and the redistribution of wealth:

The indiscriminate denunciation of the rich is mischievous … No poor man was ever made richer or happier by it. It is quite as illogical to despise a man because he is rich as because he is poor. Not what a man has, but what he is, settles his class. We cannot right matters by taking from one what he has honestly acquired to bestow upon another what he has not earned. ATTRIBUTED

We cannot afford in America to have any discontented classes, and if fair wages are paid for fair work we will have none. ATTRIBUTED

On overseas interventionism:

We Americans have no commission from God to police the world. ATTRIBUTED

On civil rights:

It seems to me that the work that is unfinished is to make that constitutional grant of citizenship, the franchise, to the colored men of the South, a practical and living reality. ATTRIBUTED

At the end of his life, Harrison feared for the future of the soul of America:

God forbid that the day should ever come when, in the American mind, the thought of man as a 'consumer' shall submerge the old American thought of man as a creature of God, endowed with 'unalienable rights.'
'THE STATUS OF ANNEXED TERRITORY AND OF ITS FREE CIVILIZED INHABITANTS', in *North American Review*, vol. 172, no. 530, January 1901

What others said
* * *

Grandfather's Hat Fits Ben! TITLE OF A REPUBLICAN CAMPAIGN SONG

The White House Iceberg … He was as glacial as a Siberian stripped of his furs.
SENATOR THOMAS PLATT, *Autobiography* (1910)

PRESIDENTIAL OPINIONS: THE 26TH ON THE 23RD
* * *
He is a cold-blooded, narrow-minded, prejudiced, obstinate, timid old psalm-singing Indianapolis politician. THEODORE ROOSEVELT

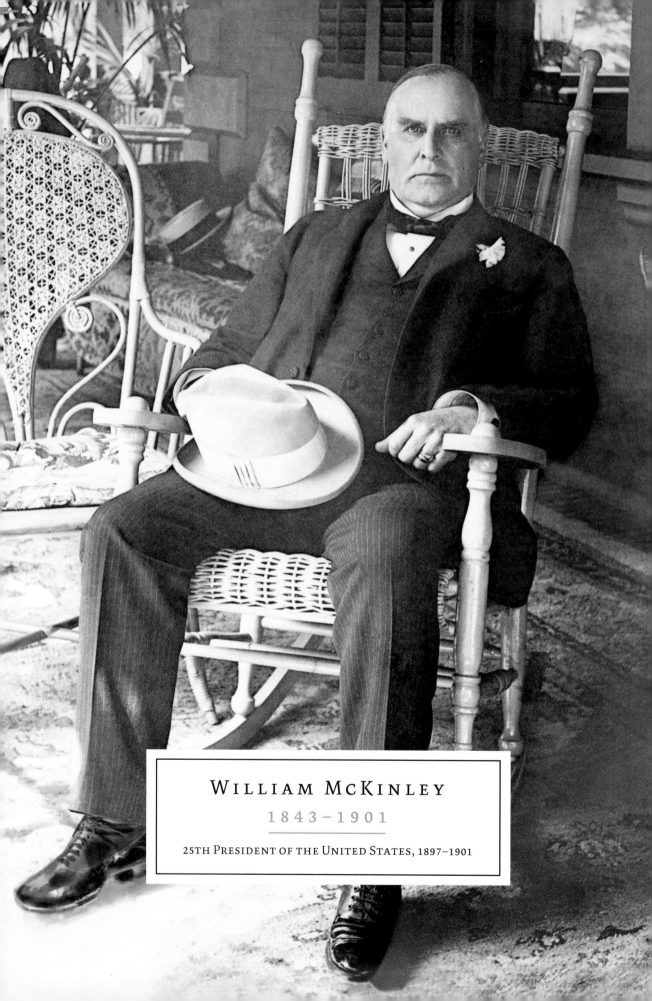

WILLIAM McKINLEY

1843–1901

25TH PRESIDENT OF THE UNITED STATES, 1897–1901

WILLIAM McKINLEY

FULL NAME: William ('Bill') McKinley, Jr
BORN: January 29, 1843, Niles, Ohio
DIED: September 14, 1901, Buffalo, New York
MARRIED: Ida Saxton
CHILDREN: Katherine, Ida (both died in infancy)
PARTY: Republican
PERIOD IN OFFICE: March 4, 1897–September 14, 1901
VICE-PRESIDENT: Garret A. Hobart (1897–9); Theodore Roosevelt (1901)
There was no vice-president from 1899 to 1901.

* * *

BORN AND RAISED IN OHIO, the son of an iron founder, McKinley was educated at Poland Seminary, Mount Union College and Allegheny College. In June 1861, shortly after the outbreak of the Civil War, he enlisted in the Union Army as a private. During the conflict he served under another future president, Rutherford B. Hayes, was commended for valor at the Battle of Antietam, and eventually attained the rank of brevet major. After the war he studied law and was admitted to the bar in 1867, opening a practise in Canton, Ohio. He entered politics as a Republican, and served in the US House of Representatives from 1871 to 1891, only failing to be re-elected in 1882 and 1890. In the latter year his sponsorship of the strongly protectionist McKinley Tariff Act – which he intended to ensure wages stayed high but which raised consumer prices – alienated many voters. McKinley then served two terms as governor of Ohio (1892–6), before securing the nomination as the Republican presidential candidate in 1896, with the support of the powerful Ohio industrialist Mark Hanna.

McKinley, a firm supporter of the gold standard, successfully stood against the populist Democratic candidate William Jennings Bryan. Initially McKinley resisted the popular clamor to intervene in Cuba, where Spain was attempting to suppress a strong independence movement, but the sinking of the USS *Maine* in Havana harbor forced his hand. By the conclusion of the short Spanish-American War of 1898, McKinley had become an enthusiastic imperialist, and the USA acquired the Philippines, Guam and Puerto Rico from Spain, while Cuba became independent. The USA also annexed Hawaii in 1898. In 1900, McKinley again defeated Bryan in the presidential election. On September 5, 1901, at the Pan-American Exposition in Buffalo, New York, McKinley announced his abandonment of protectionism in favour of free trade. The following day, at a reception, McKinley was shaking hands with a line of people, when one of them, an anarchist called Leon Czolgosz, fired at him with a revolver concealed under a handkerchief. The first shot grazed a shoulder, but the second penetrated the president's stomach, pancreas and kidney. He died eight days later.

On the sovereignty of the people:

> Unlike any other nation, here the people rule, and their will is the supreme law. It is sometimes sneeringly said by those who do not like free government, that here we count heads. True, heads are counted, but brains also. And the general sense of 63 millions of free people is better and safer than the sense of a favored few, born to nobility and ruling by inheritance. ATTRIBUTED

On wars of conquest:

We want no wars of conquest; we must avoid the temptation of territorial aggression. War should never be entered upon until every agency of peace has failed; peace is preferable to war in almost every contingency. Arbitration is the true method of settlement of international as well as local or individual differences.

First Inaugural Address, March 4, 1897

JINGO MCKINLEY
***

Shortly after taking office, McKinley remarked to Carl Schurz:

Ah, you may be sure that there will be no jingo nonsense under my administration.

Quoted in Claude M. Fuess, *Carl Schurz, Reformer, 1829–1906* (1933)

But once war with Spain had broken out, one newspaper commented:

We are all jingoes now, and the head jingo is the Hon. William McKinley.

The New York Sun, April 20, 1898

There is no desire on the part of our people to profit by the misfortunes of Spain.

Annual Message to Congress, December 6, 1897

Shortly before the war with Spain, McKinley recalled his experience in the Civil War:

I have been through one war, I have seen the dead piled up, and I do not want to see another.

Quoted in Claire Whitcomb, *Real Life at the White House* (2000)

On the USA's military intervention in the Cuban revolt against Spanish rule:

The grounds justifying that step were the interests of humanity, the duty to protect the life and property of our citizens in Cuba, the right to check injury to our commerce and people through the devastation of the island, and, most important, the need of removing at once and forever the constant menace and the burdens entailed upon our government by the uncertainties and perils of the situation caused by the unendurable disturbance in Cuba.

Annual Message to Congress, December 5, 1898

Reacting to the capture of Manila in the Philippines:

I could not have told where those damned islands were within two thousand miles.

Attributed

On the acquisition of the Philippines from Spain:

The mission of the United States is one of benevolent assimilation, substituting the mild sway of justice and right for arbitrary rule.

Letter to General Harrison Gray Otis, December 21, 1898

On the Philippine revolt against US rule, in which 200,000 Filipinos lost their lives:

Our countrymen should not be deceived. We are not waging war against the inhabitants of the Philippine Islands. A portion of them are making war against the United States. By far the greater part of the inhabitants recognize American sovereignty and welcome it as a guaranty of order and of security for life, property, liberty, freedom of conscience, and the pursuit of happiness. To them full protection will be given. They shall not be abandoned.

We will not leave the destiny of the loyal millions [of] the islands to the disloyal thousands who are in rebellion against the United States. SECOND INAUGURAL ADDRESS, March 4, 1901

On being shot, McKinley said to his secretary, George Cortelyou:

My wife, Cortelyou, be careful how you tell her, oh be careful. September 6, 1901

Cortelyou had advised the president on security grounds to cancel the reception in Buffalo where he was assassinated, to which McKinley had responded:

Why should I? No one would wish to hurt me.

Of his assassin, the anarchist Leon Czolgosz, who was being attacked by an angry crowd:

Boys! Don't let them hurt him … It must have been some poor misguided fellow.

September 6, 1901. Czolgosz went to the electric chair on October 29, 1901.

As McKinley lay dying a few days later, his wife cried, 'I want to go too, I want to go too', to which he responded:

We are all going. LAST WORDS, September 14, 1901

What others said

* * *

My opponents go at me tooth and nail, but they always apologize to William when they are going to call him names. SPEAKER TOM REED, quoted in Thomas Beer, *Hanna* (1929)

He had a way of handling men so that they thought their ideas were his own.

ELIHU ROOT, who served as secretary of war, 1899–1904

The ocean is not wide enough to hold all the sympathy that is streaming from the Old World to the New. *NEUES WEINER TAGEBLATT*, the Austrian newspaper, reacts to the assassination of McKinley.

Why, if a man were to call my dog McKinley, and the brute failed to resent to the death the damning insult, I'd drown it.

WILLIAM COWPER BRANN, owner and editor of the *Iconoclast* newspaper, Waco, Texas

THEODORE ROOSEVELT

1858–1919

26TH PRESIDENT OF THE UNITED STATES, 1901–9

THEODORE ROOSEVELT

FULL NAME: Theodore ('Teddy') Roosevelt

BORN: October 27, 1858, New York, New York

DIED: January 6, 1919, Oyster Bay, New York

MARRIED: (1) Anne Hathaway Lee, (2) Edith Kermit Carow

CHILDREN: Alice Lee (by his first wife); Theodore, Jr, Kermit,
Ethel Carow, Archibald Bulloch, Quentin (by his second wife)

PARTY: Republican

PERIOD IN OFFICE: September 14, 1901–March 4, 1909

VICE-PRESIDENT: Charles W. Fairbanks (1905–9)

There was no vice-president from 1901 to 1905.

* * *

BORN INTO AN OLD, wealthy New York family, young Roosevelt was a sickly boy, but from the age of ten he embarked on a lifelong program of intense physical activities, ranging from boxing to big-game hunting. He also spent some time working as a cowboy, and became an enthusiastic naturalist and pioneering conservationist. He studied at Harvard, and for a short time at Columbia Law School, and throughout his life was a prolific writer of history, natural history and autobiography. Through the 1880s and 1890s Roosevelt was active in New York Republican politics, and earned a reputation as both a maverick and an astute political operator. In 1896 he came out in support of William McKinley's bid for the White House, and was appointed assistant secretary of the navy the following year. An enthusiastic expansionist, he was exasperated by McKinley's reluctance to go to war with Spain over Cuba, and when war eventually came in 1898 he resigned his position to lead a squad of volunteers, the 'Rough Riders', to fight against the Spanish in Cuba. He returned to the US a national hero, and served as governor of New York (1898–1900).

McKinley named Roosevelt as his running mate in the 1900 election, and when McKinley was assassinated in September 1901, Roosevelt took over the presidency. In office he pursued what he called the 'Square Deal', promoting the interests of the working man, pursuing anti-trust cases against big business, intervening in industrial disputes, and regulating the rail and food industries. In foreign affairs, via the 'Roosevelt Corollary' (see below), he asserted US hegemony in the Americas, and used armed intervention to support the independence of Panama from Columbia, so giving the US control of the zone through which the proposed Panama Canal would pass. In 1905 Roosevelt was awarded the Nobel Peace Prize for negotiating the agreement ending the Russo-Japanese War. Roosevelt was re-elected in 1904, but declared that he would not seek what would effectively be a third term, and supported the nomination of William Howard Taft in 1908. But Roosevelt became disaffected with Taft's presidency, and unsuccessfully sought the Republican nomination in 1912. Instead, he ran as the Progressive candidate, and thus split the Republican vote, allowing the Democratic candidate, Woodrow Wilson, to win. During the First World War, Roosevelt lobbied Wilson to allow him to lead a corps of volunteers to support the Allies, but Wilson refused. Roosevelt's health began to fail after his son Quentin was killed in action in 1918, and he died on January 5, 1919.

On Native Americans:

I don't go so far as to think that the only good Indians are dead Indians, but I believe nine out of ten are, and I shouldn't inquire too closely into the cause of the tenth. The most vicious cowboy has more moral principle than the average Indian.
    Letter to Owen Wister, 1885

Roosevelt was physically tireless – and endlessly proud of it:

I wish to preach, not the doctrine of ignoble ease, but the doctrine of the strenuous life.
    Speech to the Hamilton Club, Chicago, April 10, 1899

I am as strong as a bull moose and you can use me to the limit.
    Letter to Mark Hanna, Republican national chairman, June 27, 1900. The Progressive Party that Roosevelt formed some years later became popularly known as the Bull Moose Party.

The first requisite of a good citizen in this republic of ours is that he shall be able and willing to pull his weight. Speech in New York, November 11, 1902

Roosevelt saw war as a virtuous pursuit:

No triumph of peace is quite so great as the supreme triumphs of war.
    Quoted in Henry F. Pringle, *Theodore Roosevelt* (1931)

Every man who has in him any real power of joy in battle knows that he feels it when the wolf begins to rise in his heart; he does not then shrink from blood or sweat or deem that they mar the fight; he revels in them, in the toil, the pain and the danger, as but setting off the triumph. Quoted in Edward Wagenknecht, *The Seven Worlds of Theodore Roosevelt* (1958)

This country needs a war.
    Remark to Henry Cabot Lodge in 1895, at a time of tension between the USA and Great Britain

It is a base untruth to say that happy is the nation that has no history. Thrice happy is the nation that has a glorious history. Speech, April 10, 1899

When at last he got a war, he led the famous 'San Juan charge' of the Rough Riders in Cuba:

The charge itself was great fun. Oh, but we have had a bully fight!
    Quoted in Henry F. Pringle, *Theodore Roosevelt* (1956)

On his perception of America's role in the world:

There is a homely adage which runs 'Speak softly and carry a big stick; you will go far.' If the American nation will speak softly and yet build and keep at a pitch of the highest training a thoroughly efficient navy, the Monroe Doctrine will go far.
    Speech in Chicago, April 3, 1903. Roosevelt was very fond of this adage, first using it in a letter to Henry L. Sprague, dated January 26, 1900.

Do not hit at all if it can be avoided, but never hit softly.
    Autobiography (1913)

Roosevelt coined the term 'Square Deal' to characterize his populist domestic policies, combining trust-busting with measures mildly favorable to labor:

> I fought beside the colored troops at Santiago, and I hold that if a man is good enough to be put up and shot at, then he is good enough for me to do what I can to get him a square deal.
>
> SPEECH, May 27, 1903

A man who is good enough to shed his blood for his country is good enough to be given a square deal afterwards. More than that no man is entitled to, and less than that no man shall have.

> SPEECH AT THE LINCOLN MONUMENT, Springfield, Illinois, June 4, 1903

I stand for the square deal … I mean not merely that I stand for fair play under the present rules of the game, but that I stand for having those rules changed so as to work for a more substantial equality of opportunity and of reward for equally good service.

> SPEECH, Osawatomie, Kansas, August 31, 1910

We demand that big business give the people a square deal; in return we must insist that when anyone engaged in big business honestly endeavors to do right he shall himself be given a square deal; and the first, and most elementary, kind of square deal is to give him in advance full information as to just what he can, and what he cannot, legally and properly do. It is absurd, and much worse than absurd, to treat the deliberate lawbreaker as on an exact par with the man eager to obey the law, whose only desire is to find out from some competent governmental authority what the law is, and then to live up to it. Moreover, it is absurd to treat the size of a corporation as in itself a crime.

> AUTOBIOGRAPHY (1913)

On controlling big business:

It may well be that the determination of the government … to punish certain malefactors of great wealth, has been

THE ROOSEVELT COROLLARY

* * *

Roosevelt formulated the 'Roosevelt Corollary' to the Monroe Doctrine (see p. 36):

> It is not true that the United States feels any land hunger or entertains any projects as regards the other nations of the Western Hemisphere save such as are for their welfare. All that this country desires is to see the neighboring countries stable, orderly and prosperous. Any country whose people conduct themselves well can count upon our hearty friendship. If a nation shows that it knows how to act with reasonable efficiency and decency in social and political matters, if it keeps order and pays its obligations, it need fear no interference from the United States. Chronic wrongdoing, or an impotence which results in a general loosening of the ties of civilized society, may in America, as elsewhere, ultimately require intervention by some civilized nation, and in the Western Hemisphere the adherence of the United States to the Monroe Doctrine may force the United States, however reluctantly, in flagrant cases of such wrongdoing or impotence, to the exercise of an international police power.
>
> ANNUAL MESSAGE TO CONGRESS, December 6, 1904

A year later he was predicting:

> Some time soon I shall have to spank some little brigand of a South American republic.
>
> LETTER TO DOUGLAS ROBINSON, August 31, 1905

responsible for some of the trouble [on the stock market] ... I regard this contest as one to determine who shall rule this free country – the people through their governmental agents, or a few ruthless and domineering men whose wealth makes them peculiarly formidable because they hide behind the breastworks of corporate organization. SPEECH, August 20, 1907

Combinations in industry are the result of an imperative economic law which cannot be repealed by political legislation ... The way out lies, not in attempting to prevent such combinations, but in completely controlling them in the interest of public welfare.
SPEECH, August 31, 1910

THE BULLY PULPIT
* * *
Roosevelt loved the platform that the presidency gave him:

I have got such a bully pulpit!
IN *OUTLOOK*, February 27, 1909

Many decades later, First Lady Nancy Reagan stated:

If the President has a bully pulpit, then the First Lady has a white glove pulpit ... more refined, restricted, ceremonial, but it's a pulpit all the same.
INTERVIEWED in the *New York Times*, March 10, 1988

On seeking the Republican nomination in 1912:

We stand at Armageddon, and we battle for the Lord.
SPEECH, June 17, 1912

On political corruption:

No people is wholly civilized where a distinction is drawn between stealing an office and stealing a purse.
SPEECH in Chicago, June 22, 1912

Roosevelt was always the man of action:

It is not the critic who counts, not the man who points out how the strong man stumbled, or where the doer of deeds could have done better. The credit belongs to the man who is actually in the arena; whose face is marred by the dust and sweat and blood; who strives valiantly; who errs and comes short again and again, because there is no effort without error or shortcoming; who knows the great enthusiasms, the great devotions and spends himself in a worthy cause; who at the best, knows in the end the triumph of high achievement, and who, at worst, if he fails, at least fails while daring greatly; so that his place shall never be with those cold and timid souls who know neither victory or defeat.
'CITIZENSHIP IN A REPUBLIC', speech at the Sorbonne, Paris, April 23, 1910

Roosevelt believed in a vigorous defense of principle:

The things that will destroy America are prosperity-at-any-price, peace-at-any-price, safety-first instead of duty-first, the love of soft living, and the get-rich-quickly theory of life. LETTER TO S. STANWOOD MENCKEN, January 10, 1917

On loyalty:

There can be no fifty-fifty Americanism in this country. There is room here for only one hundred percent Americanism. SPEECH in Saratoga, New York, July 19, 1918

Roosevelt's Coinages

★ ★ ★

Roosevelt coined or popularized a number of well-known phrases:

Muckrakers – a term Roosevelt applied to those investigative journalists who exposed political corruption and the exploitative practises of big business:

> The men with the muckrakes are often indispensable to the well-being of society, but only if they know when to stop raking the muck, and to look upward to the celestial crown above them ... If they gradually grow to feel that the whole world is nothing but muck their power of usefulness is gone.
>
> SPEECH in Washington DC, April 14, 1906, referring to the muckraker in *Pilgrim's Progress* who was so obsessed with scraping the floor that he never looked heavenward

Lunatic fringe:

> Every reform movement has a lunatic fringe. AUTOBIOGRAPHY (1913)

Hyphenated Americans:

> There is no room in this country for hyphenated Americanism ... The one absolutely certain way of bringing this nation to ruin, of preventing all possibility of its continuing to be a nation at all, would be to permit it to become a tangle of squabbling nationalities. SPEECH in New York, October 12, 1915

Weasel words:

> One of our defects as a nation is a tendency to use what have been called 'weasel words'. When a weasel sucks eggs the meat is sucked out of the egg. If you use a 'weasel word' after another, there is nothing left of the other.
>
> SPEECH in St Louis, May 31, 1916. The phrase originated in a story by Stewart Chaplin entitled 'Stained-glass Political Platform', which was published in the *Century Magazine* in June 1900.

> We have room in this country for but one flag, the Stars and Stripes ... We have room for but one loyalty, loyalty to the United States ... We have room for but one language, the English language. MESSAGE TO THE AMERICAN DEFENSE SOCIETY, January 3, 1919

Roosevelt was never in any doubt that it had all been enormous fun:

> No president has ever enjoyed himself as much as I have enjoyed myself, and for the matter of that I do not know of any man of my age who has had as good a time.
>
> Quoted in David C. Whitney, *The American Presidents* (1967)

What others said

★ ★ ★

On the selection of Roosevelt as McKinley's running mate in the 1900 presidential election:

> Don't any of you realize that there's only one life between this madman and the White House? MARK HANNA, Republican national chairman, at the Republican convention, June 1900

Now look, that damned cowboy is president of the United States.

MARK HANNA, following McKinley's assassination in September 1901

You must always remember that the president is about six.

CECIL SPRING RICE, British diplomat, quoted in Henry F. Pringle, *Theodore Roosevelt* (1931)

His idea of getting hold of the right end of the stick is to snatch it from the hands of someone who is using it effectively, and to hit him over the head with it.

GEORGE BERNARD SHAW

On Roosevelt's departure to hunt big game in Africa in 1909:

Health to the lions!

J.P. MORGAN, against whose Northern Securities Company Roosevelt had launched an anti-trust action in 1902

I always enjoy his society, he is so hearty, so straightforward, outspoken and, for the moment, so absolutely sincere. MARK TWAIN, *Autobiography* (1913)

I curled up in the seat opposite, and listened and wondered, until the universe seemed to be spinning around and Theodore was the spinner.

RUDYARD KIPLING, quoted in William Roscoe Thayer, *John Hay* (1915)

THE LION IS DEAD.

ARCHIE ROOSEVELT, telegram to his brothers announcing his father's death, January 5, 1919

Father always wanted to be the bride at every wedding and the corpse at every funeral.

ALICE ROOSEVELT, the president's daughter, quoted in Nicholas Roosevelt, *A Front Row Seat* (1953)

To President Roosevelt we ascribe that quality that medieval theology assigned God: he was pure act. HENRY ADAMS, *The Education of Henry Adams* (1918)

An interesting combination of St Vitus and St Paul ... Do you know the two most extraordinary things I have seen in your country? Niagara Falls and the president of the United States – both great wonders of nature!

JOHN MORLEY, the British essayist, quoted in Joseph Bishop, *Notes and Anecdotes of Many Years* (1925)

One always thinks of him as a glorified bouncer engaged eternally in cleaning out bar-rooms and not too proud to gouge when the inspiration came to him, or to bite in the clinches.

H.L. MENCKEN, *Prejudices, 2nd Series* (1920). Elsewhere Mencken wrote that Roosevelt 'hated all pretension save his own pretension.'

PRESIDENTIAL OPINIONS: THE 28TH ON THE 26TH

★ ★ ★

He is the most dangerous man of the age. WOODROW WILSON

WILLIAM HOWARD TAFT

1857–1930

27TH PRESIDENT OF THE UNITED STATES, 1909–13

WILLIAM HOWARD TAFT

FULL NAME: William Howard Taft
BORN: September 15, 1857, near Cincinnati, Ohio
DIED: March 8, 1930, Washington DC
MARRIED: Helen Louise ('Nellie') Herron
CHILDREN: Robert, Helen, Charles Phelps
PARTY: Republican
PERIOD IN OFFICE: March 4, 1909–March 4, 1913
VICE-PRESIDENT: James S. Sherman (1909–12)
There was no vice-president in 1912–13.

* * *

TAFT'S FATHER WAS A PROMINENT Republican lawyer in Cincinnati who served as secretary of war under President Ulysses S. Grant. Taft himself was brought up a Unitarian, and was educated at Yale before following his father into the law and setting up a practise in Cincinnati. In 1887 he was appointed a judge of the Ohio Superior Court, and in 1890 President Benjamin Harrison made him solicitor general of the United States. Taft went on to serve as a federal judge (1892–1900). In 1900 President McKinley asked Taft to be the first civilian governor of the Philippines, and Taft reluctantly agreed. He had not approved of the annexation of the islands, and his rule proved too equitable for President Roosevelt, who unsuccessfully tried to lure Taft back home by offering him a position on the US Supreme Court – something that Taft had long desired. Taft did return to the USA in 1904 as Roosevelt's secretary of war, a position he held until 1908, when, with Roosevelt's backing, he secured the Republican nomination, and successfully ran for president. Taft pursued Roosevelt's anti-trust policies, but lost Roosevelt's support when he raised tariffs and sacked the conservationist head of the Forestry Service, whom Roosevelt had appointed. In 1912 Roosevelt ran against Taft as a Progressive, giving the victory to Woodrow Wilson, the Democratic candidate. Taft taught law at Yale until 1921, championing international arbitration as a means of avoiding war, and supporting the League of Nations. In 1921 he was appointed chief justice of the US Supreme Court, his lifelong ambition, and served until his death in 1930.

On government:

> We are all imperfect. We cannot expect perfect government.
> SPEECH, Washington DC, May 8, 1909

On his foreign policy:

> The diplomacy of the present administration has sought to respond to modern ideas of commercial intercourse. This policy has been characterized as substituting dollars for bullets. ANNUAL MESSAGE TO CONGRESS, December 3, 1912

Taft temporized over the Fifteenth Amendment, implicitly approving the literacy tests that many Southern states used to prevent African Americans from exercising their right to vote under the Amendment:

It is clear to all that the domination of an ignorant, irresponsible element can be prevented by constitutional laws which shall exclude from voting both negroes and whites not having education or other qualifications thought to be necessary for a proper electorate. The danger of the control of an ignorant electorate has therefore passed.

INAUGURAL ADDRESS, March 4, 1909

On the limits of presidential power:

The intoxication of power rapidly sobers off in the knowledge of its restrictions and under the prompt reminder of an ever-present and not always considerate press, as well as the kindly suggestions that not infrequently come from Congress.

SPEECH TO THE LOTUS CLUB, November 16, 1912

Politics never was quite to his taste:

Politics, when I am in it, makes me sick. Quoted in Archibald W. Butt, *Taft and Roosevelt* (1930)

I'll be damned if I am not getting tired of this. It seems to be the profession of a president simply to hear other people talk. Quoted in Archibald W. Butt, *Taft and Roosevelt* (1930)

On his defeat in the 1912 presidential election:

I have one consolation. No one candidate was ever elected ex-president by such a large majority. ATTRIBUTED

Opposing socialism:

Enlightened selfishness … is at the basis of all human labor and effort, enterprise and new activity. POPULAR GOVERNMENT (1913)

Taft believed in the supremacy of law:

The battlefield as a place of settlement of disputes is gradually yielding to arbitral courts of justice. THE DAWN OF WORLD PEACE (1911)

I love judges, and I love courts. They are my ideals, that typify on earth what we shall meet hereafter in heaven under a just God. SPEECH, Pocatello, Idaho, October 5, 1911

While chief justice of the Supreme Court (1921–30) he declared:

Presidents come and go, but the Court goes on forever.

PRESIDENTIAL OPINIONS: THE 26TH ON THE 27TH

★ ★ ★

Taft meant well, but he meant well feebly.
THEODORE ROOSEVELT

A flub-dub with a streak of the second-rate and the common in him.
THEODORE ROOSEVELT

WOODROW WILSON

1856–1924

28TH PRESIDENT OF THE UNITED STATES, 1913–21

WOODROW WILSON

FULL NAME: Thomas Woodrow Wilson
BORN: December 28, 1856, Staunton, Virginia
DIED: February 3, 1924, Washington DC
MARRIED: (1) Ellen Axson, (2) Edith Galt (née Bolling;
she was the widow of Norman Galt)
CHILDREN: Margaret, Jessie, Eleanor (all by his first wife)
PARTY: Democratic
PERIOD IN OFFICE: March 4, 1913–March 4, 1921
VICE-PRESIDENT: Thomas R. Marshall

* * *

WILSON, THE SON OF A PRESBYTERIAN MINISTER of Ulster-Scots extraction, was raised in Augusta, Georgia, then in Columbia, South Carolina, before studying history and political science at Princeton. He went on to train as a lawyer, but abandoned the profession in favor of undertaking a PhD in history and political science at Johns Hopkins. He then taught at a number of universities, including Princeton, before entering politics in 1910, when he was elected Democratic governor of New Jersey. In the presidential election of 1912 he defeated Theodore Roosevelt and William Howard Taft, and as president continued the progressive agenda he had begun in New Jersey. He supported subsidies to farmers and improved rights and conditions for labor, and set up the Federal Reserve System and the Federal Trade Commission, the latter being tasked with enforcing the Clayton Anti-Trust Act of 1914.

But it was foreign affairs that dominated Wilson's two terms as president. In 1914 and again in 1916 he sent US troops to intervene in the upheavals in Mexico. On the outbreak of the First World War in August 1914, Wilson announced that the USA would remain neutral. However, German submarines attacked Allied ships trading with America, culminating in the sinking of the *Lusitania* on May 7, 1915, in which 128 US citizens drowned. Under US pressure, Germany abandoned unrestricted submarine warfare, and Wilson won the 1916 presidential election with the slogan 'He kept us out of the war'. But after Germany resumed unrestricted submarine attacks in February 1917, relations deteriorated, and were made worse on March 1 when the Zimmerman Telegram – by which Germany promised to help Mexico to recover territory lost to the USA – was made public. On April 6 Wilson obtained Congress's agreement to declare war. Wilson outlined America's war aims in the Fourteen Points, which included the establishment of a League of Nations to prevent future wars. The American Expeditionary Force sent to Europe helped to ensure Allied victory over Germany in November 1918, but, to his great disappointment, Wilson failed to achieve the necessary Senate support for the League of Nations. On September 25, 1919 Wilson suffered the first of three strokes that left him intellectually unimpaired but partially paralyzed. In retirement, Wilson continued to live in Washington, where he died and was buried in 1924.

On speech-making:

> If I am to speak for ten minutes, I need a week for preparation; if fifteen minutes, three days; if half an hour, two days; if an hour, I am ready now.
>
> Quoted in Josephus Daniels, *The Wilson Era* (1946)

On the presidential candidates in 1912:

> There is no indispensable man. The government will not collapse and go to pieces if any one of the men who are seeking to be entrusted with its guidance should be left at home.
>
> Quoted in the *New York Times Magazine*, July 10, 1956

On his election:

> God ordained that I should be the next president of the United States. Neither you nor any other mortal could have prevented that!
>
> REMARK TO WILLIAM F. MCCOMBS, chairman of the Democratic National Committee, quoted in William F. McCombs, *Making Woodrow Wilson President* (1921)

WILSON AND *THE BIRTH OF A NATION*

* * *

After viewing D.W. Griffith's white-supremacist film The Birth of a Nation *at the White House, February 18, 1915, Wilson has frequently been quoted as saying:*

> It is like writing history with lightning. And my only regret is that it is all so terribly true.

These words were in fact attributed to the president by Thomas Dixon, author of the novel and play The Clansman, *on which Griffith's film was based. Wilson's aide Joseph Tumulty was obliged to write to the Boston branch of the National Association for the Advancement of Colored People that:*

> The president was entirely unaware of the nature of the play before it was presented and at no time has expressed his approbation of it.
>
> LETTER TO DOUGLAS ROBINSON, August 31, 1905

On taking office:

> The nation has been deeply stirred ... The feelings with which we face this new age of right and opportunity sweep across our heartstrings like some air out of God's own presence.
>
> FIRST INAUGURAL ADDRESS, March 4, 1913

On the monopolistic practises of the big corporations:

> When all the combinations are combined ... then there is something that even the government of the nation itself might come to fear – something for the law to pull apart, and gently, but firmly and persistently, dissect.
>
> THE NEW FREEDOM (1913). In fact, once in office Wilson did little in the way of trust-busting.

On office-holders:

> Every man who takes office in Washington either grows or swells, and when I give a man office I watch him carefully to see whether he is growing or swelling.
>
> SPEECH, May 15, 1916

On international justice:

> No nation is fit to sit in judgment upon any other nation. SPEECH in New York, April 20, 1915

On the USA's position in the First World War:

> The Unites States must be neutral in fact as well as in name during these days that are to try men's souls. We must be impartial in thought as well as in action.
>
> SPEECH, August 19, 1914, shortly after the outbreak of war in Europe. It was Thomas Paine who in a pamphlet in December 1776 had famously written 'These are the times that try men's souls.'

Our whole duty, for the present, at any rate, is summed up in the motto, 'America First'. Let us think of America before we think of Europe, in order that America may be fit to be Europe's friend when the day of tested friendship comes. April 20, 1915

There is no such thing as a man being too proud to fight.
SPEECH in Philadelphia, May 10, 1915, soon after the sinking of the *Lusitania*

We have stood apart, studiously neutral. It was our manifest duty to do so. Not only did we have no part or interest in the policies which seem to have brought the conflict on; it was necessary, if a universal catastrophe was to be avoided, that a limit should be set to the sweep of destructive war and that some part of the great family of nations should keep the processes of peace alive, if only to prevent collective economic ruin and the breakdown throughout the world of the industries by which its populations are fed and sustained.
ANNUAL MESSAGE TO CONGRESS, December 7, 1915

America cannot be an ostrich with its head in the sand ... There is a price which is too great to pay for peace, and that price can be put into one word. Once cannot pay the price of self-respect. SPEECH in Des Moines, Iowa, February 1, 1916

It must be a peace without victory ... Victory would mean peace forced upon the loser, a victor's terms imposed upon the vanquished. It would be accepted in humiliation, under duress, at an intolerable sacrifice, and would leave a sting, a resentment, a bitter memory upon which terms of peace would rest, not permanently, but only as upon quicksand. Only a peace between equals can last. SPEECH TO THE US SENATE, January 22, 1917

On the right of national self-determination:

Every people should be left free to determine its own policy, its own way of development, unhindered, unthreatened, unafraid, the little along with the great and powerful ... These are American principles. SPEECH TO THE US SENATE, January 22, 1917

Self-determination is not a mere phrase. It is an imperative principle which statesmen will henceforth ignore at their peril. ADDRESS TO CONGRESS, February 11, 1918

On April 1, 1917, Wilson was reported (perhaps inaccurately) by the journalist Frank Cobb as saying:

Once lead this people into war and they will forget there ever was such a thing as tolerance. To fight you must be brutal and ruthless, and the spirit of ruthless brutality will enter into the very fiber of our national life, infecting Congress, the courts, the policeman on the beat, the man on the street ... If there is any alternative, for God's sake, let's take it.

The next day, April 2, 1917, Wilson called on Congress to declare war on Germany and its allies:

Armed neutrality is ineffectual enough at best; in such circumstances and in the face of such pretensions it is worse than ineffectual: it is likely only to produce what it was meant to prevent; it is practically certain to draw us into the war without either the rights or the effectiveness of belligerents. There is one choice we cannot make, we are incapable of making: we will not choose the path of submission and suffer the most sacred rights of our nation and our people to be ignored or violated. The wrongs against which we now array ourselves are no common wrongs; they cut to the very roots of human life.
ADDRESS TO CONGRESS, April 2, 1917

The world must be made safe for democracy. Its peace must be planted upon the tested foundations of political liberty. [*At this point, Senator John Sharp Williams of Mississippi began to clap and continued to do so until all those present joined in.*] We have no selfish ends to serve. We desire no conquest, no dominion. We seek no indemnities for ourselves, no material compensation for the sacrifices we shall freely make. We are but one of the champions of the rights of mankind. We shall be satisfied when those rights have been made as secure as the faith and the freedom of nations can make them.

Just because we fight without rancor and without selfish object, seeking nothing for ourselves but what we shall wish to share with all free peoples, we shall, I feel confident, conduct our operations as belligerents without passion and ourselves observe with proud punctilio the principles of right and of fair play we profess to be fighting for.

ADDRESS TO CONGRESS, April 2, 1917

It is a fearful thing to lead this great peaceful people into war, into the most terrible and disastrous of all wars, civilization itself seeming to be in the balance. But the right is more precious than peace, and we shall fight for the things which we have always carried nearest our hearts – for democracy, for the right of those who submit to authority to have a voice in their own governments, for the rights and liberties of small nations, for a universal dominion of right by such a concert of free peoples as shall bring peace and safety to all nations and make the world itself at last free.

ADDRESS TO CONGRESS, April 2, 1917

Later that day he remarked:

My message today was a message of death for our young men. How strange it seems to applaud that.

On the need for national mobilization:

It is not an army we must train for war: it is a nation.

SPEECH in Washington DC, May 12, 1917

On the League of Nations:

There must be a League of Nations and this must be virile, a reality, not a paper League.

REMARK, 1918, quoted in A. Willert, *The Road to Safety: A Study in Anglo-German Relations* (1953)

Why has Jesus Christ so far not succeeded in inducing the world to follow His teaching in these matters? It is because He taught the ideal without devising any practical scheme to carry out His aims.

Quoted in David Lloyd George, *Memoirs of the Peace Conference* (1939)

There is only one power to put behind the liberation of mankind, and that is the power of mankind. It is the power of the united moral forces of the world, and in the Covenant of the League of Nations the moral forces of the world are mobilized.

SPEECH at Pueblo, Colorado, September 25, 1919

There seems to me to stand between us and the rejection or qualification of this treaty [the Treaty of Versailles, which incorporated the covenant of the League of Nations] the serried ranks of those boys in khaki, not only these boys who came home, but those dear ghosts that still deploy upon the fields of France.

> SPEECH at Pueblo, Colorado,
> September 25, 1919

On refusing to accept Senator Henry Cabot Lodge's reservations on the League of Nations in the Versailles Treaty:

> Better to go down fighting than to dip your colors to dishonorable compromise.

> Quoted in Edith Bolling Wilson,
> *My Memoir* (1938)

On the Russian Civil War that followed the Bolshevik Revolution:

> A lot of impossible folk fighting among themselves.

> REMARK, autumn 1918. Russia did not participate in the Paris Peace Conference.

On the newly formed Kingdom of Serbs, Croats and Slovenes (later renamed Yugoslavia):

> It will be a turbulent nation as they are a turbulent people.

> REMARK following the proclamation of the new state on December 1, 1918

On the French demands at the Paris Peace Conference:

> My opinion is that if they had their way the world would go to pieces in a very short while.

> REMARK TO HIS PHYSICIAN, DR GRAYSON, April 1919. Many historians have blamed the harsh terms of the Treaty of Versailles, insisted upon by the French, at least in part for the rise of the Nazis and the outbreak of the Second World War.

THE FOURTEEN POINTS
✴ ✴ ✴

On January 8, 1918, Wilson outlined the USA's war aims to a joint session of Congress. These were his famous 'Fourteen Points', which included:

> 1. Open covenants of peace must be arrived at, after which there will surely be no private international action or rulings of any kind, but diplomacy shall proceed always frankly and in the public view.
> 2. Absolute freedom of navigation upon the seas, outside territorial waters, alike in peace and in war …
> 3. The removal, so far as possible, of all economic barriers and the establishment of an equality of trade conditions among all the nations consenting to the peace …
> 4. Adequate guarantees given and taken that national armaments will be reduced to the lowest points consistent with domestic safety.
> 5. A free, open-minded, and absolutely impartial adjustment of all colonial claims …
> 14. A general association of nations must be formed under specific covenants for the purpose of affording mutual guarantees of political independence and territorial integrity to great and small states alike.

Georges Clemenceau, prime minister of France, was not impressed:

> Mr Wilson bores me with his Fourteen Points; why, God Almighty has only ten.

In the end, Wilson concluded:

> America is the only idealistic nation in the world.

> SPEECH at Sioux Falls, South Dakota, September 8, 1919

He never lost his belief that he was the instrument of Providence:

> I have seen fools resist Providence before, and I have seen their destruction … That we shall prevail is as sure as God reigns.
>
> Quoted in Edith Bolling Wilson, *My Memoir* (1938)

Shortly before his death he stated:

> You can't fight God!
>
> REMARK TO RAYMOND FOSDICK, quoted by Fosdick in *Harper's*, December 1956

PRESIDENTIAL OPINIONS:
THE 26TH AND 27TH ON THE 28TH
★ ★ ★

A Byzantine logothete. THEODORE ROOSEVELT

[That] infernal skunk in the White House. THEODORE ROOSEVELT

He is a silly doctrinaire at times and an utterly selfish and cold-blooded politician always. THEODORE ROOSEVELT

I regard him as a ruthless hypocrite and as an opportunist, who has not convictions he would not barter at once for votes. WILLIAM HOWARD TAFT

That mulish enigma, that mountain of egotism and selfishness who lives in the White House. WILLIAM HOWARD TAFT

I feel certain that he would not recognize a generous impulse if he met it on the street. WILLIAM HOWARD TAFT

What others said
★ ★ ★

Of Wilson's handshake:

> Like a ten-cent pickled mackerel in brown paper. WILLIAM ALLEN WHITE, *Autobiography* (1946)

> The air currents of the world never ventilated his mind.
>
> WALTER HINES PAGE, US ambassador to Great Britain during the First World War

> Like Odysseus, he looked wiser when seated.
>
> JOHN MAYNARD KEYNES, *The Economic Consequences of the Peace* (1919). The British economist was at the Paris Peace Conference with Wilson, and the allusion is to Odysseus and Menelaus, whose visit to Troy to negotiate the return of Helen failed, resulting in the Trojan War.

At the Paris Peace Conference, French prime minister Georges Clemenceau explained to André Tardieu why he had given in to the British premier Lloyd George's demands:

> What do you expect when I'm between two men of whom one [Lloyd George] thinks he is Napoleon and the other [Wilson] thinks he is Jesus Christ?
>
> Quoted by the British diplomat Harold Nicolson in a letter to his wife, May 20, 1919

WARREN HARDING

1865–1923

29TH PRESIDENT OF THE UNITED STATES, 1921–3

WARREN HARDING

FULL NAME: Warren Gamaliel Harding
BORN: November 2, 1865, Blooming Grove, Ohio
DIED: August 2, 1923, San Francisco
MARRIED: Florence ('Flossie') Mabel Kling (who was
divorced from Henry Athenton DeWolfe)
CHILDREN: none (though he had a stepson,
Marshall Eugene DeWolfe)
PARTY: Republican
PERIOD IN OFFICE: March 4, 1921–August 2, 1923
VICE-PRESIDENT: Calvin Coolidge

* * *

HARDING WAS BORN IN RURAL OHIO, the son of a farmer who later became a physician. After an indifferent schooling, Harding learnt the basics of journalism on a weekly newspaper that his father had bought, and continued in the profession while studying at Ohio Central College. In 1884 he moved to Marion, Ohio, and bought the failing *Marion Daily Star*, and in 1891 married Florence Kling DeWolfe, an older divorcée who had pursued him in the face of his reluctance and her father's strong opposition. Her determination and business acumen helped to transform the *Daily Star* into one of the most successful newspapers in the county. She also gave her husband the impetus to enter Republican Party politics, and his distinguished looks and amiability, rather than any innate talent, led to his election as state senator (1899–1903), lieutenant governor (1903–5) and US senator (1915–21). At the Republican Party convention in Chicago in June 1920 he was said to be everybody's second choice, but after a late-night session in the original 'smoke-filled room' at the Blackstone Hotel he emerged as the preferred candidate. On the conservative wing of the Republican Party, he supported big business and opposed the League of Nations, and this and his stated desire to return America to 'normalcy' after the First World War brought him a landslide victory in the subsequent presidential election. His time in office saw some notable achievements, such as the Washington Naval Conference and the creation of the Budget Bureau, but these were overshadowed by a succession of corruption scandals, notably the Teapot Dome Scandal, in which Harding's secretary of the interior was jailed for accepting bribes. Harding died in San Francisco on August 2, 1923, either from a heart attack or a stroke, precipitated by food poisoning.

On himself:

> I like to go out into the country and bloviate.
>
> Quoted in Francis Russell, *The Shadow of Blooming Grove* (1968). 'Bloviate' was contemporary slang, meaning to sound off, talk loudly and at length, especially deploying orotund and meaningless rhetoric.

Bloviating turned out to be Harding's forte, as this sample illustrates:

> Progression is not proclamation nor palaver. It is not pretense nor play on prejudice. It is not of personal pronouns, nor perennial pronouncement. It is not the perturbation of a people passion-wrought, nor a promise proposed. Progression is everlastingly lifting the

standards that marked the end of the world's march yesterday and planting them on new and advanced heights today.

Harding's big appeal to the electorate was his promise of a return to 'normalcy' after the upheavals of the First World War:

America's present need is not heroics, but healing; not nostrums but normalcy; not revolution, but restoration; not agitation, but adjustment; not surgery, but serenity; not the dramatic, but the dispassionate; not experiment, but equipoise; not submergence in internationality, but sustainment in triumphant nationality.

SPEECH in Boston, May 14, 1920. Even though Harding had intended to say 'normality', not 'normalcy', the sentiment chimed with the electorate. Previously the word 'normalcy' had only been used in mathematical contexts. As G.N. Clark wrote in 1929, 'If … "normalcy" is ever to become an accepted word it will presumably be because the late President Harding did not know any better.'

Harding was good at getting his words and his concepts mixed up:

The United States should adopt a protective tariff of such a character as will help the struggling industries of Europe to get on their feet.

Quoted in Francis Russell, *The Shadow of Blooming Grove* (1968)

Harding could on occasion be more coherent. Here he is on the duties of the citizen:

In the great fulfilment we must have a citizenship less concerned about what the government can do for it and more anxious about what it can do for the nation.

ADDRESS TO THE REPUBLICAN CONVENTION, 1916. Compare Kennedy's famous appeal to the nation, p. 159 ('Ask not what your country …')

Our most dangerous tendency is to expect too much of government, and at the same time do for it too little. INAUGURAL ADDRESS, March 4, 1921

On a return to American isolationism:

We seek no part in directing the destinies of the world. INAUGURAL ADDRESS, March 4, 1921

On revolution:

If revolution insists upon overturning established order, let other peoples make the tragic experiment. There is no place for it in America … When revolution threatens we unfurl the flag of law and order. INAUGURAL ADDRESS, March 4, 1921

On voting rights:

Let the black man vote when he is fit to vote; prohibit the white man voting when he is unfit to vote. SPEECH in Birmingham, Alabama, October 27, 1921

On the League of Nations:

The League is not for us. ADDRESS TO CONGRESS, February 2, 1923

Harding was aware of his limitations:

I am not fit for this office and never should have been here.

Quoted in Nicholas Murray Butler, *Across the Busy Years* (1939)

I don't know what to do or where to turn in this taxation matter. Somewhere there must be a book that tells all about it, where I could go to straighten it out in my mind. But I don't know where the book is, and maybe I couldn't read it if I found it. And there must be a man in the country somewhere who could weigh both sides and know the truth. Probably he is in some college or other. But I don't know where to find him. I don't know who he is, and I don't know how to get him. My God, this is a hell of a place for a man like me to be!

> REMARK TO JUDSON WELLIVER, one of his secretaries, quoted in Francis Russell, *The Shadow of Blooming Grove* (1968)

When Senator Frank B. Brandegee asked him how he liked being president, he replied:

Frank, it is hell! No other word can describe it.

> Quoted in Francis Russell, *The Shadow of Blooming Grove* (1968)

On friends and enemies:

I have no trouble with my enemies. I can take care of my enemies in a fight. But my friends, my goddamned friends, they're the ones who keep me walking the floor at nights!

> REMARK TO WILLIAM ALLEN WHITE, editor of the *Emporia Gazette*

PRESIDENTIAL OPINIONS: THE 28TH ON THE 29TH
* * *

He has a bungalow mind.

> WOODROW WILSON, quoted in Thomas A. Bailey, *Woodrow Wilson and the Great Betrayal* (1945)

What others said
* * *

A tin horn politician with the manner of a rural corn doctor and the mien of a ham actor.

> H.L. MENCKEN, in the *Baltimore Evening Sun*, June 15, 1920

Keep Warren at home. Don't let him make any speeches. If he goes on tour somebody's sure to ask him questions, and Warren's just the sort of damned fool that will try to answer them.

> SENATOR BOIES PENROSE of Pennsylvania

He writes the worst English that I have ever encountered. It reminds me of a string of wet sponges; it reminds me of tattered washing on the line, it reminds me of stale bean soup, of college yells, of dogs barking idiotically through endless nights. It is so bad that a sort of grandeur creeps into it. It drags itself out of a dark abyss ... of pish, and crawls insanely up the topmost pinnacle of posh. It is rumble and bumble. It is flap and doodle. It is balder and dash.

> H.L. MENCKEN, in the *Baltimore Evening Sun*, March 7, 1921. Mencken characterized Harding's version of English as 'Gamalielese'.

Harding was not a bad man. He was just a slob.

> ALICE ROOSEVELT LONGWORTH, *Crowded Hours* (1933)

CALVIN COOLIDGE

1872–1933

30TH PRESIDENT OF THE UNITED STATES, 1923–9

CALVIN COOLIDGE

FULL NAME: John Calvin Coolidge
BORN: July 4, 1872, Plymouth, Vermont
DIED: January 5, 1933, Northampton, Massachusetts
MARRIED: Grace Anna Goodhue
CHILDREN: John, Calvin Jr
PARTY: Republican
PERIOD IN OFFICE: August 2, 1923–March 4, 1929
VICE-PRESIDENT: Charles G. Dawes (1925–9)
There was no vice-president 1923–5.

* * *

COOLIDGE, the son of a village storekeeper and notary public, was brought up to respect the Puritan virtues of hard work, thrift and honesty. After graduating from Amherst College, Coolidge trained as a lawyer with a law firm in Northampton, Massachusetts. He was admitted to the bar in 1897 and started his own practise in Northampton the following year. By this time he had already become involved in the local Republican Party, and as his political career flourished he abandoned his earlier progressive beliefs in favour of pro-business conservatism. He served as a Massachusetts state senator (1911–15), and then as lieutenant governor (1915–18) and governor (1919–21) of the state, in which role he attracted national attention by suppressing the 1919 Boston police strike. Largely because of his strong stance against organized labor, he was selected as Warren Harding's running-mate in the 1920 presidential election, and on Harding's death he was sworn in, by his father, as president. Coolidge succeeded in restoring public trust in the presidency after the scandals of the Harding era. He believed in big business and small government, cutting taxes for the rich, opposing federal intervention in the economy, refusing to subsidize struggling farmers, and maintaining a position of isolationism in international affairs. In 1924, amidst growing prosperity, Coolidge was re-elected, running under the slogan 'Keep cool and keep Coolidge'. At the time, as business boomed, many in the country welcomed his laissez-faire approach, but his lack of activity has been blamed by some for failing to reign in the speculation that culminated in the Wall Street Crash of 1929. By this time Coolidge had left office, having declined to run in the 1928 election. He retired to Northampton, where he wrote a syndicated newspaper column and his autobiography.

On himself:

I think the American people wants a solemn ass as a president. And I think I'll go along with them. REMARK TO ETHEL BARRYMORE, quoted in *Time*, May 16, 1955

On industrial action:

There is no right to strike against the public safety by anybody, anywhere, any time.
TELEGRAM TO SAMUEL GOMPERS, president of the American Federation of Labor, September 14, 1919, during the Boston police strike

On the primacy of the law:

One with the law is a majority.
ACCEPTING THE VICE-PRESIDENTIAL NOMINATION at the Republican convention, July 27, 1920

Silent Cal
* * *

Coolidge, known as 'Silent Cal', was notably taciturn, hence the following (probably apocryphal) exchange. Coolidge had been asked by his wife what a sermon had been about:

> COOLIDGE: Sin.
> MRS COOLIDGE: Well, what did he say about sin?
> COOLIDGE: He was against it.
>> Quoted in John H. McKee, *Coolidge: Wit and Wisdom* (1933)

On hearing of the death of President Harding:

> Guess we'd better have a drink. AUGUST 3, 1923

On another occasion a guest at the White House told Coolidge she had just wagered that she could get more than three words out the president, to which he replied:

> You lose. Quoted in Gamaliel Bradford, *The Quick and the Dead* (1931)

Exchange during the 1924 presidential campaign:

> REPORTERS: Have you any statement on the campaign?
> COOLIDGE: No.
> REPORTERS: Can you tell us something about the world situation?
> COOLIDGE: No.
> REPORTERS: Any information about Prohibition?
> COOLIDGE: No. *[pause]* Now, remember – don't quote me.

On another occasion he said:

> If you don't say anything, you can't be called on to repeat it.

After he left office, he advised his successor, Herbert Hoover, on how to deal with garrulous visitors:

> If you keep dead still they will run down in three or four minutes.
>> Quoted in Herbert Hoover, *Memoirs* (1952)

On capitalism:

> Civilization and profits go hand in hand. SPEECH in New York, November 27, 1920

> The chief business of the American people is business.
>> SPEECH to the American Society of Newspaper Editors, Washington DC, January 17, 1925

> The man who builds a factory builds a temple; the man who works there worships there.
>> Quoted in William E. Leuchtenburg, *The Perils of Prosperity 1914–1929* (1958)

> Prosperity is only an instrument to be used, not a deity to be worshipped.
>> SPEECH in Boston, June 11, 1928

On the war debts of Great Britain and others:

> Well, they hired the money, didn't they?
>> Quoted in John H. McKee, *Coolidge: Wit and Wisdom* (1933)

On persistence:

> Nothing in the world can take the place of persistence. Talent will not; nothing is more common than unsuccessful men with talent. Genius will not; unrewarded genius is almost a proverb. Education will not; the world is full of educated derelicts. Persistence and determination are omnipotent. The slogan 'press on' has solved and always will solve the problems of the human race.
>> Quoted in the program for a memorial service for Coolidge in 1933

On patriotism:

> Patriotism is easy to understand in America; it means looking out for yourself while looking out for your country. ATTRIBUTED

On refusing to stand again in 1928:

> I do not choose to run.
>> The full press release that he handed out to journalists on August 27, 1927, read: 'I do not choose to run for president in 1928.'

The onset of the Great Depression moved him to understatement:

> The country is not in good condition. ATTRIBUTED, January 1931

What others said

★ ★ ★

Democracy is that system of government under which the people, having 35,717,342 native-born adult whites to choose from, including thousands who are handsome and many whom are wise, pick out a Coolidge to be head of state. H.L. MENCKEN

He looks as if he had been weaned on a pickle. ALICE LEE LONGWORTH, *Men of Destiny* (1927)

Mr Coolidge's genius for inactivity is developed to a very high point. It is far from being an indolent activity. It is a grim, determined, alert inactivity which keeps Mr Coolidge occupied constantly. Nobody has ever worked harder at inactivity, with such force of character, with such unremitting attention to detail, with such conscientious devotion to the task. WALTER LIPPMANN, *Men of Destiny* (1927)

On being told that Coolidge was dead:

> How can they tell? DOROTHY PARKER

HERBERT HOOVER

1874–1964

31ST PRESIDENT OF THE UNITED STATES, 1929–33

HERBERT HOOVER

FULL NAME: Herbert Clark Hoover
BORN: August 10, 1874, West Branch, Iowa
DIED: October 20, 1964, New York, New York
MARRIED: Louise Henry
CHILDREN: Herbert Clark, Alan Henry
PARTY: Republican
PERIOD IN OFFICE: March 4, 1929–March 4, 1933
VICE-PRESIDENT: Charles Curtis

* * *

Hoover's father was of German and Swiss descent, and worked as a blacksmith and dealer of farm machinery. His mother, a Quaker, was from Canada. By the time he was nine, both his parents were dead, and Hoover then lived with an uncle and aunt in Oregon. He studied geology at Stanford University, and then made a fortune as a mining engineer in Australia, China and Burma. During the First World War he established his humanitarian and organizational credentials as head of the Commission for Relief in Belgium, and after the war headed the American Relief Administration that delivered food to millions in Europe threatened with starvation. The proven abilities of the 'Great Engineer' prompted President Harding to make him secretary of commerce, in which role he also served Harding's successor, Calvin Coolidge. Unlike many other leading Republicans of the time, Hoover supported the League of Nations, was sympathetic to organized labor, and believed in a degree of government regulation of industry. Once nominated as the Republican candidate to run in the 1928 presidential election, he espoused the 'American system of rugged individualism' as opposed to European 'state socialism'.

The economic prosperity of the 1920s helped Hoover to a landslide victory over the Democratic candidate, Al Smith, but within a few months of taking office Wall Street had crashed, ushering in the Great Depression. Against the promptings of more conservative, laisser-faire Republicans, Hoover took a number of initiatives to try to counter the dire effects of the Depression, including the establishment of the Reconstruction Finance Corporation, but the economy failed to respond, and unemployment soared. Hoover opposed federal welfare payments, and many thought he did too little to alleviate the sufferings of the poor, who called their shanty towns 'Hoovervilles'. In the 1932 presidential election Hoover was swept out of office by Franklin Delano Roosevelt, and thereafter became a fierce critic of Roosevelt's New Deal policies, and an ardent isolationist and anti-communist.

On words and deeds:

Words without action are the assassins of idealism.
Quoted in the *New York Tribune*, April 29, 1920

On Prohibition:

Our country has deliberately undertaken a great social and economic experiment, noble in motive and far-reaching in purpose. LETTER TO SENATOR W.H. BORAH, February 23, 1928

On big government:

Bureaucracy is ever desirous of spreading its influence and its power. You cannot extend the mastery of the government over the daily working life of a people without at the same time making it the master of the people's souls and thoughts.

SPEECH in New York, October 22, 1928

A year before the Wall Street Crash and the onset of the Great Depression:

We in America today are nearer to the final triumph over poverty than ever before in the history of any land. The poorhouse is vanishing from among us.

SPEECH at Stanford University, August 11, 1928

The slogan of progress is changing from the full dinner pail to the full garage.

SPEECH in New York, October 22, 1928

Four months later he was still blithely optimistic:

In no nation are the fruits of accomplishment more secure … I have no fears for the future of our country. It is bright with hope. INAUGURAL ADDRESS, March 4, 1929

Even after disaster struck, he insisted:

Prosperity is just around the corner. ATTRIBUTED

Hoover believed the federal government should play no part in alleviating poverty:

This is not an issue as to whether people shall go hungry or cold in the United States … It is a question as to whether the American people, on the one hand, will maintain the spirit of charity and mutual self-help through voluntary giving and the responsibility of local government as distinguished, on the other hand, from appropriations out of the Federal Treasury. February 1931, quoted in *The Memoirs of Herbert Hoover*, vol. 3 (1953)

On proposals 'to reduce the protective tariff to a competitive tariff for revenue':

The grass will grow in the streets of a hundred cities, a thousand towns.

SPEECH, October 31, 1932. Hoover had borrowed the phrase from William Jennings Bryan's famous 'Cross of Gold' speech (July 8, 1898).

RUGGED INDIVIDUALISM
* * *

Hoover used this famous phrase in a speech in New York, October 22, 1928:

We are challenged with a peacetime choice between the American system of rugged individualism and a European philosophy of diametrically opposed doctrines – doctrines of paternalism and state socialism.

Six years later he admitted:

While I can make no claim for having introduced the term 'rugged individualism', I should have been proud to have invented it. It has been used by American leaders for over half a century in eulogy of those God-fearing men and women of honesty whose stamina and character and fearless assertion of rights led them to make their own way in life.

Out of office, he had no time for FDR's policy of spending his way out of the Depression:

Blessed are the young, for they shall inherit the national debt.

SPEECH in Lincoln, Nebraska, January 16, 1936

On war:

Older men declare war. But it is youth who must fight and die.

SPEECH AT THE REPUBLICAN CONVENTION in Chicago, June 27, 1944

On his time in the White House:

The thing I enjoyed most were visits from children. They did not want public office.

ON GROWING UP: LETTERS TO AMERICAN BOYS AND GIRLS (1962)

On being a politician:

Being a politician is a poor profession. Being a public servant is a noble one.

ON GROWING UP: LETTERS TO AMERICAN BOYS AND GIRLS (1962)

Asked how he dealt with those who blamed him for the Great Depression:

I outlived the bastards. Quoted in William O. Douglas, *The Court Years 1939-75* (1980)

PRESIDENTIAL OPINIONS:
THE 30TH AND 32ND ON THE 31ST
★ ★ ★

The wunduh boy.

Calvin Coolidge, under whom Hoover served as secretary of commerce, quoted in David C. Whitney, THE AMERICAN PRESIDENTS (1967)

He is certainly a wonder, and I wish we could make him president of the United States. There couldn't be a better one.

FRANKLIN DELANO ROOSEVELT, quoted in Louis W. Koenig, *The Chief Executive* (1964). This was when Hoover was heading up the American effort to administer relief in Europe at the end of the First World War. Roosevelt was to change his mind about Hoover.

What others said
★ ★ ★

Hoover, if elected, will do one thing that is almost incomprehensible to the human mind: he will make a great man out of Coolidge.

CLARENCE DARROW, during the 1928 presidential election campaign

He wouldn't commit himself to the time of day from a hatful of watches.

WESTBROOK PEGLER, *Pegler: Angry Man of the Press* (1963)

Such a little man could not have made such a big depression.

NORMAN THOMAS, six times presidential candidate for the Socialist Party of America, letter to Murray B. Seidler, August 3, 1960

FRANKLIN D. ROOSEVELT

1882–1945

32ND PRESIDENT OF THE UNITED STATES, 1933–45

FRANKLIN D. ROOSEVELT

FULL NAME: Franklin Delano Roosevelt

BORN: January 30, 1882, Hyde Park, New York

DIED: April 12, 1945, Warm Springs, Georgia

MARRIED: Anna Eleanor Roosevelt

CHILDREN: Anna Eleanor, James, Elliott, Franklin, John

PARTY: Democratic

PERIOD IN OFFICE: March 4, 1933–April 12, 1945

VICE-PRESIDENTS: John N. Garner (1933–41), Henry A. Wallace (1941–5),
Harry S. Truman (1945)

* * *

FRANKLIN D. ROOSEVELT – known universally as FDR – was born into one of the oldest, richest and most influential families in New York state. He was a fifth cousin of Theodore Roosevelt, the 26th president, and his paternal grandmother was a first cousin of Elizabeth Kortright Monroe, wife of the 5th president. In 1905, during his final year at Harvard, he married Theodore Roosevelt's niece, Eleanor Roosevelt, who opened his eyes to the appalling poverty in the slums of New York city. In 1907 he was admitted to the New York bar, and in 1911 he became a New York state senator. Between 1913 and 1920 he served as Woodrow Wilson's assistant secretary of the navy, resigning to run (unsuccessfully) as vice-presidential candidate with the Democratic nominee, James M. Cox. In 1921 his political career almost came to an end when he contracted polio, which lost him the use of his legs – although with formidable will power, dedicated exercise and the support of his wife he was, with the aid of iron braces and sticks, able to walk a few steps for appearances in public, although in private he used a wheelchair. He campaigned for Al Smith, the Democratic presidential candidate, in 1924 and 1928, and in the latter year became governor of New York. He stood himself for president in 1932, at the head of a 'New Deal' coalition, and after taking office launched a massive programme of public spending to deal with the miseries of the Great Depression.

With the advent of war in Europe in 1939, Roosevelt pledged to maintain American neutrality, knowing the isolationist sentiments of the majority of the electorate, while following a policy of 'preparedness'. He turned the USA into what he called 'the arsenal of democracy', and, by the Lend-Lease Act, provided Britain with much needed military aid. The Japanese attack on Pearl Harbor in December 1941 brought the USA unequivocally into the Second World War. Roosevelt worked effectively with the other main Allied leaders, Churchill and Stalin, and his mobilization of American industry proved a key factor in the eventual Allied victory. He won an unprecedented fourth term in 1944, but died of a cerebral haemorrhage on April 12, 1945, less than a month before Germany's unconditional surrender.

On his battle with polio:

If you had spent two years in bed trying to wiggle your big toe, after that anything else would seem easy.

On the 'forgotten man':

These unhappy times call for the building of plans that rest upon the forgotten, the unorganized but the indispensable units of economic power, for plans ... that build from the bottom up and not from the top down, that put their faith once more in the forgotten man at the bottom of the economic pyramid. RADIO ADDRESS, Albany, New York, April 7, 1932

Roosevelt felt that economic theory could have a dehumanizing effect:

Men and women are becoming mere units in statistics. People aren't cattle, you know!
Quoted in Earle Looker, *This Man Roosevelt* (1932)

The advent of the New Deal:

Throughout the nation men and women, forgotten in the political philosophy of the government, look to us here for guidance and for more equitable opportunity to share in the distribution of national wealth. On the farms, in the large metropolitan areas, in the smaller cities and in the villages, millions of our citizens cherish the hope that their old standards of living and of thought have not gone forever. Those millions cannot and shall not hope in vain. I pledge you, I pledge myself, to a new deal for the American people. Let us all here assembled constitute ourselves prophets of a new order of competence and of courage. It is more than a political campaign. It is a call to arms. Give me your help, not to win votes alone, but to win in this crusade to restore America to its own people.
SPEECH TO THE DEMOCRATIC CONVENTION, July 2, 1932, accepting the presidential nomination. The term 'new deal' had been coined by Stuart Chase in the title of his book, *A New Deal*, published earlier that year.

FDR's first Inaugural Address was the occasion for one of his most famous phrases:

This great nation will endure as it has endured, will revive and will prosper. So, first of all, let me assert my firm belief that the only thing we have to fear is fear itself – nameless, unreasoning, unjustified terror which paralyzes needed efforts to convert retreat into advance. FIRST INAUGURAL ADDRESS, March 4, 1933

During the same speech, he announced the 'good neighbor' approach to relations with other countries (particularly those of Latin America):

In the field of world policy I would dedicate this nation to the policy of the good neighbor – the neighbor who resolutely respects himself and, because he does so, respects the rights of others – the neighbor who respects his obligations and respects the sanctity of his agreements in and with a world of neighbors. FIRST INAUGURAL ADDRESS, March 4, 1933

Of the Nicaraguan dictator Anastasio Tacho Somoza:

He may be a son of a bitch, but he's our son of a bitch. REMARK, 1938

On the National Industrial Recovery Act:

No business which depends for existence on paying less than living wages to its workers has any right to continue in this country.
STATEMENT, June 16, 1933

On the dangers of excessive corporate power:

Americans must forswear that conception of the acquisition of wealth which, through excessive profits, creates undue private power over private affairs and, to our misfortune, over public affairs as well.
STATE OF THE UNION ADDRESS, January 4, 1935

On the bottom line of government responsibility:

> While it isn't written in the Constitution, nevertheless it is the inherent duty of the federal government to keep its citizens from starvation.
>
> Quoted in Charles Beard and Mary Beard, *America in Midpassage* (1939)

> The test of our progress is not whether we add more to the abundance of those who have much; it is whether we provide enough for those who have too little.
>
> SECOND INAUGURAL ADDRESS, January 20, 1937

On pluralism:

> Why do we have to be 'socialist' or 'capitalist'? The United States is a big enough country to have several systems going at once. It has brains and tolerance enough to accommodate them. We don't have to force everything into some doctrinaire model.
>
> REMARK TO ADOLF BERLE, after the Tennessee Valley Authority, which FDR had set up, was attacked for being 'socialistic'. Quoted in Berle, 'Dreams and the Possible', *The New Leader*, February 1, 1965.

> YOUNG REPORTER: Mr President, are you a communist?
> FDR: No.
> YOUNG REPORTER: Are you a capitalist?
> FDR: No.
> YOUNG REPORTER: Are you a socialist?
> FDR: No.
> YOUNG REPORTER: What then is your philosophy?
> FDR: Philosophy? Philosophy? I am a Christian and a Democrat – that's all.
>
> Quoted in Frances Perkins, *The Roosevelt I Knew* (1946)

On liberalism:

> I am reminded of four definitions. A radical is a man with both feet firmly planted – in the air. A conservative is a man with two perfectly good legs who, however, has never learned to walk forward. A reactionary is a somnambulist walking backwards. A liberal is a man who uses his legs and his hands at the behest of his head.
>
> RADIO ADDRESS to the *New York Herald Tribune Forum*, October 26, 1939

On immigrants and revolutionaries:

> Remember, remember always, that all of us, and you and I especially, are descended from immigrants and revolutionists.
>
> ADDRESS TO THE DAUGHTERS OF THE AMERICAN REVOLUTION, quoted in Arthur Schlesinger Jr, *The Politics of Upheaval* (1960)

On the great tasks ahead:

> There is a mysterious cycle in human events. To some generations much is given. Of other generations much is expected. This generation has a rendezvous with destiny.
>
> SPEECH TO THE DEMOCRATIC CONVENTION, June 26, 1936, accepting the presidential nomination

The following day he outlined his commitment to government action:

> Better the occasional faults of a government that lives in a spirit of charity than the consistent omissions of a government frozen in the ice of its own indifference.
>
> SPEECH, Philadelphia, June 27, 1936

His Second Inaugural Address reinforced the magnitude of the challenge:

> I see millions of families trying to live on incomes so meager that the pall of family disaster hangs over them day by day. I see millions whose daily lives in city and on farm [*sic*] continue under conditions labeled indecent by a so-called polite society half a century ago. I see millions denied education, recreation and the opportunity to better their lot and the lot of their children. I see millions lacking the means to buy the products of farm and factory and by their poverty denying work and productiveness to many other millions.
>
> I see one-third of a nation ill-housed, ill-clad, ill-nourished.
>
> It is not in despair that I paint you that picture. I paint it for you in hope …
>
> Second Inaugural Address, January 20, 1937

On war:

> I have seen war … I hate war.
>
> Speech at Chautauqua, New York, August 14, 1936

> When peace has been broken anywhere, the peace of all countries everywhere is in danger.
>
> 'Fireside Chat' radio broadcast, September 3, 1939. This was the day Britain declared war on Germany, following the latter's invasion of Poland two days earlier.

> Your boys are not going to be sent into any foreign wars.
>
> Speech in Boston, October 30, 1940

But the Japanese attack on Pearl Harbor was to change all that:

> Yesterday, December 7, 1941 – a date which will live in infamy – the United States of America was suddenly and deliberately attacked by naval and air forces of the Empire of Japan … I ask that the Congress declare that since the unprovoked and dastardly attack by Japan on Sunday, December 7, 1941, a state of war has existed between the United States and the Japanese Empire.
>
> Address to Congress, December 8, 1941, requesting a declaration of war

---

FDR Unbuttoned
★ ★ ★

On less formal occasions, FDR was a generous host, and liked to press a second or a third cocktail on his guests, asking:

> How about another little sippy?

When the novelist Fanny Hurst, who had been on a diet, wanted to impress the president with the result, FDR asked her to turn around, and then commented:

> The Hurst may have changed, but it's the same old fanny.
>
> Quoted in the *New York Times*, February 24, 1968

His advice to speech makers:

> Be sincere, be brief, be seated.

If he suspected any guest at the White House was not paying attention to his words, he would say:

> I murdered my grandmother this morning.
>
> Quoted in Diana McClellan, *Ear on Washington* (1982)

To Winston Churchill, who had congratulated him on his 60th birthday, he replied:

> It is fun to be in the same decade with you.
>
> Quoted in Winston Churchill, *The Hinge of Fate* (1950)

FDR had already indicated which side he was in the global conflict:

We must be the great arsenal of democracy. For us this is an emergency as serious as war itself. We must apply ourselves to our task with the same resolution, the same sense of urgency, the same spirit of patriotism and sacrifice as we would show were we at war.

We have furnished the British great material support and we will furnish far more in the future ...

'FIRESIDE CHAT' RADIO BROADCAST, December 29, 1940

THE FOUR FREEDOMS

* * *

In a message to Congress, January 6, 1941, Roosevelt outlined the values for which America would be fighting, the famous 'four freedoms':

In the future days, which we seek to make secure, we look forward to a world founded upon four essential human freedoms.

The first is freedom of speech and expression – everywhere in the world.

The second is freedom of every person to worship God in his own way – everywhere in the world.

The third is freedom from want, which, translated into world terms, means economic understandings which will secure to every nation a healthy peacetime life for its inhabitants – everywhere in the world.

The fourth is freedom from fear, which, translated into world terms, means a worldwide reduction of armaments to such a point and in such a thorough fashion that no nation will be in a position to commit an act of physical aggression against any neighbor – anywhere in the world.

On books as weapons:

We all know that books burn – yet we have the greater knowledge that books cannot be killed by fire. People die, but books never die. No man and no force can abolish memory ... In this war, we know, books are weapons.

MESSAGE TO THE AMERICAN BOOKSELLERS ASSOCIATION, May 6, 1942

On the war aims of the USA and Great Britain:

Nothing less than the unconditional surrender of Germany, Italy and Japan.

STATEMENT TO THE PRESS at the Casablanca Conference, January 24, 1943

On running for office for an unprecedented fourth term in 1944:

If anyone says that's unorthodox lay it onto me. They already have me tagged. But it's doing the country good.

REMARK TO FRANCES PERKINS, secretary of labor, quoted by her in *The Roosevelt I Knew* (1946)

Eight days before his death, FDR was asked how he felt:

You know how I really feel? I feel like a baseball team going into the ninth inning with only eight men left to play. REMARK TO CLARK GRIFFITH, April 4, 1945

At his death he left the draft of a speech he was to give the following day, Jefferson Day, April 13, 1945:

The work, my friend, is peace. More than an end of this war – an end to the beginnings of all wars.

What others said
* * *

A second-class intellect – but a first-class temperament!

SUPREME COURT JUSTICE OLIVER WENDELL HOLMES JR, quoted in Arthur Schlesinger Jr, *The Coming of the New Deal* (1959)

Franklin D. Roosevelt is no crusader. He is no tribune of the people. He is no enemy of entrenched privilege. He is a pleasant man who, without any important qualifications for the office, would very much like to be president.

WALTER LIPPMANN, in the *New York Herald Tribune*, January 1932

He would rather follow public opinion than lead it.

ATTRIBUTED TO HARRY HOPKINS, one of FDR's closest advisers and director of the Works Progress Administration

I'd rather be right than Roosevelt. HEYWOOD BROUN

The man who started more creations since Genesis – and finished none.

GENERAL HUGH JOHNSON, director of the National Recovery Administration under FDR, quoted in George Wolfskill and John Hudson, *All But the People: F.D. Roosevelt and His Critics* (1969)

If he became convinced tomorrow that coming out for cannibalism would get him the votes he so sorely needs, he would begin fattening a missionary on the White House backyard come Wednesday.

H.L. MENCKEN, quoted in *Franklin D. Roosevelt: A Profile,* W.E. Leuchtenberg, ed. (1967)

Two-thirds mush and one-third Eleanor. ALICE ROOSEVELT LONGWORTH

If anything happened to that man, I couldn't stand it. He is the truest friend; he has the farthest vision; he is the greatest man I have ever known.

WINSTON CHURCHILL, remark to a US diplomat, 1943

HARRY S. TRUMAN

1884–1972

33RD PRESIDENT OF THE UNITED STATES, 1945–53

Harry S. Truman

Full name: Harry S. Truman (the 'S.' did not stand for anything)
Born: May 8, 1884, Lamar, Missouri
Died: December 26, 1972, Kansas City, Missouri
Married: Elizabeth ('Bess') Virginia Wallace
Children: Margaret
Party: Democratic
Period in office: April 12, 1945–January 20, 1953
Vice-presidents: Alben Barkley (1949–53)
There was no vice-president 1945–9.

* * *

THE SON OF A FARMER AND LIVESTOCK DEALER, Truman grew up in rural Missouri. After high school he worked at a number of clerical jobs in Kansas City before returning to the family farm, the running of which he took over on his father's death in 1914. During the First World War he served as an artillery captain on the Western Front. On his return to Kansas City he opened a haberdashery, but this went bust in the recession of 1921. The following year, with the backing of the boss of the local Democratic Party, Truman was elected a county judge. His incorruptibility set him apart from the local Democratic politicians, and he served two terms as presiding judge of the county court. In 1934 he was elected to the US Senate, and during the Second World War served as chairman of the Senate committee overseeing defense expenditure, highlighting billions of dollars worth of wastage. Elected vice-president in 1944, Truman succeeded to the presidency on Roosevelt's death the following April, and won a surprise victory over Thomas Dewey in the presidential election of 1948.

In August 1945 Truman authorized the dropping of the atomic bombs on Hiroshima and Nagasaki, thus bringing the Second World War to an end. But just as that conflict closed, the Cold War commenced. Truman supported the Marshall Plan, under which massive amounts of aid were sent to war-torn Western Europe, partly with the aim of averting a communist takeover. Truman also enunciated the Truman Doctrine, by which the USA pledged to support governments that were resisting communist influence. When communist North Korea invaded South Korea in 1950, he sent US forces to fight the North under a United Nations mandate. At home, he introduced his 'Fair Deal' program of social reforms, but his proposals to raise the minimum wage, extend social security, protect civil rights, introduce national health insurance and increase spending on science and education were largely rejected by Congress. However, he did achieve support for programs of urban renewal, and abolished racial segregation in the armed forces. With his poll ratings low, in 1952 he declared that he would not run again for president. However, during his retirement his reputation steadily grew.

On the First World War:

> It was said in the First World War that the French fought for their country, the British fought for freedom of the seas, and the Americans fought for souvenirs.
>
> Quoted in Margaret Truman, *Harry S. Truman* (1973)

TRUMAN AND THE BOMB
* * *

Following the dropping of an atomic bomb on Hiroshima:

This is the greatest thing in history.
REMARK, August 6, 1945

On a visit to the Oval Office, Robert Oppenheimer, who had led the team that developed the atomic bomb, said, wringing his hands:

I have blood on my hands.

Afterwards, Truman exploded:

Never bring that f–ing cretin in here again. He didn't drop the bomb. I did. That kind of weepiness makes me sick.
Quoted in Jean-Jacques Salomon, *Science et Politique* (1970)

On the Nazi invasion of the Soviet Union, prior to America's entry into the war:

If we see that Germany is winning the war we ought to help Russia, and if Russia is winning we ought to help Germany, and in that way let them kill as many as possible.
Quoted in the *New York Times*, July 24, 1941

On hearing that Roosevelt wanted him as his running-mate:

Tell him to go to hell. REMARK, July 21, 1944

On succeeding to the presidency:

I don't know whether you fellows ever had a load of hay fall on you, but when they told me yesterday what had happened, I felt like the moon, the stars and all the planets had fallen on me. If you fellows pray, pray for me. REMARK TO JOURNALISTS, April 13, 1945

On fighting the war:

I want peace and I'm willing to fight for it.
DIARY, May 22, 1945

Introducing the 'Fair Deal':

Every segment of our population, and every individual, has a right to expect from his government a fair deal. SPEECH TO CONGRESS, September 6, 1945

On the new threat:

Unless Russia is faced with an iron fist and strong language, another war is in the making. Only one language do they understand – 'How many divisions have you?' … I'm tired of babying the Soviets. TO SECRETARY OF STATE JAMES BYRNES, January 5, 1946

On liberals:

No professional liberal is intellectually honest. That's a real indictment – but true as the Ten Commandments. Professional liberals aren't familiar with the Ten Commandments or the Sermon on the Mount. REMARK, 1948, quoted in Margaret Truman, *Harry S. Truman* (1973)

On being president:

If you can't stand the heat, get out of the kitchen.
ATTRIBUTED TO TRUMAN by Major General Harry Vaughan in *Time*, April 28, 1952

All the president is, is a glorified public relations man who spends his time flattering, kissing and kicking people to get them to do what they are supposed to do anyway.
LETTER TO HIS SISTER, November 14, 1947

It is ignorance that causes most mistakes. The man who sits here ought to know his American history, at least.

> Quoted in Laurin L. Henry, *Presidential Transitions* (1960)

Do your duty, and history will do you justice.

> ATTRIBUTED by Edward T. Roybal in a memorial tribute in the House of Representatives, January 3, 1973

The buck stops here.

> MOTTO on a sign on Truman's desk in the Oval Office. (To 'pass the buck' in poker is to pass on the deck of cards to the next dealer.)

On the public:

I never give them hell. I just tell the truth, and they think it is hell.   Quoted in *Look*, April 3, 1956

After winning the 1948 presidential election:

The biggest mistake in politics is to take your friends for granted and try to buy your enemies.   Quoted in the *Observer* (London), July 7, 1996

On economists:

Give me a one-handed economist! All my economists say, 'On the one hand ... on the other.'
> ATTRIBUTED

On politicians vs statesmen:

A politician is a man who understands government, and it takes a politician to run a government. A statesman is a politician who's been dead ten or fifteen years.

> Quoted in the *New York World Telegram and Sun*, April 12, 1958

On recession vs depression

It's a recession when your neighbor loses his job; it's a depression when you lose yours.

> Quoted in the *Observer* (London), April 13, 1958. Ronald Reagan, while campaigning for the presidency in 1980, repeated the epigram, adding, 'Recovery will be when Jimmy Carter loses his.'

Looking back at his time in office:

Some of the presidents were great and some of them weren't. I can say that because I wasn't one of the great presidents; but I had a good time trying to be one.

> INTERVIEWED April 27, 1959, quoted in Mark Goodman, ed., *Give 'Em Hell, Harry* (1975)

THE TRUMAN DOCTRINE

* * *

At the present moment in world history nearly every nation must choose between alternative ways of life. The choice is too often not a free one. One way of life is based upon the will of the majority, and is distinguished by free institutions, representative government, free elections, guarantees of individual liberty, freedom of speech and religion, and freedom from political oppression. The second way of life is based upon the will of a minority forcibly imposed upon the majority. It relies upon terror and oppression, a controlled press and radio; fixed elections, and the suppression of personal freedoms. I believe it must be the policy of the United States to support free peoples who are resisting attempted subjugation by armed minorities or by outside pressures.

> SPEECH TO CONGRESS, March 12, 1947

MUSIC CRITICISM

* * *

On December 5, 1950, the president's daughter Margaret gave a public singing recital that attracted the following unfavorable review from Paul Hume, music critic of the Washington Post:

> Miss Truman cannot sing very well. She is flat a good deal of the time … She communicates almost nothing of the music she presents … There are a few moments during her recital when one can relax and feel confident that she will make her goal, which is the end of the song.

Furious, Margaret's father dashed off a note to Hume:

> I have just read your lousy review buried in the back pages. You sound like a frustrated old man who never made a success, an eight-ulcer man on a four-ulcer job, and all four ulcers working. I have never met you, but if I do you'll need a new nose and plenty of beefsteak and perhaps a supporter below.

On the pitfalls of life:

> Three things ruin a man – power, money and women. I never wanted power, I never had any money, and the only woman in my life is up at the house right now.
>
> STATEMENT TO REPORTERS on his 75th birthday, May 8, 1959

What others said

* * *

The captain with the mighty heart. DEAN ACHESON, *Present at the Creation* (1970)

Harry Truman proves the old adage that any man can become president of the United States.
> NORMAN THOMAS, six-times presidential candidate for the Socialist Party of America, quoted in Murray B. Seidler, *Norman Thomas, Respectable Rebel* (1967)

He is a man totally unfitted for the position. His principles are elastic, and he is careless with the truth. He has no special knowledge of any subject, and he is a malignant, scheming sort of individual who is dangerous not only to the United Mine Workers, but dangerous to the United States of America.
> JOHN L. LEWIS, labor leader, speech to the United Mine Workers convention, 1948

Give 'em hell, Harry! VOICE FROM THE CROWD during the 1948 election campaign

DEWEY BEATS TRUMAN
> THE *CHICAGO DAILY TRIBUNE*, November 3, 1948, famously jumps the gun on the result of that year's election

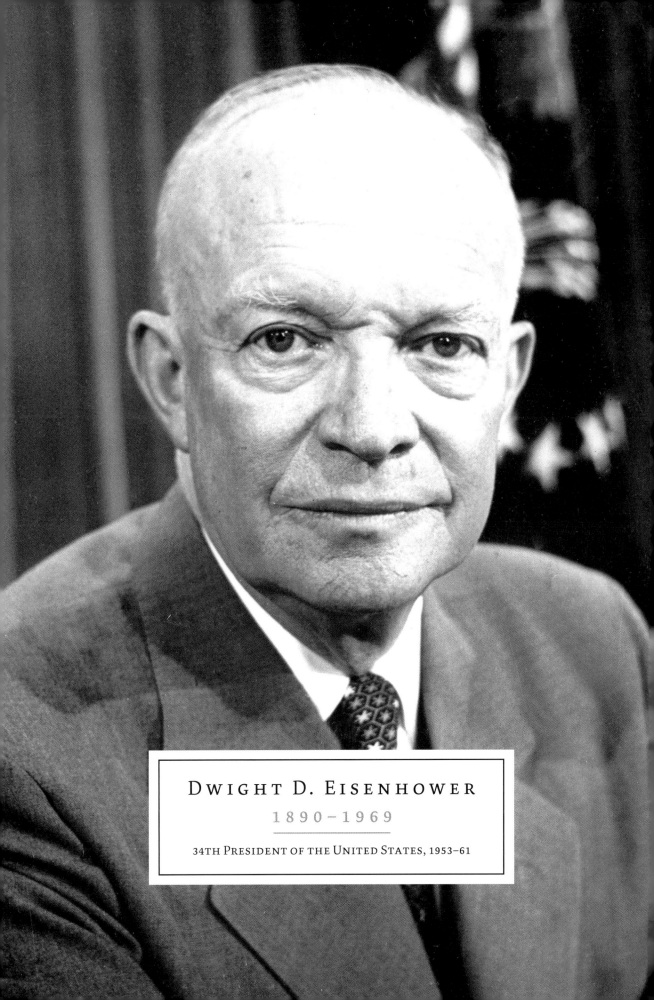

DWIGHT D. EISENHOWER

1890–1969

34TH PRESIDENT OF THE UNITED STATES, 1953–61

Dwight D. Eisenhower

FULL NAME: Dwight David Eisenhower
BORN: October 14, 1890, Denison, Texas
DIED: March 28, 1969, Washington DC
MARRIED: Mamie Geneva Doud
CHILDREN: Doud Dwight, John Sheldon David
PARTY: Republican
PERIOD IN OFFICE: January 20, 1953–January 20, 1961
VICE-PRESIDENT: Richard Nixon

* * *

ALTHOUGH BORN IN TEXAS, Eisenhower was only a baby when he moved with his parents to Abilene, Kansas, where his father, a trained engineer, was employed in a creamery. After high school Eisenhower worked to support his brother at college before entering West Point, from where he graduated in 1915 and joined the army. Eisenhower – still only a major in 1936 – was rapidly promoted following the outbreak of war in Europe, and by the middle of 1941 he was chief of staff of the Third Army. On America's entry into the war, Eisenhower – by now a brigadier general, and admired for his organizational skills, grasp of strategy and ability to get on with a wide range of people – was put in charge of developing plans for the invasion of mainland Europe. From September 1942 he was commander of US forces in Europe, overseeing the invasions of northwest Africa, Sicily and Italy, and in September 1943 he was made supreme commander of the Allied Expeditionary Force that undertook the D-Day landings and pushed on into Germany itself. After the Allied victory Eisenhower returned to America a hero, and was chief of staff of the army until leaving active duty in 1948 to become president of Columbia University. In 1950 he was appointed supreme commander of NATO. After being wooed for years by both parties, in 1952 he agreed to run as the Republican candidate in that year's presidential election. Riding on the slogan 'I like Ike', he won a landslide victory over Adlai Stevenson, and, in an era of domestic prosperity, was re-elected in 1956. At a time of heightened Cold War anxiety, Eisenhower propounded the Domino Theory and the Eisenhower Doctrine (see below). However, he opposed the anti-communist witch-hunting excesses of Senator Joe McCarthy, and in 1957 sent in federal troops to enforce school desegregation in Little Rock, Arkansas. He also oversaw the passage of the Civil Rights Acts of 1957 and 1960. In retirement he wrote two volumes of memoirs.

Addressing troops on D-Day, June 6, 1944:

The eyes of the world are upon you. The hopes and prayers of liberty-loving people everywhere march with you.

On politics and statesmanship:

The opportunist thinks of me and today. The statesman thinks of us and tomorrow.
SPEECH AT LAFAYETTE COLLEGE, Easton, Pennsylvania, November 1, 1946

Politics is a profession; a serious, complicated and, in its true sense, a noble one.
LETTER TO LEONARD V. FINDER, January 22, 1948

To a reporter in 1948, when there was increasing clamor for Eisenhower to run for president:

Look, son, I cannot conceive of any circumstance that could drag out of me permission to consider me for any political post from dogcatcher to Grand High Supreme King of the Universe. Quoted in Merlo J. Pusey, *Eisenhower, the President* (1956)

On privileges vs principles:

A people that values its privileges above its principles soon loses both.
FIRST INAUGURAL ADDRESS, January 20, 1953

On hopes for the future:

Whatever America hopes to bring to pass in the world must first come to pass in the heart of America.
FIRST INAUGURAL ADDRESS, January 20, 1953

On freedom:

History does not long entrust the care of freedom to the weak or the timid.
FIRST INAUGURAL ADDRESS, January 20, 1953

The history of free men is never really written by chance but by choice – their choice.
SPEECH in Pittsburgh, October 9, 1956

THE EISENHOWER DOCTRINE
* * *

Applying the Truman Doctrine (p. 149) specifically to the Middle East, Eisenhower promised to employ US armed forces:

To secure and protect the territorial integrity and political independence of such nations, requesting such aid, against overt armed aggression from any nation controlled by International Communism.
SPECIAL MESSAGE TO CONGRESS, January 5, 1957

On the New Deal policies of the Roosevelt–Truman era:

I believe that for the past twenty years there has been a creeping socialism spreading in the United States.
STATEMENT, June 11, 1953, quoted in Robert Donovan, *Eisenhower: The Inside Story* (1956)

On being president:

There is one thing about being president – nobody can tell you when to sit down.
Quoted in the *Observer* (London), 'Sayings of the Week', August 9, 1953

Now look, this idea that all wisdom is in the president, in me, that's baloney … I don't believe this government was set up to be operated by anyone acting alone; no one has a monopoly on the truth and on the facts that affect this country … We must work together.
Quoted in Elmo Richardson, *The Presidency of Dwight D. Eisenhower* (1979)

On leadership:

It's long, slow, tough work. Quoted in Peter Lyon, *Eisenhower: Portrait of the Hero* (1974)

On refusing to take on Senator Joe McCarthy in public:

I will not get in the gutter with that guy!
Quoted in Robert J. Donovan, *Eisenhower: The Inside Story* (1956)

On the arms race:

Every gun that is made, every warship launched, every rocket fired signifies, in the final sense, a theft from those who hunger and are not fed, those who are cold and are not clothed. This world in arms is not spending money alone. It is spending the sweat of its laborers, the genius of its scientists, the hopes of its children.

SPEECH in Washington DC, April 16, 1953

THE MILITARY-INDUSTRIAL COMPLEX
* * *

On leaving office, Eisenhower famously warned over the dangers presented by an over-powerful 'military-industrial complex':

In the councils of government, we must guard against the acquisition of unwarranted influence, whether sought or unsought, by the military-industrial complex. The potential for the disastrous rise of misplaced power exists and will persist. We must never let the weight of this combination endanger our liberties or democratic processes.

FAREWELL ADDRESS, January 17, 1961. This passage owes much to Eisenhower's chief speech writer Malcolm Moos.

Harry Truman, no admirer of Eisenhower, astutely commented:

I think somebody must have written it for him, and I'm not sure he understood what he was saying. But it's true.

As the French colonial power faced defeat by the communist Viet Minh in Indo-China, Eisenhower outlined the Domino Theory, by which it was feared that if one country fell to communism, all its neighbors would too:

You have broader considerations that might follow what you might call the 'falling domino' principle. You have a row of dominoes set up. You knock over the first one, and what will happen to the last one is that it will go over very quickly. So you have the beginning of a disintegration that would have the most profound of influences.

STATEMENT AT A PRESS CONFERENCE, April 7, 1954. The theory dominated US strategy in Southeast Asia for a generation.

On Washington DC:

There are a number of things wrong with Washington. One of them is that everyone has been too long away from home.

STATEMENT AT A PRESS CONFERENCE, May 11, 1955

Referring to the role of Britain and France in the Suez Crisis:

There can be no law if we were to invoke one code of international conduct for those who oppose us and another for our friends. RADIO BROADCAST, October 31, 1956

On peace:

I think that the people want peace so much that one of these days governments had better get out of the way and let them have it.

TV DISCUSSION with British Prime Minister Harold Macmillan, August 31, 1959

On his criteria in decision-making:

I have only one yardstick by which I test every major problem and that yardstick is: Is it good for America? Unlike presidential administrations, problems rarely have terminal dates. STATE OF THE UNION ADDRESS, January 12, 1961

On planning:

In preparing for battle, I have always found that plans are useless but planning is indispensable. Quoted in Richard Nixon, *Six Crises* (1962)

On intellectuals:

An intellectual is a man who takes more words than necessary to tell you more than he knows. Attributed

On his speech-writers:

Gosh, someone around here is always feeding me all these 'folksy' phrases. Well, I'm folksy enough as it is, without their trying to make matters worse.

Quoted in Emmet John Hughes, *The Ordeal of Power: A Political Memoir of the Eisenhower Years* (1963)

PRESIDENTIAL OPINIONS: THE 33RD ON THE 34TH
* * *
He's a good man. The only trouble was, he had a lot of damn fool Republicans around him.

Harry S. Truman, remark, December 1963

What others said
* * *

I doubt very much if a man whose main literary interests were in works by Mr Zane Grey ... is particularly well-equipped to be chief executive of this country, particularly where Indian affairs are concerned.

Dean Acheson, secretary of state (1949–53) under President Truman

Eisenhower is the most completely opportunistic and unprincipled politician America has ever raised to high office ... insincere, vindictive, hypocritical, and a dedicated, conscious agent of the communist conspiracy.

Robert H. Weichler, founder of the John Birch Society, an ultra-conservative pressure group

Roosevelt proved that a president could serve for life; Truman proved anybody could be president; Eisenhower proved that your country can be run without a president.

Nikita Khrushchev, the Soviet leader, in 1960

Perhaps his peculiar contribution to the art of politics was to make politics boring at a time when the people wanted any excuse to forget public affairs.

Arthur Schlesinger Jr, in *Esquire*, January 1965

Eisenhower was a subtle man, and no fool, though in pursuit of his objectives he did not like to be thought of as brilliant; people of brilliance, he thought, were distrusted.

David Halberstam, *The Best and the Brightest* (1969)

JOHN F. KENNEDY

1917–1963

35TH PRESIDENT OF THE UNITED STATES, 1961–3

JOHN F. KENNEDY

FULL NAME: John ('Jack') Fitzgerald Kennedy
BORN: May 29, 1917, Brookline, Massachusetts
DIED: November 22, 1963, Dallas, Texas
MARRIED: Jacqueline ('Jackie') Lee Bouvier
CHILDREN: Arabella, Caroline Bouvier, John Fitzgerald Jr, Patrick Bouvier
PARTY: Democratic
PERIOD IN OFFICE: January 20, 1961–November 22, 1963
VICE-PRESIDENT: Lyndon B. Johnson

* * *

KENNEDY WAS BORN INTO A PROSPEROUS Irish Catholic family in Massachusetts. His father Joseph was a successful businessman who did much to build the political career of his sons in the Democratic Party. When Kennedy was ten, he moved with his family to New York, and was educated at private schools before going on to Harvard, where he studied international affairs. In September 1941 he volunteered for the navy, and went on to serve in the Pacific as a lieutenant in command of a motor torpedo (PT) boat. In August 1943 his boat, PT-109, was sunk by a Japanese destroyer. Despite being injured, Kennedy led his men to safety, and he himself swam three miles towing a badly burnt crewman. After the war, Kennedy entered politics, representing Massachusetts in the US House of Representatives (1947–53) and Senate (1953–61). He was selected as the Democratic presidential nominee in 1960, and won a close victory over the Republican candidate, Richard Nixon. The first Catholic president, and the youngest after Theodore Roosevelt, Kennedy assumed office during a tense period of the Cold War. Presenting America with the challenges of the 'New Frontier', and vowing that America would 'pay any price' to defend freedom, he promised to send men to the moon, authorized the disastrous Bay of Pigs invasion of Cuba, increased US military commitment to South Vietnam, and faced down the Soviets in the Cuban Missile Crisis. At home, he did not manage to achieve all that he had hoped, and it was left to his successor to push through a comprehensive program of civil rights legislation and social reform. Kennedy's youth, charm and liberal values entranced millions all around the world, and there was great shock and sense of loss when he was assassinated in Dallas on November 22, 1963. The official Warren Commission concluded that he was the victim of a single gunman, Lee Harvey Oswald, acting alone. However, countless conspiracy theories have pointed the finger at suspects as diverse as the Mafia, the Soviet Union, supporters or opponents of Cuban president Fidel Castro, and even the FBI and the CIA.

On being asked by a schoolboy how he became a war hero:

It was involuntary. They sank my boat.
    Quoted in Arthur Schlesinger Jr, *A Thousand Days* (1965)

Joking about his notoriously corrupt father, Joseph Kennedy:

I just received the following wire from my generous Daddy – Don't buy a single vote more than necessary. I'll be damned if I'm going to pay for a landslide.
    Kennedy read out the message – almost certainly his own invention – at a dinner in Washington, March 15, 1958.

On politicians:

Mothers all want their sons to grow up to become president, but they don't want them to become politicians in the process. ATTRIBUTED

On being told by a friend that he had a good chance of gaining the vice-presidential nomination in 1960:

Let's not talk so much about vice. I'm against vice in any form.
Quoted in Bill Adler, ed., *The Complete Kennedy Wit* (1967)

On the 'New Frontier':

I stand tonight facing west on what was once the last frontier. From the lands that stretch three thousand miles behind me, the pioneers of old gave up their safety, their comfort and sometimes their own lives to build a new world here in the West ... Today some would say that those struggles are all over – that all the horizons have been explored – that all the battles have been won – that there is no longer an American frontier. But I trust that no one in this vast assemblage will agree with those sentiments. For the problems are not all solved and the battles are not all won – and we stand today on the edge of a New Frontier – the frontier of the 1960s – a frontier of unknown opportunities and perils, a frontier of unfulfilled hopes and threats ... The New Frontier of which I speak is not a set of promises, it is a set of challenges. It sums up not what I intend to offer the American people, but what I intend to ask of them. It appeals to their pride, not to their pocketbook – it holds out the promise of more sacrifice instead of more security.
SPEECH accepting the Democratic nomination in Los Angeles, July 15, 1960

Kennedy used his Inaugural Address, delivered during a tense period of the Cold War, to reinforce America's role as the defender of freedom around the world:

Let the word go forth from this time and place, to friend and foe alike, that the torch has been passed to a new generation of Americans – born in this century, tempered by war, disciplined by a hard and bitter peace, proud of our ancient heritage – and unwilling to witness or permit the slow undoing of those human rights to which this nation has always been committed, and to which we are committed today at home and around the world. Let every nation know, whether it wishes us well or ill, that we shall pay any price, bear any burden, meet any hardship, support any friend, oppose any foe to assure the survival and the success of liberty. INAUGURAL ADDRESS, January 20, 1961

On America's obligations:

To those peoples in the huts and villages of half the globe struggling to break the bonds of mass misery, we pledge our best efforts to help them help themselves, for whatever period is required – not because the communists may be doing it, not because we seek their votes, but because it is right. If a free society cannot help the many who are poor, it cannot save the few who are rich. INAUGURAL ADDRESS, January 20, 1961

On dealing with the Soviet Bloc:

Only when our arms are sufficient beyond doubt can we be certain beyond doubt that they will never be employed ... Let us never negotiate out of fear. But let us never fear to negotiate. INAUGURAL ADDRESS, January 20, 1961

On the task ahead:

All this will not be finished in the first hundred days. Nor will it be finished in the first thousand days, nor in the life of this administration, nor even perhaps in our lifetime on this planet. But let us begin.

INAUGURAL ADDRESS, January 20, 1961

On appointing his younger brother Robert as attorney general:

I can't see that it's wrong to give him a little legal experience before he goes out to practice law.

Quoted in *Time*, February 3, 1961

On his ambitions in space:

I believe that this nation should commit itself to achieving the goal, before this decade is out, of landing a man on the moon and returning him safely to earth.

ADDRESS to a joint session of Congress
May 25, 1961

ASK NOT WHAT YOUR COUNTRY …

* * *

Towards the end of his Inaugural Address, Kennedy made a famous appeal:

And so, my fellow Americans: ask not what your country can do for you – ask what you can do for your country. My fellow citizens of the world: ask not what America will do for you, but what together we can do for the freedom of man.

INAUGURAL ADDRESS, January 20, 1961

This passage echoes a speech made by Oliver Wendell Holmes in Keene, New Hampshire, on May 30, 1884:

We pause to … recall what our country has done for each of us and to ask ourselves what we can do for our country in return.

We choose to go to the moon in this decade and do the other things, not because they are easy, but because they are hard.

SPEECH AT RICE UNIVERSITY, September 12, 1962

On his popularity after the Bay of Pigs fiasco of April 1961:

The worse I do, the more popular I get.

Quoted in D. Wallenchinsky, *The People's Almanac* (1962)

On the chances of US–Soviet rapprochement:

It's going to be a cold winter.

REMARK TO SOVIET LEADER NIKITA KHRUSHCHEV in Vienna, June 4, 1961

On time:

We must use time as a tool, not as a couch.

Quoted in the *Observer* (London), 'Sayings of the Week', December 10, 1961

On war and peace:

Mankind must put an end to war or war will put an end to mankind.

SPEECH TO THE UNITED NATIONS GENERAL ASSEMBLY, September 25, 1961

Arms alone are not enough to keep the peace – it must be kept by men.

Quoted in the *Observer* (London), 1962, 'Sayings of the Decade'

If we cannot end now our differences, at least we can make the world safe for diversity. For, in the final analysis, our most basic common link is that we all inhabit this small planet. We all breathe the same air. We all cherish our children's future. And we are all mortal.

SPEECH AT THE AMERICAN UNIVERSITY, Washington DC, June 10, 1963

The war against hunger is truly mankind's war of liberation.

SPEECH AT THE WORLD FOOD CONGRESS, June 4, 1963

On the stationing of Soviet missiles on Cuba:

This urgent transformation of Cuba into an important strategic base – by the presence of these large, long-range and clearly offensive weapons of sudden mass-destruction – constitutes an explicit threat to the peace and security of all the Americas. STATEMENT, October 22, 1962

As the Cuban Missile Crisis developed:

I guess this is the week I earn my salary.

Quoted in M. Ringo, *Nobody Said It Better* (1962)

On equality:

It's very hard in military or personal life to assure complete equality. Life is unfair.

REMARK AT A NEWS CONFERENCE, March 23, 1962

ICH BIN EIN BERLINER

★ ★ ★

At a speech in City Hall, West Berlin, June 26, 1963, Kennedy expressed solidarity with the people of Berlin, recently divided by the Berlin Wall:

Freedom has many flaws and our democracy is imperfect, but we have never had to put up a wall to keep our people in. Two thousand years ago the proudest boast was '*Civis Romanus sum*'. Today, in the world of freedom, the proudest boast is '*Ich bin ein Berliner*' ... All free men, wherever they may live, are citizens of Berlin, and, therefore, as a free man, I take pride in the words '*Ich bin ein Berliner*'.

It was Cicero who had famously declared '*Civis Romanus sum*'. '*Ein Berliner*' is a doughnut.

On civil rights:

It ought to be possible for American consumers of any color to receive equal service in places of public accommodation, such as hotels and restaurants and theaters and retail stores, without being forced to resort to demonstrations in the street, and it ought to be possible for American citizens of any color to register and to vote in a free election without interference of fear of reprisal ... In short, every American ought to have the right to be treated as he would wish to be treated, as one would wish his children to be treated. But this not the case. TELEVISED ADDRESS TO THE NATION, June 10, 1963

No one has been barred on account of his race from fighting or dying for America – there are no 'white' or 'colored' signs on the foxholes or graveyards of battle.

MESSAGE TO CONGRESS, June 19, 1963

On Winston Churchill:

He mobilized the English language and sent it into battle.

SPEECH at a ceremony granting Churchill honorary US citizenship, April 9, 1963

On art and artists:

> In free society art is not a weapon ... Artists are not engineers of the soul.
>
> SPEECH AT AMHERST COLLEGE, Massachusetts, October 26, 1963. It was Stalin who had described writers as 'engineers of human souls'.

On Washington DC:

> Washington is a city of Southern efficiency and Northern charm.
>
> Quoted in William Manchester, *Portrait of a President* (1967)

On his legacy:

> I had plenty of problems when I came into office. But wait until the fellow who follows me sees what he will inherit.
>
> Quoted in Hugh Sidey, *John F. Kennedy, President: A Reporter's Inside Story* (1963)

A FATEFUL DAY IN DALLAS
* * *

> Dallas is a very dangerous place. I wouldn't go there. Don't you go.
>
> SENATOR WILLIAM FULBRIGHT, remark to President Kennedy, October 3, 1963

> We're nothing but sitting ducks in a shooting gallery.
>
> JACQUELINE KENNEDY, remark to a Secret Service man, November 22, 1963

> Jackie, if somebody wants to shoot me from a window with a rifle, nobody can stop it, so why worry about it?
>
> PRESIDENT KENNEDY, remark to his wife, 8 a.m., November 22, 1963

What others said
* * *

The liberals like his rhetoric and the conservatives like his inaction.

NORMAN THOMAS, US socialist leader

The chickens are coming home to roost. And you live in the chicken house.

GENERAL DOUGLAS MACARTHUR, remark to Kennedy, late 1961

There is something very 18th-century about this young man. He is always on his toes during our discussions, but in the evening there will be music and wine and pretty women.

HAROLD MACMILLAN, British prime minister, quoted in the *New York Journal American*, January 21, 1962

PRESIDENTIAL OPINIONS: THE 33RD AND 36TH ON THE 35TH
* * *

I'm not against the Pope. I'm against the Pop.

HARRY S. TRUMAN, referring to Kennedy's Catholicism and his famously corrupt father Joseph Kennedy

The enviable attractive nephew who sings an Irish ballad for the company and then winsomely disappears before the table-clearing and dishwashing begin.

LYNDON B. JOHNSON

LYNDON B. JOHNSON

1908–1973

36TH PRESIDENT OF THE UNITED STATES, 1963–9

LYNDON B. JOHNSON

FULL NAME: Lyndon Baines Johnson
BORN: August 27, 1908, Stonewall, Gillespie County, Texas
DIED: January 22, 1973, Stonewall, Gillespie County, Texas
MARRIED: Claudia Alta ('Lady Bird') Taylor
CHILDREN: Lynda Bird, Luci Baines
PARTY: Democratic
PERIOD IN OFFICE: November 22, 1963–January 20, 1969
VICE-PRESIDENT: Hubert Humphrey (1965–9)
There was no vice-president in 1963–5.

* * *

JOHNSON WAS RAISED IN SOUTHERN TEXAS, the son of a businessman and member of the Texas House of Representatives who had fallen on hard times. After high school Johnson worked in a variety of odd jobs before enrolling in 1926 in Southwest Texas State Teachers' College. He graduated in 1930, having spent a formative spell teaching impoverished children at a predominantly Mexican American school in Cotulla, Texas. Soon afterwards he entered politics, going to Washington as the legislative assistant of a Democratic congressman. A supporter of Roosevelt's New Deal, in 1935–7 he was director of the National Youth Administration in Texas, creating employment and training opportunities for young people. Apart from six months active service in the Pacific in 1941–2, during which he won the Silver Star for gallantry, he sat in the US House of Representatives from 1937 to 1949, when he entered the US Senate. In 1955, having built up a formidable reputation as a political persuader, he became Senate majority leader, and set himself apart from most Southern Democrats by supporting the Civil Rights Acts of 1957 and 1960.

J.F. Kennedy selected Johnson to be his running-mate in the presidential election of 1960, but as vice-president, the folksy, down-to-earth Southerner found himself at odds with the elite East Coast liberal Ivy Leaguers who surrounded Kennedy, and he was frustrated at the president's failure to push domestic reforms through Congress. On succeeding to the presidency after Kennedy's assassination, Johnson went on to win the 1964 presidential election on the back of his program of 'Great Society' reforms, which included the Civil Rights Act of 1964 (outlawing all forms of racial discrimination), the Voting Rights Act of 1965, and massively increased spending on welfare in his 'war on poverty'. Johnson's nemesis was the Vietnam War, to which he committed ever-increasing quantities of men and resources to little apparent effect, apart from a growing anti-war movement at home. The bitter divisions thus created in American society – together with a deterioration in race relations marked by inner-city riots – persuaded Johnson not to stand in the presidential election of 1968, and he retired to his ranch in Texas, dying a few days before a treaty was signed in Paris to end the Vietnam War.

On his identity:

I am a free man, an American, a United States senator and a Democrat, in that order.

In *TEXAS QUARTERLY*, Winter 1958

On politics:

> If you're in politics and you can't tell when you walk into a room who's for you and who's against you, then you're in the wrong line of work.
>
> Quoted in B. Mooney, *The Lyndon Johnson Story* (1956)

> Come now, let us reason together.
>
> FREQUENT PLEA TO POLITICAL OPPONENTS, quoting Isaiah 1:18

On the vice-presidency:

> Not being able to do anything will wear you down sooner than hard work.
>
> REMARK TO HIS BROTHER, Sam Houston Johnson, and quoted by the latter in *My Brother, Lyndon* (1970)

Following the assassination of President Kennedy:

> Yesterday is not ours to recover, but tomorrow is ours to win or lose.
>
> ADDRESS TO THE NATION, November 28, 1963

> All I have I would have given gladly not to be standing here today.
>
> ADDRESSING CONGRESS for the first time as president, November 27, 1963

On becoming president:

> I do not think that I will ever get credit for anything I do, because I did not go to Harvard.
>
> Quoted in Hugh Sidey, *A Very Personal Presidency* (1968)

On his civil rights program:

> We have talked long enough in this country about equal rights. We have talked for a hundred years or more. It is time now to write the next chapter, and to write it in the books of law. SPEECH TO CONGRESS, November 27, 1963

Following violent attacks by white racists on a civil rights march in Selma, Alabama:

> At times history and fate meet at a single time in a single place to shape a turning point in man's unending search for freedom. So it was at Lexington and Concord. So it was a century ago at Appomattox. So it was last week in Selma, Alabama ... There is no Negro problem. There is no Southern problem. There is no Northern problem. There is only an American problem ... Many of the issues of civil rights are very complex and most difficult. But about this there can and should be no argument. Every American citizen must have the right to vote ... Yet the harsh fact is that in many places in this country men and women are kept from voting simply because they are Negroes ... There is no Constitutional issue here. The command of the Constitution is plain. There is no moral issue. It is wrong – deadly wrong – to deny any of your fellow Americans the right to vote in this country. There is no issue of states' rights or national rights. There is only the struggle for human rights.
>
> SPEECH TO CONGRESS, March 15, 1965, introducing the Voting Rights Act

Declaring war on poverty:

> This administration here and now declares unconditional war on poverty in America.
>
> STATE OF THE UNION MESSAGE, January 8, 1964

THE GREAT SOCIETY

∗ ∗ ∗

In 1964, Johnson outlined his vision of the 'Great Society':

Your imagination, your initiative and your indignation will determine whether we build a society where progress is the servant of our needs, or a society where old values and new visions are buried under unbridled growth. In your time we have the opportunity to move not only toward the rich society and the powerful society, but upward to the Great Society. The Great Society rests on abundance and liberty for all. It demands an end to poverty and racial injustice, to which we are totally committed in our time. But that is just the beginning. The Great Society is a place where every child can find knowledge to enrich his mind and to enlarge his talents. It is a place where leisure is a welcome chance to build and reflect, not a feared cause of boredom and restlessness. It is a place where the city of man serves not only the needs of the body and the demands of commerce but the desire for beauty and the hunger for community. It is a place where man can renew contact with nature. It is a place which honors creation for its own sake and for what it adds to the understanding of the race. It is a place where men are more concerned with the quality of their goals than the quantity of their goods. But most of all, the Great Society is not a safe harbor, a resting place, a final objective, a finished work. It is a challenge constantly renewed, beckoning us toward a destiny where the meaning of our lives matches the marvelous products of our labor.

> SPEECH at the University of Michigan, May 22, 1964. The phrase 'Great Society' was coined by speechwriter Richard N. Goodwin in early March 1964.

I am going to build the kind of nation that President Roosevelt hoped for, President Truman worked for, and President Kennedy died for.

> SPEECH, December 1964

If you looked at my record, you would know that I am a Roosevelt New Dealer. As a matter of fact, to tell the truth, John F. Kennedy was a little too conservative to suit my taste.

> REMARKS, November 23, 1963, the day after Kennedy's assassination, quoted in William E. Leuchtenburg, *In the Shadow of FDR* (1993 edn)

On his hopes for peace:

We hope that the world will not narrow into a neighborhood before it has broadened into a brotherhood.

> SPEECH AT THE LIGHTING OF THE NATION'S CHRISTMAS TREE, December 22, 1963

On Vietnam:

We Americans know, although others appear to forget, the risks of spreading conflict. We still seek no wider war. RADIO AND TELEVISION BROADCAST, August 4, 1964

I didn't just screw Ho Chi Minh. I cut his pecker off.

> REMARK referring to the North Vietnamese leader, 1964

We are not about to send American boys nine or ten thousand miles away from home to do what Asian boys ought to be doing for themselves.

SPEECH at Akron University, October 21, 1964

LBJ's People Skills
★ ★ ★

When things haven't gone well for you, call in a secretary or a staff man and chew him out. You will sleep better and they will appreciate the attention.

Quoted in *People*, February 2, 1987

I don't want loyalty. I want *loyalty*. I want him to kiss my ass in Macy's window at high noon and tell me it smells like roses. I want his pecker in my pocket.

On appointing a new assistant, quoted in David Halberstam, *The Best and the Brightest* (1972)

I don't have ulcers. I give 'em.

Quoted in Franck Cormier, *LBJ: The Way He Was* (1977)

There are no favorites in my office. I treat them all with the same general inconsideration.

Quoted in Alfred Steinberg, *Sam Johnson's Boy: A Close-up of the President from Texas* (1968)

I do not find it easy to send the flower of our youth, our finest young men, into battle.

REMARK AT A NEWS CONFERENCE, July 28, 1965

You let a bully come into your front yard, the next day he'll be on your porch.

AN OFT-REPEATED OBSERVATION, quoted in *Time*, April 15, 1984

The kids were right. I blew it.

REMARK ON VIETNAM late in life, quoted in *Parade*, October 19, 1980

After authorizing the invasion of the Dominican Republic, ostensibly to prevent a communist takeover:

We don't propose to sit here in our rocking chair with our hands folded and let the communists set up any government in the western hemisphere. STATEMENT, May 3, 1965

On J. Edgar Hoover, director of the FBI:

Better to have him inside the tent pissing out than outside pissing in.

Quoted in David Halberstam, *The Best and the Brightest* (1972)

On economists:

Did y'ever think, Ken, that making a speech on economics is a lot like pissing down your leg? It seems hot to you, but it never does to anyone else.

REMARK TO J.K. GALBRAITH, quoted in the latter's *A Life in Our Times* (1981)

An economist is a man who couldn't tell the difference between chicken salad and chicken shit. ATTRIBUTED

To an officer who told him that he was walking towards the wrong helicopter with the words 'That's your helicopter over there, sir':

Son, they are all my helicopters. Quoted in Hugh Sidey, *A Very Personal Presidency* (1968)

Announcing that he would not stand in the 1968 presidential election:

It is true that a house divided against itself is a house that cannot stand. There is a division in the American house now and believing this as I do, I have concluded that I should not permit the presidency to become involved in the partisan divisions that are developing in this political year. Accordingly, I shall not seek, and I will not accept, the nomination of my party for another term as your president.

> TV BROADCAST, March 31, 1968. The 'division' he was referring to was the split in America over the rights and wrongs of the Vietnam War. The biblical 'divided house' metaphor – one famously deployed by Lincoln in 1858 (see pp. 73–4) – was drawn from Mark 3:25.

On his legacy:

I don't want to be remembered as a can't-do man.

> Quoted in Frank Cormier, *LBJ: The Way He Was* (1977)

I do not want to be the president who built empires, or sought grandeur, or extended dominions … I want to be the president who educated young children … who helped to feed the hungry … who helped the poor to find their own way and who protected the right of every citizen to vote in every election.

> Quoted in Doris Kearns, *Lyndon Johnson and the American Dream* (1976)

I knew from the start that if I left the woman I really loved – the Great Society – in order to fight that bitch of a war … then I would lose everything at home. All my hopes … my dreams …

> REMARK TO DORIS KEARNS, who helped him with his autobiography, quoted in the *New York Times Magazine*, November 2, 1980

PRESIDENTIAL OPINIONS: THE 37TH ON THE 36TH
★ ★ ★
People said that my language was bad, but Jesus, you should have heard LBJ!

RICHARD NIXON, in 1976

What others said
★ ★ ★

Johnson's instinct for power is as primordial as a salmon's going upstream to spawn.

> THEODORE WHITE, *The Making of the President, 1964* (1965)

Hey, hey, LBJ,
How many kids did you kill today? ANTI-WAR SLOGAN

He wanted everyone with him all the time, and when they weren't, it broke his heart.

> MAX FRANKEL of the *New York Times*, quoted in Richard Harwood and Haynes Johnson, *Lyndon* (1973)

Kennedy promised, Johnson delivered.

> ARTHUR SCHLESINGER JR, in the *Observer* (London), November 20, 1983

RICHARD M. NIXON

1913–1994

37TH PRESIDENT OF THE UNITED STATES, 1969–74

RICHARD M. NIXON

FULL NAME: Richard Milhous Nixon
BORN: January 9, 1913, Yorba Linda, California
DIED: April 22, 1994, New York, New York
MARRIED: Thelma Catherine ('Pat') Ryan
CHILDREN: Tricia, Julie
PARTY: Republican
PERIOD IN OFFICE: January 20, 1969–August 9, 1974
VICE-PRESIDENTS: Spiro Agnew (1969–73), Gerald Ford (1973–4)
There was no vice-president October–December 1973.

* * *

NIXON WAS BORN AND RAISED A QUAKER IN CALIFORNIA, where his father, after his ranch failed, ran a grocery store. After high school Nixon attended Whittier College, living at home and paying his way by working in his father's store. He went on to study law at Duke University, North Carolina, graduating in 1937 and then practicing law in Whittier. After serving as an aviation ground officer in the navy (1942–6), he won a seat in the US House of Representatives, where he took a strongly anti-communist stance. In 1950 he was elected to the US Senate, and in 1952 Eisenhower chose him as his running-mate in that year's presidential election. Nixon was almost dropped after allegations that he was benefitting from a secret fund set up by Californian businessmen, but in the eyes of many he vindicated himself in the televised 'Checkers Speech' (see below). He served as Eisenhower's vice-president from 1953 to 1961, and in 1960 was selected as the Republicans' presidential candidate, being narrowly defeated in that year's election by John F. Kennedy.

In 1968 Nixon made a successful comeback, winning the Republican nomination and the presidential election, partly on the basis of a promise to end the Vietnam War. To this end, he began peace talks in Paris, while maintaining the military pressure in Southeast Asia. Although anti-war demonstrations continued at home, Nixon genuinely regarded himself as a peacemaker, and initiated a policy of détente towards China and the Soviet Union. His administration was rocked when his vice-president, Spiro Agnew, resigned to avoid corruption charges. This was followed by the unraveling of the Watergate scandal, in which it was gradually revealed that the president's closest advisers had been involved in all kinds of illegal and unconstitutional 'dirty tricks' against his political enemies, and that the president himself was deeply implicated in the subsequent cover-up. Faced with impeachment, Nixon resigned, and was issued with an unconditional pardon by his successor, Gerald Ford. In retirement, Nixon emerged as something of an elder statesman, meeting with many foreign leaders, including Mikhail Gorbachev, and being consulted on foreign affairs by both President Reagan and President Carter.

Of the gift to his daughters of a spaniel called Checkers:

> I just want to say this, right now, that regardless of what they say about it, we are going to keep it ... I don't believe I ought to quit, because I am not a quitter.
>
> TV BROADCAST (the famous 'Checkers Speech'), September 23, 1952, following accusations that he had been the beneficiary of a secret fund

After losing the 1962 election for governor of California:

Just think how much you're going to be missing. You won't have Nixon to kick around any more, because, gentlemen, this is my last press conference.

STATEMENT TO THE PRESS, November 7, 1962

Of his aspirations as president:

Let us begin by committing ourselves to the truth – to see it as it is, and tell it like it is – to find the truth, to speak the truth, and to live the truth.

SPEECH ACCEPTING THE REPUBLICAN NOMINATION in Miami, 1968

THE NIXON DOCTRINE
★ ★ ★

This signposted that the USA would no longer use massive deployments of ground troops in Southeast Asia to counter the spread of communism:

Except for the threat of a major power, involving nuclear weapons ... the United States is going to encourage and has a right to expect that this problem will be increasingly handled by, and the responsibility for it taken by, the Asian nations themselves.

STATEMENT, July 25, 1969

This isn't going to be a good country for any of us to live in until it's a good country for all of us to live in.

Quoted in the *Observer* (London), 'Sayings of the Week', September 29, 1968

On Vietnam:

I have a secret plan to end the war.

REMARK attributed to Nixon during the 1968 presidential election campaign

Nixon popularized the phrase 'the silent majority', applying it to those Americans who did not join in anti-war demonstrations:

Let historians not record that when America was the most powerful nation in the world we passed on the other side of the road and allowed the last hopes for peace and freedom of millions of people to be suffocated by the forces of totalitarianism. And so tonight – to you, the great silent majority of my fellow Americans – I ask for your support. TV BROADCAST, November 3, 1969

On détente:

We look at each country in terms of its own conduct rather than lumping them all together and saying that because they have this kind of philosophy they are all in utter darkness.

ADDRESSING THE CHINESE PREMIER ZHOU ENLAI in Beijing, February 1972

On the first manned moon landing:

This certainly has to be the most historic phone call ever made.

TALKING TO THE APOLLO 11 ASTRONAUTS on the moon, July 20, 1969

For years politicians have promised the moon. I'm the first one to be able to deliver it.

ATTRIBUTED REMARK, July 20, 1969

This is the greatest week in the history of the world since the Creation.

WELCOMING THE RETURN TO EARTH of the Apollo astronauts aboard the *USS Hornet*, July 24, 1969. He was later castigated for exaggeration by Billy Graham.

On self-help:

> Let each of us ask – not just what government can do for me but what can I do for myself ?
>
> SPEECH, January 20, 1973, rebutting Kennedy's famous injunction (p. 159), 'Ask not what your country can do for you. Ask what you can do for your country.'

Of the incendiary situation in the Middle East:

> It was like a ghastly game of dominoes, with a nuclear war waiting at the end.
>
> REMARK, September 20, 1970. Nixon was referring specifically to the conflict in Jordan between the government and the PLO, and the dangers of the USA and the Soviet Union being drawn in.

PRESIDENTIAL OPINIONS: THE 33RD, 34TH, 35TH, 36TH AND 38TH ON THE 37TH

* * *

Richard Nixon is a no-good lying bastard. He can lie out of both sides of his mouth at the same time and if he ever caught himself telling the truth he'd lie just to keep his hand in. HARRY S. TRUMAN

On the nomination of Vice-President Nixon as the Republican presidential candidate in 1960:

> You don't set a fox to watching the chickens just because he has a lot of experience in the hen house. HARRY S. TRUMAN, remark, October 30, 1960

Asked to sum up Nixon's contribution as vice-president:

> Well, if you give me two weeks. DWIGHT D. EISENHOWER

> Do you realize the responsibility I carry? I'm the only person standing between Nixon and the White House. JOHN F. KENNEDY, during the 1960 presidential campaign

> Boys, I may not know much, but I know chicken shit from chicken salad.
> LYNDON B. JOHNSON, after hearing Nixon make a speech

On issuing a pardon to Nixon:

> The tranquility to which this nation has been restored by the events of recent weeks could be irreparably lost by the prospects of bringing to trial a former president of the United States. The prospects of such trial will cause prolonged and divisive debate over the propriety of exposing to further punishment and degradation a man who has already paid the unprecedented penalty of relinquishing the highest elective office of the United States. GERALD FORD, Proclamation 4311, September 8, 1974

On Watergate:

> I want you to know beyond the shadow of a doubt that during my term as president, justice will be pursued fairly, fully and impartially, no matter who is involved. This office is a sacred trust and I am determined to be worthy of that trust ... There can be no whitewash at the White House. RADIO AND TV BROADCAST, April 30, 1973

However, the subsequent release of taped conversations in the White House showed that there had been a cover-up, and that Nixon had directed it from the start:

You open that scab there's a hell of a lot of things and we just feel that it would be very detrimental to have this thing go any further ... Play it rough. That's the way they play it and that's the way we are going to play it.

> To H.R. Haldeman, White House chief of staff, June 23, 1972

I don't give a shit what happens. I want you all to stonewall it, let them plead the Fifth Amendment, cover-up or anything else, if it'll save it, save the plan.

> To his personal lawyer, John Dean, March 22, 1973

I want to say this to the television audience. I made my mistakes, but in all of my years of public life, I have never profited, never profited from public service. I have earned every cent. And in all of my years of public life, I have never obstructed justice. And I think, too, that I can say that in my years of public life, that I welcome this kind of examination because people have got to know whether or not their president's a crook. Well, I'm not a crook. I've earned everything I've got.

> Televised press conference, November 17, 1973

You fellows, in your business, you have a way of handling problems like this. Somebody leaves a pistol in the drawer. I don't have a pistol.

> Remark to General Alexander Haig, August 7, 1974, the day before he announced his resignation

I have never been a quitter. To leave office before my term is completed is abhorrent to every instinct in my body. But as president I must put the interests of America first ... Therefore, I shall resign the presidency, effective at noon tomorrow. Broadcast, August 8, 1974

This country needs good farmers, good businessmen, good plumbers ...

> Farewell address at the White House, August 9, 1974. Ironically, the team that broke into the Watergate Hotel, and others involved in 'dirty tricks' on behalf of the president, had been codenamed 'the Plumbers'.

A month later, on accepting a pardon from his successor:

No words can describe the depth of my regret and pain at the anguish my mistakes over Watergate have caused this nation. Quoted in Gerald R. Ford, *A Time to Heal* (1979)

I let down my friends, I let down my country, I let down our system of government.

> Quoted in the *Observer* (London), 'Sayings of the Week', May 8, 1977

Well, when the president does it that means that it is not illegal.

> TV interview with David Frost, May 19, 1977

I brought myself down. I gave them a sword. And they stuck it in, and they twisted it with relish. And I guess if I had been in their position, I'd have done the same thing.

> TV interview with David Frost, May 19, 1977

What others said

* * *

Of Nixon's 'Checkers Speech':

The most tremendous performance I've ever seen!

> HOLLYWOOD PRODUCER DARRYL ZANUCK, in a phone call to Nixon after the broadcast

Would you buy a second-hand car from this man? MORT SAHL, attributed

Inexplicable, strange, hard to understand.

> H.R. HALDEMAN, Nixon's chief of staff at the White House

Nixonland is a land of slander and scare, of sly innuendo, of a poison pen and the anonymous telephone call, and hustling, pushing and thieving, the land of smash and grab and anything to win.

> ADLAI STEVENSON, speaking as Democratic presidential candidate in 1952

Nixon is the kind of politician who would cut down a redwood tree and then mount the stump to make a speech for conservation. ADLAI STEVENSON

I believe there really is a 'new Nixon', a maturer and mellower man who is no longer clawing his way to the top. WALTER LIPPMANN in 1968, quoted in David Abrahamsen, *Nixon vs Nixon* (1977)

A man with no soul, no inner convictions, with the integrity of a hyena and the style of a poison toad. The Nixon I remembered was absolutely humorless; I couldn't imagine him laughing at anything except maybe a paraplegic who wanted to vote Democratic but couldn't quite reach the lever on the voting machine.

> HUNTER S. THOMPSON, in *Pageant*, July 1968

If he wants to do his country a favor, he'll stay over there.

> REPUBLICAN SENATOR BARRY GOLDWATER, during Nixon's 1972 visit to China

Nixon's motto was if two wrongs don't make a right, try three.

> NORMAN COUSINS, newspaper editor and peace activist

He has a deeper concern for his place in history than for the people he governs. And history will not fail to note that fact. SHIRLEY CHISHOLM, *The Good Fight* (1973)

History buffs probably noted the reunion at a Washington party a few weeks ago of three ex-presidents, Carter, Ford and Nixon: See No Evil, Hear No Evil, and Evil.

> SENATOR BOB DOLE, March 26, 1983

Others had different perceptions. In 1971, while still a young boy, John F. Kennedy Jr was invited with his mother and sister to a dinner party in the White House, and recalls of Nixon:

He was very warm and he was a wonderful host ...

> Interviewed by Chris Matthews, February 5, 1996

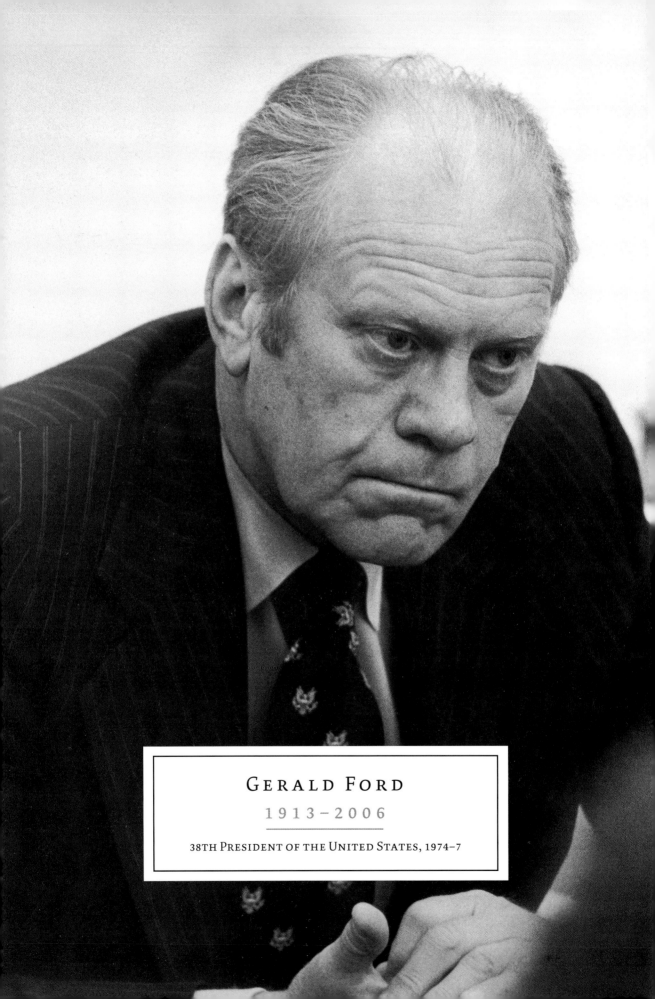

GERALD FORD

1913–2006

38TH PRESIDENT OF THE UNITED STATES, 1974–7

GERALD FORD

FULL NAME: Gerald ('Jerry') Rudolph Ford Jr (born Leslie Lynch King Jr)
BORN: July 14, 1913, Omaha, Nebraska
DIED: December 26, 2006, Rancho Mirage, California
MARRIED: Elizabeth ('Betty') Anne Bloomer (who had previously
been married to and divorced from William G. Warren)
CHILDREN: Michael Gerald, Jon Gardner, Steven Meigs, Susan Elizabeth
PARTY: Republican
PERIOD IN OFFICE: August 9, 1974–January 20, 1977
VICE-PRESIDENT: Nelson Rockefeller (1974–7)
There was no vice-president August–December 1974.

* * *

FORD WAS BORN LESLIE LYNCH KING, the son of a wool trader of the same name. His parents separated shortly after his birth, and he moved with his mother to Grand Rapids, Michigan. In 1916 she married a salesman called Gerald Rudolff Ford, who adopted Leslie Jr, and gave him his own name (although Ford Jr later changed the spelling of his middle name). At the University of Michigan Ford was a star football player, and after graduating in 1935 he studied law at Yale while working as a football coach. He gained his law degree in 1941, then served in the navy in the Second World War, rising to the rank of lieutenant commander. He saw considerable action in the South Pacific aboard the aircraft carrier USS *Monterey*, and in 1944 was almost lost overboard during a typhoon. Entering politics as a moderate conservative, Ford sat in the US House of Representatives from 1949 to 1973, becoming House minority leader in 1965. After Vice-President Spiro Agnew resigned in disgrace in 1973, President Nixon made Ford his vice-president. Following Nixon's own resignation, Ford became president – thus becoming the only man to occupy the White House without being elected either as vice-president or president. Ford set out to heal the divisions in America brought about by the Vietnam War and the Watergate scandal, announcing a conditional amnesty for draft-dodgers and deserters, and a catch-all pardon to ex-President Nixon. This latter act was particularly unpopular, and – combined with Ford's perceived verbal and physical clumsiness and the dire state of the economy – led to his narrow defeat by Jimmy Carter in the presidential election of 1976. In 1980 he refused to stand as Ronald Reagan's vice-presidential running-mate, and retired from public life.

Of himself:

Disgustingly sane. Quoted in Jerald F. terHorst, *Gerald Ford and the Future of the Presidency* (1978)

I am a Ford, not a Lincoln. My addresses will never be as eloquent as Mr Lincoln's. But I will do my very best to equal his brevity and his plain speaking.
ON TAKING THE OATH AS VICE-PRESIDENT, December 6, 1973

It's the quality of the ordinary, the straight, the square, that accounts for the great stability and success of our nation. It's a quality to be proud of. But it's a quality that many people seem to have neglected. Quoted in *Time*, January 28, 1974

On assuming the presidency:

> I guess it proves that in America anyone can become president.
>
> Quoted in Richard Reeves, *A Ford, Not a Lincoln* (1977)

> I believe that truth is the glue that holds government together, not only our government but civilization itself ... Our long national nightmare is over. Our Constitution works; our great Republic is a government of laws and not of men. Here, the people rule.
>
> ON BEING SWORN IN AS PRESIDENT, August 9, 1974. He was quoting John Adams's phrase, 'a government of laws, not of men' (see p. 18); the 'long national nightmare' phrase was coined by speechwriter Bob Hartman.

On Watergate:

> The political lesson of Watergate is this: Never again must America allow an arrogant, elite guard of political adolescents to by-pass the regular party organization and dictate the terms of a national election. Quoted in the *New York Times*, March 31, 1974

On pardoning Nixon:

> America needed recovery, not revenge. The hate had to be drained and the healing begun.
>
> *A TIME TO HEAL* (1979)

On big government:

> A government big enough to give you everything you want is a government big enough to take away everything you have.
>
> ADDRESS TO CONGRESS, August 12, 1974. Ford first said something along these lines many years earlier, as recorded in John F. Parker, *If Elected* (1960).

Ford betrayed a shaky grasp of foreign affairs:

> There is no Soviet domination of Eastern Europe and there never will be under a Ford administration.
>
> TV DEBATE WITH JIMMY CARTER, October 6, 1976, during the presidential election campaign

Among many 'Fordisms', apocryphal or otherwise, is this:

> If Abraham Lincoln were alive today he'd be turning in his grave.
>
> ATTRIBUTED in *Time*, February 17, 1967

PRESIDENTIAL OPINIONS:
THE 36TH AND 39TH ON THE 38TH
* * *

Gerry Ford is so dumb that he can't fart and chew gum at the same time ... A nice guy, but he played too much football with his helmet off ... He's so dumb he couldn't tip shit out of a boot if the instructions were written on the heel.

LYNDON B. JOHNSON, remarks on various occasions

For myself and for our nation, I want to thank my predecessor for all he has done to heal our land. JIMMY CARTER, INAUGURAL ADDRESS, January 20, 1977

JIMMY CARTER

1924 –

39TH PRESIDENT OF THE UNITED STATES, 1977–81

JIMMY CARTER

FULL NAME: James Earl Carter Jr
BORN: October 1, 1924, Plains, Georgia
MARRIED: Rosalynn Smith
CHILDREN: John William, James Earl III, Donnel Jeffrey, Amy Lynn
PARTY: Democratic
PERIOD IN OFFICE: January 20, 1977–January 20, 1981
VICE-PRESIDENT: Walter Mondale

* * *

CARTER WAS BORN IN RURAL GEORGIA, where his father was a successful peanut farmer and his mother a registered nurse (who in her late sixties worked as a Peace Corps volunteer in India). Carter studied at Georgia Southwestern College, the Georgia Institute of Technology and the US Naval Academy at Annapolis, from where he graduated in 1946 and went on to become a career officer in the navy. He resigned his commission on the death of his father in 1953 to take over the family peanut business. He served in the Georgia Senate (1963–7) and as governor of Georgia (1971–5), in which role he reorganized the state government on more efficient lines, and opened up positions to women and African Americans. He had become a born-again Christian in the 1960s, and, with his promise to restore trust in government after the Watergate scandal, emerged as a dark-horse candidate at the Democratic convention in 1976. On becoming president the following year, he continued the policy of détente of his predecessors, while placing a new emphasis on human rights around the world. His greatest achievement in foreign affairs was the Camp David Agreement, ending the state of war between Israel and Egypt. However, this was overshadowed by two events: the failure of a military mission to free the US hostages held in Tehran, and the Soviet invasion of Afghanistan. In the 1980 presidential election, with inflation and unemployment running high, the down-beat Carter was overwhelmingly defeated by the up-beat Ronald Reagan. Since leaving office, Carter has been active on behalf of a range of humanitarian causes, and has been involved in attempts to resolve conflicts in various parts of the world.

On government:

> A simple and proper function of government is just to make it easy for us to do good and difficult for us to do wrong.
>
> ACCEPTING THE DEMOCRATIC NOMINATION, New York, July 15, 1976

Retreating from the ideals of the New Deal:

> Government cannot solve our problems. It cannot define our vision. Government cannot eliminate poverty, or provide a bountiful economy, or reduce inflation, or save our cities, or cure illiteracy, or provide energy.
>
> Quoted by Arthur Schlesinger Jr in *New Republic*, April 12, 1980

On America as a 'melting pot':

> We become not a melting pot but a beautiful mosaic. Different people, different beliefs, different yearnings, different hopes, different dreams.
>
> SPEECH in Pittsburgh, October 27, 1976

To the electorate:

I have been accused of being an outsider. I plead guilty. Unfortunately, the vast majority of Americans ... are also outsiders.

Quoted in Billy Adler, ed., *The Wit and Wisdom of Jimmy Carter* (1977)

Show me a good loser, and I'll show you a loser. *Why Not the Best* (1975)

Carter was not shy about his beliefs:

We should live our lives as though Christ were coming this afternoon. Speech, March 1976

Yet he realized it was politically expedient to dilute his image as a narrow-minded Southern Baptist:

I've looked on a lot of women with lust. I've committed adultery in my heart many times. This is something that God recognizes that I will do – and I have done it – and God forgives me for it. Interviewed in *Playboy*, November 1976

On the Soviet invasion of Afghanistan, December 27, 1979:

History teaches perhaps few lessons. But surely one such lesson learned by the world at great cost is that aggression unopposed becomes a dangerous disease.

Broadcast to the nation, January 4, 1980

On the perceived 'crisis of confidence':

THE CARTER DOCTRINE

* * *

An attempt by any outside force to gain control of the Persian Gulf region will be regarded as an assault on the vital interests of the United States of America, and such an assault will be repelled by any means necessary, including military force.

Statement, January 23, 1980

I want to talk to you right now about a fundamental threat to American democracy ... The threat is nearly invisible in ordinary ways. It is *a crisis of confidence*. It is a crisis that strikes at the very heart and soul and spirit of our national will. We can see this crisis in the growing doubt about the meaning of our own lives and in the loss of a unity of purpose for our nation. The erosion of our confidence in the future is threatening to destroy the social and the political fabric of America.

Broadcast to the nation, July 15, 1979. Some days later he spoke of a 'national malaise'. This negative talk did not go down well with the electorate.

On being told it took 20 years to build the Great Pyramid:

I'm surprised that a government organization could do it that quickly.

Remark during a visit to Egypt, quoted in *Time*, March 19, 1979

On lawyers:

We have the heaviest concentration of lawyers on Earth – one for every 500 Americans; three times as many as are in England, four times as many as are in West Germany, 21 times as many as there are in Japan. We have more litigation, but I am not sure that we have more justice. No resources of talent and training in our own society, even including the medical care, is more wastefully or unfairly distributed than legal skills. Ninety per cent of our lawyers serve ten per cent of our people. We are over-lawyered and under-represented.

Speech at the centenary celebration of the Los Angeles County Bar Association, May 4, 1978

On a visit to Poland:

I desire the Poles carnally.

> This was the translation into Polish of Carter's words 'I have come to learn your opinions and understand your desires for the future.'

Paying tribute to Hubert Horatio Humphrey, the Democratic candidate defeated by Nixon in 1968:

The great president who might have been – Hubert Horatio Hornblower.

> SPEECH in New York, accepting the Democratic nomination, August 15, 1980

Conceding defeat in the 1980 election:

I promised you four years ago that I would never lie to you, so I can't stand here and say it doesn't hurt. I've wanted to serve as president because I love this country and because I love the people of this nation. Just one more word. Finally, let me say that I am disappointed tonight but I have not lost either love.

> Quoted in *Newsweek*, November 17, 1980

Our American values are not luxuries, but necessities – not the salt in our bread, but the bread itself.

> FAREWELL ADDRESS, January 20, 1981

I can't deny I'm a better ex-president than I was a president.

> SPEECH in Washington DC, November 3, 2005

PRESIDENTIAL OPINIONS: THE 40TH ON THE 39TH
✶✶✶

On Carter's foreign policy:

Like the sorry tapping of Neville Chamberlain's umbrella on the cobblestones of Munich. RONALD REAGAN, attributed

---

What others said
✶✶✶

Sometimes when I look at my children I say to myself, 'Lillian, you should have stayed a virgin.' LILLIAN CARTER, the president's mother, quoted in *Woman* magazine, April 9, 1977

Carter is your typical smiling, brilliant, back-stabbing, bullshitting Southern nut-cutter.
LANE KIRKLAND, president of the AFL-CIO 1979–95

I would not want Jimmy Carter and his men put in charge of snake control in Ireland.
EUGENE McCARTHY, attributed

RONALD REAGAN

1911–2004

40TH PRESIDENT OF THE UNITED STATES, 1981–9

RONALD REAGAN

FULL NAME: Ronald Wilson Reagan
BORN: February 6, 1911, Tampico, Illinois
DIED: June 5, 2004, Bel Air, Los Angeles
MARRIED: (1) Jane Wyman (born Sarah Jane Mayfield; previously
married to Ernest Eugene Wyman and Myron Futterman),
(2) Nancy Davis (stage name of Anne Frances Robbins)
CHILDREN: Maureen, Christine, Michael (with his first wife;
Christine died in infancy and Michael was adopted);
Patti, Ron (by his second wife)
PARTY: Republican
PERIOD IN OFFICE: January 20, 1981–January 20, 1989
VICE-PRESIDENT: George H.W. Bush

* * *

REAGAN HAD A SOMEWHAT UNSETTLED CHILDHOOD, moving from town to town as his alcoholic father moved from job to job. In 1920 the family settled in Dixon, Illinois, where Reagan attended high school, before going on to Eureka College, from where he graduated in 1932 with a degree in economics and sociology. A keen football player, he then embarked on a career as a radio sportscaster, and in 1937 moved to California to become an actor. He went on to appear in numerous, mostly low-budget movies, and during the Second World War he worked with an army film unit based in Los Angeles. He served two stints as president of the Screen Actors Guild, and cooperated with Senator McCarthy's investigation into suspected communist sympathizers in Hollywood. Originally a Democrat, Reagan became increasingly conservative and formally switched to the Republicans in 1962. He served as governor of California from 1967 to 1975. In 1968 and 1976 he failed to secure the Republican nomination to run for president, but in 1980 won the nomination and the presidential election. He repeated this success in 1984, his amiability, jokiness and optimism having won him immense popularity as 'the Great Communicator'.

Reagan cut taxes, reduced business regulation and slashed government spending on welfare, but by the end of his presidency he had doubled the budget deficit via a massive increase in defense spending, notably on the Strategic Defense Initiative ('Star Wars'). This space-based missile defense system was aimed at ending the nuclear stalemate with the Soviet Union, which found it could no longer afford to compete in the escalated arms race. After 1985 Reagan worked successfully with Mikhail Gorbachev, the reform-minded new Soviet leader, to bring about an easing of tensions, and is credited by many with ending the Cold War. Reagan was not averse to using military force, invading Grenada in 1983 and bombing Libya in 1986. His second term was dominated by the Iran-Contra Scandal, in which it was revealed that his administration had been involved in illegally selling arms to Iran to fund the right-wing Contra rebels in Nicaragua. Reagan was 77 when he left office, and in 1994 he announced that he had been diagnosed with Alzheimer's disease; he died ten years later.

His catchphrase:

Win one for the Gipper.

> Reagan first spoke these lines when he played the American footballer George Gipp in the 1940 film *Knute Rockne, All American*. In real life Gipp had himself spoken these words.

On government:

Government is like a baby: an alimentary canal with a big appetite at one end and no responsibility at the other.

> REMARK while campaigning for the governorship of California, quoted in the *New York Times Magazine*, November 14, 1965

On politics:

Politics is supposed to be the second oldest profession. I have come to realize that it bears a very close resemblance to the first.

> REMARKS at a business conference in Los Angeles, March 2, 1977

Politics is just like show business. You have a hell of an opening, coast for a while, and then have a hell of a close. REMARK TO STUART SPENCER, 1966

On Vietnam:

We could pave the whole country and put parking stripes on it and still be home for Christmas. INTERVIEW in the *Fresno Bee*, October 10, 1965

On hippies:

A hippie is someone who looks like Tarzan, walks like Jane and smells like Cheetah.
ATTRIBUTED

On liberals:

Sadly I have come to the conclusion that many so-called liberals aren't liberal – they will defend to the death your right to agree with them. *WHERE'S THE REST OF ME?* (1965)

The masquerade is over, it's time to ... use the dreaded L-word; to say the policies of our opposition ... are liberal, liberal, liberal. Quoted in the *New York Times*, August 16, 1988

On his favourite foodstuff:

You can tell a lot about a man's character by his way of eating jelly beans.
> Quoted in the *New York Times*, January 15, 1981

To Jimmy Carter, who had delivered a lengthy critique of Reagan's position on Medicare:

There you go again! PRESIDENTIAL DEBATE, October 28, 1980

On his core values:

At the heart of our message should be five simple familiar words. No big economic theories. No sermons on political philosophy. Just five short words: family, work neighborhood, freedom, peace. Quoted in Richard Harwood, ed., *The Pursuit of the Presidency* (1980)

The Shining City on a Hill

* * *

Reagan used this image (inspired by Matthew 5:14) for his vision of America on several occasions:

A troubled and afflicted mankind looks to us, pleading for us to keep our rendezvous with destiny; that we will uphold the principles of self-reliance, self-discipline, morality, and, above all, responsible liberty for every individual; that we will become that shining city on a hill.

ANNOUNCING THAT HE WOULD RUN FOR THE PRESIDENCY, November 13, 1979

I've spoken of the shining city all my political life, but I don't know if I ever quite communicated what I saw when I said it. But in my mind it was a tall proud city built on rocks stronger than oceans, wind-swept, God-blessed, and teeming with people of all kinds living in harmony and peace, a city with free ports that hummed with commerce and creativity, and if there had to be city walls, the walls had doors and the doors were open to anyone with the will and the heart to get here. That's how I saw it and see it still. FAREWELL ADDRESS, January 11, 1989

When being wheeled into theatre after a failed assassination attempt:

Please assure me that you are all Republicans!

REMARK TO THE WAITING SURGEONS, March 30, 1981

To his wife, while in hospital:

Honey, I forgot to duck.

The boxer Jack Dempsey had used these words after losing the World Heavyweight title, September 23, 1926.

During a Republican primary debate in Nashua, New Hampshire:

Don't you cut me off. I am paying for this microphone.

February 23, 1980, borrowing a line of Spencer Tracy's in the 1948 film, *State of the Union*: 'Don't you shut me off, I'm paying for this broadcast'.

On American 'exceptionalism':

I have long believed that there was a divine plan that placed this land here to be found by people of a special kind, that we have a rendezvous with destiny. CAMPAIGN LETTER, 1976

Characterizing the Soviet Union as 'an evil empire':

Yes, let us pray for the salvation of all of those who live in that totalitarian darkness – pray they will discover the joy of knowing God. But until they do, let us be aware that while they preach the supremacy of the state, declare its omnipotence over individual man, and predict its eventual domination of all peoples on the earth, they are the focus of evil in the modern world … I urge you [not] to ignore the facts of history and the aggressive impulses of an evil empire, to simply call the arms race a giant misunderstanding and thereby remove yourself from the struggle between right and wrong and good and evil.

SPEECH TO THE NATIONAL ASSOCIATION OF EVANGELICALS in Orlando, Florida, March 8, 1983. Many have suggested that Reagan got the idea for the phrase from the 'evil galactic empire' of the *Star Wars* films.

My fellow Americans, I am pleased to tell you I have signed legislation which outlaws Russia for ever. We begin bombing in five minutes.

> TESTING A MICROPHONE, not realizing he was being broadcast live, August 11, 1984

At the Berlin Wall:

Mr Gorbachev, open the gate! Mr Gorbachev, tear down this wall!

> SPEECH in West Berlin, June 12, 1987

On 'rogue' states:

We are especially not going to tolerate these attacks from outlaw states run by the strangest collection of misfits, Looney Tunes and squalid criminals since the advent of the Third Reich. BROADCAST, July 8, 1985, following the hijack of an American plane

On Colonel Gaddafi of Libya:

Not only a barbarian, but flaky. ATTRIBUTED

On the Iran-Contra scandal:

As a matter of fact, I was very definitely involved in the decisions about the support to the freedom fighters. It was my idea to begin with.

> May 5, 1987. The president's spokespeople were obliged to issue a rapid 'clarification'.

His slogan while running for re-election in 1984:

You ain't seen nothing yet.

> Reagan was quoting the famous line spoken by Al Jolson in the first 'talkie', *The Jazz Singer* (1927).

I will not make age an issue of this campaign. I am not going to exploit for political purposes my opponent's youth and inexperience.

> REFERRING TO WALTER MONDALE, his opponent in the 1984 presidential election

Eulogizing the crew of the Challenger, *who died when the space shuttle broke up shortly after lift-off:*

We will never forget them, nor the last time we saw them – this morning, as they prepared for their journey, and waved goodbye, and 'slipped the surly bonds of earth' to 'touch the face of God.'

> BROADCAST FROM THE OVAL OFFICE, January 28, 1986. The quotations are from the poem 'High Flight' by John Gillespie Magee, an airman killed in action in the Second World War.

Joking about his grasp of economics:

The deficit is big enough to take care of itself. Quoted in *Newsweek*, November 21, 1988

Revealing that he had Alzheimer's disease:

I now begin the journey that will lead me into the sunset of my life. I know that for America there will always be a bright dawn ahead.

> OPEN LETTER TO THE AMERICAN PEOPLE, November 5, 1994

PRESIDENTIAL OPINIONS: THE 37TH, 38TH, 39TH, 41ST, 42ND, 43RD AND 44TH ON THE 40TH

* * *

The political landscape is littered with those who underestimated Ronald Reagan.
RICHARD M. NIXON

Ronald Reagan doesn't dye his hair, he's just prematurely orange. GERALD FORD, in 1974

On Reagan's economic policies:

Voodoo economics. GEORGE H.W. BUSH, while vying for the Republican nomination in 1980

Reagan's death brought forth a number of eulogies:

[He] provided ... unshakable beliefs and was able to express them effectively, both in America and abroad. JIMMY CARTER

History will give Reagan great credit for standing for principles. GEORGE BUSH SR

He believed that freedom was a universal value ... that people everywhere wished to be free. BILL CLINTON

He leaves behind a nation he restored and a world he helped save ... because of his leadership, the world laid to rest an era of fear and tyranny. GEORGE W. BUSH

When the Berlin Wall came tumbling down, I had to give the old man his due, even if I never gave him my vote. BARACK OBAMA

What others said

* * *

He doesn't make snap decisions, but he doesn't over-think either. NANCY REAGAN

Reagan is the most popular figure in the history of the US. No candidate we put up would have been able to beat Reagan this year. TIP O'NEILL, Democratic politician, in 1984

When you meet the president, you ask yourself: 'How did it ever occur to anyone that he should be governor, much less president?' HENRY KISSINGER, in *US*, June 2, 1986

Washington couldn't tell a lie. Nixon couldn't tell the truth. Reagan couldn't tell the difference. MORT SAHL

I take the death of Ronald Reagan very hard. He was a man whom fate set by me in perhaps the most difficult years at the end of the 20th century ... It was his goal and his dream to ... enter history as a peacemaker. MIKHAIL GORBACHEV, 2004

Ronald Reagan had a higher claim than any other leader to have won the Cold War for liberty, and he did it without a shot being fired. MARGARET THATCHER, 2004

GEORGE BUSH SR

1924 –

41ST PRESIDENT OF THE UNITED STATES, 1989–93

GEORGE BUSH SR

FULL NAME: George Herbert Walker Bush
BORN: June 12, 1924, Milton, Massachusetts
MARRIED: Barbara Pierce
CHILDREN: George Walker (43rd president), Pauline Robinson,
John Ellis, Neil Mallon, Marvin Pierce, Dorothy
PARTY: Republican
PERIOD IN OFFICE: January 20, 1989–January 20, 1993
VICE-PRESIDENT: Dan Quayle

* * *

BUSH WAS BORN INTO AN AFFLUENT NEW ENGLAND FAMILY, the son of an investment banker and US senator. After attending private schools, he saw action in the Second World War as a carrier-based pilot in the Pacific. He then studied at Yale, before moving to Texas to start a career in the oil business. Having entered Republican politics, he twice failed to win a seat in the US Senate, but sat in the US House of Representatives from 1967 to 1971. President Nixon appointed him ambassador to the United Nations (1971–3), and President Ford made him US representative to China (1974–5) and then director of the CIA (1975–7). Bush campaigned for the Republican presidential nomination, but was beaten by Ronald Reagan, who made him his vice-president (1981–9). Bush won the Republican nomination in 1988 and went on to beat the Democratic candidate, Michael Dukakis. As president, Bush was obliged to renege on his promise not to increase taxes, but much of his attention was taken up with foreign affairs. In 1989 he authorized the invasion of Panama to overthrow the corrupt dictator Manuel Noriega, and in 1991 US forces led an international coalition to end the Iraqi invasion of Kuwait. In the meantime, however, America was suffering economic difficulties, and these were largely responsible for Bush's defeat by Bill Clinton in the 1992 presidential election. Bush's son, George W., became the 43rd president of the United States.

On himself:

> Let others have the charisma. I've got the class.
> Quoted in the *Guardian* (London), December 3, 1988

On being asked to consider the longer term:

> Oh, the vision thing.
> REMARK WHILE SEEKING THE REPUBLICAN NOMINATION, quoted in *Time*, January 26, 1987

On occasion, he did try to pin down 'the vision thing':

> I will keep America moving forward, always forward – for a better America, for an endless enduring dream and a thousand points of light.
> SPEECH ACCEPTING THE REPUBLICAN NOMINATION, in New Orleans, August 18, 1988

> America is never wholly herself unless she is engaged in high moral purpose. We as a people have such a purpose today. It is to make kinder the face of the nation and gentler the face of the world. INAUGURAL ADDRESS, January 20, 1989

I know what I've told you I'm going to say, I'm going to say. And what else I say, well, I'll take some time to figure out – figure that out.

REMARK AT A PRESS CONFERENCE, December 4, 1990

Bush quite often 'mis-spoke':

America's freedom is the example to which the world expires. SPEECH in Detroit, 1988

I have opinions of my – own strong opinions – but I don't always agree with them.

ATTRIBUTED

'My country, right or wrong':

I will never apologize for the United States – I don't care what the facts are ... I'm not an apologize-for-America kind of guy. STATEMENT at a campaign function, August 2, 1988

His most famous campaign pledge:

My opponent won't rule out raising taxes, but I will. And the Congress will push me to raise taxes. and I'll say no, and they'll push again. And I'll say to them, read my lips: no new taxes.

SPEECH ACCEPTING THE REPUBLICAN NOMINATION, in New Orleans, August 18, 1988

On America's role in the world:

When America is stronger, the world is safer. ADDRESS TO CONGRESS, February 9, 1989

On the Gulf War:

A line has been drawn in the sand.

STATEMENT, August 8, 1990, following the Iraqi invasion of Kuwait

On the end of the Cold War:

We have before us the opportunity to forge for ourselves and for future generations a new world order, a world where the rule of law, not the law of the jungle, governs the conduct of nations.

REMARKS IN THE OVAL OFFICE, January 16, 1991, shortly after the commencement of air strikes against Iraq

On green vegetables:

I do not like broccoli and I haven't liked it since I was a little kid. I am president of the United States and I am not going to eat it any more. ATTRIBUTED, March 1990

What others said

* * *

Gerald Ford without the pizzazz. PAT PAULSEN

Every woman's first husband. BARBARA EHRENREICH AND JANE O'REILLY

Poor George. He can't help it. He was born with a silver foot in his mouth.

ANN RICHARDS, former governor of Texas, address to the Democratic convention, July 18, 1988

BILL CLINTON

1946 –

42ND PRESIDENT OF THE UNITED STATES, 1993–2001

BILL CLINTON

FULL NAME: William Jefferson Clinton (born William Jefferson Blythe III)
BORN: August 19,1946, Hope, Arkansas
MARRIED: Hillary Rodham
CHILDREN: Chelsea
PARTY: Democratic
PERIOD IN OFFICE: January 20, 1993–January 20, 2001
VICE-PRESIDENT: Al Gore

* * *

CLINTON'S FATHER WAS KILLED in an automobile accident three months before he was born. His mother then married Roger Clinton, whose name her son took, despite the fact that his stepfather was an abusive alcoholic. Clinton was inspired to enter politics when, at the age of 16, he was introduced to President J.F. Kennedy. He went on to study international relations at Georgetown University, where he graduated in 1968 and then spent time as a Rhodes Scholar at Oxford University. In 1970 he began to study law at Yale, where he met his future wife, Hillary Rodham. In 1976 he was elected attorney general for Arkansas, and went on to serve as governor (1979–81, 1983–92). In 1992, presenting himself as a middle-of-the-road figure, he won the Democratic nomination to run for president. Despite allegations of an extramarital affair, student pot-smoking and dodging the draft, he went on to defeat sitting President George Bush. Clinton's attempt to introduce universal health insurance was blocked by Congress, though he successfully pushed through a number of other reforms, and signed the North American Free Trade Agreement.

In 1994 an official investigation began into the affairs of the Whitewater Land Development Corporation in Arkansas, but no conclusive evidence of wrongdoing on the part of the Clintons was produced. In November that year the Republicans gained control of both houses of Congress, leaving Clinton as something of a lame duck, although he went on to win the 1996 presidential election. His second term in office was dominated by the Monica Lewinsky scandal, in which the president was accused of persuading a young White House intern to deny under oath that she had had an affair with him. This eventually led to Clinton being impeached for perjury and obstruction of justice, although he was acquitted of both charges in 1999. After leaving office, Clinton involved himself in a range of global issues, such as AIDS and climate change, while supporting his wife's unsuccessful bid to gain the Democratic nomination in 2008.

On his youth:

I experimented with marijuana a time or two. And I didn't like it, and I didn't inhale.

Quoted in the *Washington Post*, March 30, 1992

On himself:

The comeback kid!

After coming second in the New Hampshire primary in the run-up to the 1992 presidential election. Since 1952 all successful presidential candidates had won the New Hampshire primary.

It's the economy, stupid!

> Although coined by James Carville, Clinton's campaign manager, the phrase became inextricably associated with Clinton.

On 'healing' America:

For too long politicians have told the most of us that are doing all right that what's really wrong with America is the rest of us. Them. Them, the minorities. Them, the liberals. Them, the poor. Them, the homeless. Them, the people with disabilities. Them, the gays. We've gotten to where we've nearly them-ed ourselves to death. Them and them and them. But this is America. There is no them; there's only us.

> SPEECH AT THE DEMOCRATIC CONVENTION, July 16, 1992

On the opportunity for national renewal:

Our democracy must be not only the envy of the world but the engine of our own renewal. There is nothing wrong with America that cannot be cured by what is right with America.

> FIRST INAUGURAL ADDRESS, January 20, 1993

The light may be fading on the 20th century, but the sun is still rising on America.

> ADDRESS TO THE NATION, December 31, 1999

THE LEWINSKY AFFAIR
✳ ✳ ✳

On Monica Lewinsky:

I want to say one thing to the American people. I want you to listen to me ... I did not have sexual relations with that woman, Miss Lewinsky. I never told anybody to lie, not a single time, never. These allegations are false, and I need to go back to work for the American people.

> STATEMENT AT A PRESS CONFERENCE, January 26, 1998

No one wants to get this matter behind us more than I do – except maybe all the rest of the American people.

> STATEMENT AT A PRESS CONFERENCE, July 31, 1998

It depends on what the meaning of the word 'is' is. If 'is' means 'is and never has been', that is one thing. If it means 'there is none', that was a completely true statement ... Now, if someone had asked me on that day, are you having any kind of sexual relations with Ms. Lewinsky, that is, asked me a question in the present tense, I would have said no. And it would have been completely true.

> TESTIMONY BEFORE A GRAND JURY, August 17, 1998

I did have a relationship with Ms Lewinsky that was not appropriate. In fact, it was wrong. It constitutes a critical lapse in judgment and a personal failure on my part for which I am solely and completely responsible.

> BROADCAST TO THE AMERICAN PEOPLE, August 18, 1998

On the post-Cold War world:

We must not let the Iron Curtain be replaced with a veil of indifference.

SPEECH TO NATO, January 10, 1994

On the Bosnian war:

History has shown that you can't allow the mass extermination of people, and just sit by and watch it happen.

Quoted in *Time*, October 3, 1994

On Northern Ireland:

Peace is no longer a dream. It is a reality.

STATEMENT after the 1998 referendum in Northern Ireland had endorsed the Good Friday Agreement

On the unveiling of his official portrait in the White House:

I felt like a pickle stepping into history. REMARK, June 14, 2004

On his role after leaving office:

What are the needs of the world? What can I do that won't be done if I don't do it?

TV INTERVIEW during the opening of the presidential library at Little Rock, Arkansas, November 2004

On ideology:

The problem with ideology is, if you've got an ideology, you've already got your mind made up. You know all the answers and that makes evidence irrelevant and arguments a waste of time. You tend to govern by assertion and attacks. SPEECH, October 18, 2006

PRESIDENTIAL OPINIONS: THE 41ST ON THE 42ND (AND HIS VICE-PRESIDENT)

* * *

My dog Millie knows more about foreign affairs than these two bozos.

GEORGE H.W. BUSH, October 1992

We're not running against the comeback kids, we're running against the Karaoke Kids – they'd sing any tune to get elected.

GEORGE H.W. BUSH, 1992

What others said

* * *

Bill Clinton does not have the moral fiber to be a mass murderer.

HENRY KISSINGER, attributed

We have never said to the press that Clinton is a philandering, pot-smoking draft dodger.

MARY MATALIN, Republican political consultant, 1992

When it is all about himself, he is cunningly smart.

RALPH NADER, quoted in the *Washington Times*, January 28, 2008

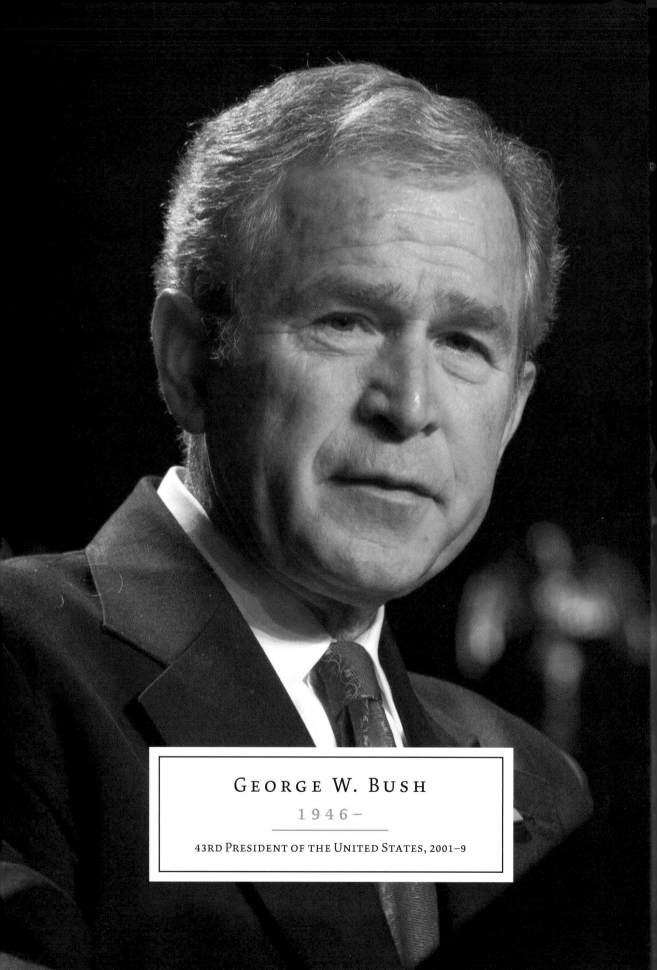

GEORGE W. BUSH

1946–

43RD PRESIDENT OF THE UNITED STATES, 2001–9

GEORGE W. BUSH

FULL NAME: George Walker Bush
BORN: July 6, 1946, New Haven, Connecticut
MARRIED: Laura Lane Welch
CHILDREN: Barbara Pierce, Jenna Welch
PARTY: Republican
PERIOD IN OFFICE: January 20, 2001–January 20, 2009
VICE-PRESIDENT: Dick Cheney

* * *

BUSH WAS BORN INTO A PRIVILEGED NEW ENGLAND FAMILY, and his father, George H.W. Bush, became 41st president of the United States. Brought up in Texas and educated at a private school in Massachusetts, Bush went on to study history at Yale, where he proved an unexceptional student. After graduating from Yale in 1968 he enlisted in the Texas Air National Guard, thus avoiding service in Vietnam. He was given an early discharge in 1973 to study at Harvard Business School. Graduating with an MBA in 1975, he followed his father into the Texas oil business. A heavy drinker as a young man, Bush gave up alcohol after becoming a bornagain Christian in the mid-1980s. After helping his father's presidential campaign, in 1994 he ran successfully for the governorship of Texas, a position he held until 2000. That year he was selected as the Republican presidential candidate, and in a highly controversial election he narrowly defeated the Democratic candidate, Vice-President Al Gore. Bush pushed through massive tax cuts, allowed more federal lands to be opened up to mining and oil and gas extraction, and abolished various environmental-protection regulations.

In foreign affairs, his administration adopted a unilateralist approach, rejecting the Kyoto Protocol on reducing greenhouse-gas emissions, withdrawing from the 1972 Anti-Ballistic Missile Treaty and refusing to recognize the jurisdiction of the International Criminal Court. But Bush's two terms as president were dominated by the al-Qaeda terrorist attacks of September 11, 2001, and their aftermath. By the end of 2001 US forces were deployed in Afghanistan, where the Taliban government had provided al-Qaeda with training bases. In 2003, having controversially linked al-Qaeda with Saddam Hussein's regime in Iraq, which he accused of developing weapons of mass destruction, Bush ordered US forces to invade Iraq. Bush's military responses to 9/11 initially proved popular at home, and he was re-elected in 2004. However, he was accused of an inadequate response to Hurricane Katrina, which devastated New Orleans in 2005, and his popularity declined further as the country entered recession at the end of 2007. After leaving office, Bush returned to Texas, and began work on a book.

On becoming president:

> And to the C students, I say you too can be president of the United States.
> COMMENCEMENT ADDRESS at Yale University, May 21, 2001

> It's amazing I won. I was running against peace, prosperity and incumbency.
> REMARK TO SWEDISH PRIME MINISTER GÖRAN PERSSON, June 14, 2001, unaware that the TV cameras were still rolling

On the Republicans losing control of the Senate:

A dictatorship would be a heck of a lot easier, there's no question about it.

REMARK, July 26, 2001

On being 'born again':

You know, I had a drinking problem. Right now I should be in a bar in Texas, not the Oval Office. There is only one reason I am in the Oval Office and not in a bar. I found faith. I found God. I am here because of the power of prayer.

ADDRESSING CHRISTIAN, JEWISH AND MUSLIM LEADERS, September 2002, quoted in David Frum, *The Right Man* (2003)

Speaking in the immediate aftermath of 9/11:

The pictures of airplanes flying into buildings, fires burning, huge structures collapsing have filled us with disbelief, terrible sadness, and a quiet, unyielding anger. These acts of mass murder were intended to frighten our nation into chaos and retreat. But they have failed. Our country is strong.

A great people has been moved to defend a great nation. Terrorist attacks can shake the foundations of our biggest buildings, but they cannot touch the foundation of America. These acts shatter steel, but they cannot dent the steel of American resolve. America was targeted for attack because we're the brightest beacon for freedom and opportunity in the world. And no one will keep that light from shining. Today, our nation saw evil – the very worst of human nature – and we responded with the best of America.

BROADCAST TO THE NATION FROM THE OVAL OFFICE on the evening of September 11, 2001

Introducing the 'war on terror' in the wake of 9/11:

Our war on terror begins with al-Qaeda, but it does not end there. It will not end until every terrorist group of global reach has been found, stopped and defeated.

ADDRESS TO CONGRESS, September 20, 2001. In his broadcast on 9/11 itself, he had used the phrase 'war on terrorism'.

On the 'axis of evil' supposedly linking Iran, Iraq and North Korea:

States like these, and their terrorist allies, constitute an axis of evil, arming to threaten the peace of the world. By seeking weapons of mass destruction, these regimes pose a grave and growing danger. They could provide these arms to terrorists, giving them the means to match their hatred. They could attack our allies or attempt to blackmail the United States. In any of these cases, the price of indifference would be catastrophic.

STATE OF THE UNION ADDRESS, January 29, 2002. Speechwriter David Frum had come up with 'axis of hatred', but this was changed to 'axis of evil' by chief speechwriter Michael Gerson.

Delivering an ultimatum to Iraq:

All the decades of deceit and cruelty have now reached an end. Saddam Hussein and his sons must leave Iraq within 48 hours. Their refusal to do so will result in military conflict, commenced at a time of our choosing.

BROADCAST TO THE NATION, March 17, 2003

Declaring the conclusion of the war with Iraq:

Major combat operations in Iraq have ended. In the battle of Iraq, the United States and our allies have prevailed.

> Speaking on the deck of the aircraft carrier USS *Abraham Lincoln*, May 2, 2003

Unless reading from a script, Bush was no master of oratory:

I think the American people – I hope the American – I don't think, let me – I hope the American people trust me.

> REMARKS, December 18, 2002

There's an old saying in Tennessee – I know it's in Texas, probably in Tennessee – that says, fool me once, shame on – [pause] – shame on you. Fool me – You can't get fooled again.

> SPEAKING in Nashville, Tennessee, September 17, 2002

THE BUSH DOCTRINE
* * *

Either you are with us, or you are with the terrorists.

> ADDRESS TO CONGRESS, September 20, 2001

Early the following year, Bush was declaring:

My hope, of course, is that nations make the right choice. And I believe some nations are doing just that by being steadfast with our coalition and our friends and allies, that nations choose a peaceful course, that they reject terror. And as I say, many nations are realizing when we say you're either with us or against us, we mean it.

> SPEECH in Atlanta, Georgia, January 31, 2002

On a dispute in Oregon between farmers' irrigation rights and Native Americans' fishing rights:

I know the human being and the fish can coexist peacefully.

> SPEECH in Saginaw, Michigan, September 29, 2000

To British Prime Minister Tony Blair:

Yo, Blair, how are you doin'?

> REMARK AT THE G8 SUMMIT, July 17, 2006, unaware that his microphone was on

On war and peace:

I just want you to know that, when we talk about war, we're really talking about peace.

> SPEECH in Washington DC, June 18, 2002

Sometimes we must fight terror with tyranny.

> REMARK AT A PRESS CONFERENCE, November 7, 2007, referring to Pakistan

What others said
* * *

He struggles to exude authority. He furrows his brow, trying to look more sagacious, but he ends up looking as if he has indigestion. Appearing confused at his own speech, he seems like a first-grade actor in a production of *James and the Giant Peach*. Are his blinks Morse code for 'Oh, man, don't let that teleprompter break'?

> MAUREEN DOWD, in the *New York Times*, November 29, 2000

I don't believe he went in there for oil. We didn't go in there for imperialist or financial reasons. We went in there because he bought the Wolfwitz-Cheney analysis that the Iraqis would be better off, we could shake up the authoritarian Arab regimes in the Middle East, and our leverage to make peace between the Palestinians and Israelis would be increased.

BILL CLINTON, interviewed in *Time*, June 2004

I'm proud of the fact that I stood up early and unequivocally in opposition to Bush's foreign policy. That opposition hasn't changed.

BARACK OBAMA, letter to the *Black Commentator*, June 19, 2003

This goofy child president we have on our hands now ...

HUNTER S. THOMPSON, 'Welcome to the Big Darkness' (July 2003)

He's as smart as he wants to be.

UNNAMED CONGRESSMAN, quoted in Fred I. Greenstein, ed., *The George W. Bush Presidency: An Early Assessment* (2003)

George W. Bush *does* have the 'vision thing,' not because he is an aficionado of policy, but because he holds that if a leader does not set his own goals, others will set them for him.

FRED I. GREENSTEIN, 'The Leadership Style of George W. Bush', in Fred I. Greenstein, ed., *The George W. Bush Presidency: An Early Assessment* (2003)

One of the myths about George Bush is that he's stupid. He's not. But he is not curious; that's not a myth. That's absolutely true. He wants to know about as much as he needs to know to make a decision and then move on.

WAYNE SLATER, Austin bureau chief of the *Dallas Morning News*, on pbs.org, 2004

He does not believe that God told him to run for president. He does not believe that God told him he would win, and he certainly does not believe that God told him to drop bombs anywhere in the world.

REV. KIRBYJON CALDWELL, a friend of Bush, quoted in the *Pittsburgh Post-Gazette*, September 11, 2004

There's an old John Anderson song, and it's entitled 'You Either Stand For Something Or You'll Fall For Anything'. And that describes the then-governor and now president. He's not bashful about his positions. He doesn't regret decisions that he makes. He wants people to know exactly what he stands for, exactly where he's headed, exactly where he's coming from, so there'll be no guessing ...

JOE ALLBAUGH, top aide to Bush during his governorship, and then director of Bush's 2000 presidential campaign, commenting on pbs.org in 2004

BARACK OBAMA

1961–

44TH PRESIDENT OF THE UNITED STATES, 2009–

BARACK OBAMA

FULL NAME: Barack Hussein Obama II
BORN: August 4, 1961, Honolulu, Hawaii
MARRIED: Michelle LaVaughn Robinson
CHILDREN: Malia Ann, Natasha (Sasha)
PARTY: Democratic
PERIOD IN OFFICE: January 20, 2009–
VICE-PRESIDENT: Joe Biden

* * *

OBAMA IS THE CHILD OF A WHITE AMERICAN MOTHER, Ann Dunham, and a Kenyan father, Barack Obama Sr, who rose from humble beginnings to became a senior government economist. His parents met when they were students in Honolulu, where they married in 1962, but the marriage ended two years later, and his father returned to Kenya. His mother then married an Indonesian student, Lolo Soetoro, and the family lived in Indonesia for some years. Obama returned to Hawaii in 1971, and in 1983 graduated with a degree in political science from Columbia University in New York. He then worked for the Business International Corporation and the Public Interest Research Group, before moving to Chicago, where for three years he was director of a church-based community organization in a poor area of the South Side. In 1988 he enrolled at Harvard Law School, from where he graduated in 1991, having been the first African American to serve as president of the *Harvard Law Review*. He then returned to Chicago, where he worked as a civil rights lawyer and a university lecturer in constitutional law, and became involved in Democratic politics. He was elected to the Illinois state Senate in 1996 and the US Senate in 2004, in which year he came to national prominence when he made the keynote address at the Democratic convention.

In 2008 he narrowly beat Hillary Rodham Clinton for the Democratic nomination, and went on to defeat the Republican candidate, John McCain, to become the first African American president in US history. As president he inherited a dire economic situation, following the collapse of a number of US banks and other financial institutions. In response, the administration put forward a massive economic stimulus package and helped to bail out the troubled automotive giants Chrysler and General Motors. In foreign affairs, Obama announced an end to the unilateralism of the Bush era, held out the hand of friendship to the Muslim world, and announced a timetable for the end of the US combat mission in Iraq (which he had opposed from the start). In contrast, he announced an increase in troop strength in Afghanistan. At home, his attempt to introduce a major reform of health care has met with strong opposition. In October 2009 Obama was awarded the Nobel Peace Prize.

On his youth:

> I was trying to raise myself to be a black man in America, and beyond the given of my appearance, no one around me seemed to know exactly what that meant.
>
> *DREAMS FROM MY FATHER* (1995)

Refusing to adopt the Clinton get-out (see p. 191):

> I inhaled – that was the point.
>
> INTERVIEW WITH DAVID REMNICK at the American Magazine Conference, October 23, 2006, referring to his teenage drug use

On his birth:

> Contrary to the rumors that you've heard, I was not born in a manger. I was actually born on Krypton and sent here by my father, Jor-el, to save the planet Earth.
>
> SPEECH in New York, October 17, 2008

On himself:

> I am reminded every day of my life, if not by events, then by my wife, that I am not a perfect man. SPEECH in Mitchell, South Dakota, June 1, 2008

On his parentage:

> I stand here today, grateful for the diversity of my heritage, aware that my parents' dreams live on in my two precious daughters. I stand here knowing that my story is part of the larger American story, that I owe a debt to all of those who came before me, and that, in no other country on earth, is my story even possible.
>
> KEYNOTE ADDRESS AT THE DEMOCRATIC CONVENTION, July 27, 2004

On fatherhood:

> If we want to pass on high expectations to our children, we have to have higher expectations for ourselves. *THE AUDACITY OF HOPE* (2006)

On his faith:

> My faith is one that admits some doubt.
>
> SPEAKING on 'This Week with George Stephanopoulos', August 15, 2004

> Evolution is more grounded in my experience than angels.
>
> INTERVIEW WITH DAVID REMNICK at the American Magazine Conference, October 23, 2006

On attacks from the right:

> In truth, being called names is not such a bad deal. *THE AUDACITY OF HOPE* (2006)

On the law:

> The law is also memory; the law also records a long-running conversation, a nation arguing with its conscience. *DREAMS FROM MY FATHER* (1995)

On the perpetrators of the 9/11 attacks:

> My powers of empathy, my ability to reach into another's heart, cannot penetrate the blank stares of those who would murder innocents with abstract, serene satisfaction.
>
> PREFACE to the 2004 edition of *Dreams from My Father*

Opposing the proposed war with Iraq:

I don't oppose all wars. What I am opposed to is a dumb war. What I am opposed to is a rash war ... A dumb war. A rash war. A war based not on reason but on passion, not on principle but on politics. REMARKS, October 2, 2002

THE QUIET HEROES

* * *

On his grandmother, and America's other 'quiet heroes':

She was somebody who was a very humble person and a very plain-spoken person. She's one of those quiet heroes that we have all across America ... They're not famous, their names aren't in the newspapers. But, each and every day, they work hard. They look after their families. They sacrifice for their children and their grandchildren. They aren't seeking the limelight. All they try to do is just do the right thing. And in this crowd, there are a lot of quiet heroes like that ...

SPEECH in Charlotte, North Carolina, November 3, 2008

On living in a democracy:

Our democracy might work a bit better if we recognized that all of us possess values that are worthy of respect: if liberals at least acknowledged that the recreational hunter feels the same way about his gun as they feel about their library books, and if conservatives recognized that most women feel as protective of their right to reproductive freedom as evangelicals do of their right to worship.

THE AUDACITY OF HOPE (2006)

On the electoral system:

Without money, and the television ads that consume all the money, you are pretty much guaranteed to lose.

THE AUDACITY OF HOPE (2006)

On the can-do spirit of America:

When we have faced down impossible odds, when we've been told that we're not ready, or that we shouldn't try, or that we can't, generations of Americans have responded with a simple creed that sums up the spirit of a people: Yes we can.

SPEAKING on the night of the New Hampshire primary, January 8, 2008

On wealth:

I think when you spread the wealth around, it's good for everybody.

REMARK at a campaign stop in Ohio, October 13, 2008

Speaking on the night of his election victory:

It's been a long time coming, but tonight, because of what we did on this date in this election at this defining moment, change has come to America ... The road ahead will be long. Our climb will be steep. We may not get there in one year or even in one term. But, America, I have never been more hopeful than I am tonight that we will get there. I promise you, we as a people will get there ... Tonight we proved once more that the true strength of our nation comes not from the might of our arms or the scale of our wealth, but from the enduring power of our ideals: democracy, liberty, opportunity and unyielding hope ... And where we are met with cynicism and doubts and those who tell us that we can't, we will respond with that timeless creed that sums up the spirit of a people: Yes, we can.

SPEECH in Chicago, November 4, 2008

On the tasks ahead:

In reaffirming the greatness of our nation, we understand that greatness is never a given. It must be earned ... Starting today, we must pick ourselves up, dust ourselves off, and begin again the work of remaking America. INAUGURAL ADDRESS, January 20, 2009

On government:

The question we ask today is not whether our government is too big or too small, but whether it works. INAUGURAL ADDRESS, January 20, 2009

On America's enemies:

We will not apologize for our way of life, nor will we waver in its defense, and for those who seek to advance their aims by inducing terror and slaughtering innocents, we say to you now that our spirit is stronger and cannot be broken; you cannot outlast us, and we will defeat you ... To those leaders around the globe who seek to sow conflict, or blame their society's ills on the West – know that your people will judge you on what you can build, not what you destroy. To those who cling to power through corruption and deceit and the silencing of dissent, know that you are on the wrong side of history; but that we will extend a hand if you are willing to unclench your fist. INAUGURAL ADDRESS, January 20, 2009

On America's global responsibilities:

We can no longer afford indifference to suffering outside our borders; nor can we consume the world's resources without regard to effect. INAUGURAL ADDRESS, January 20, 2009

Ditching the unilateralism of the Bush years:

Make no mistake: this cannot be solely America's endeavor. Those who used to chastise America for acting alone in the world cannot now stand by and wait for America to solve the world's problems alone ... Now is the time for all of us to take our share of responsibility for a global response to global challenges.
SPEECH TO THE UNITED NATIONS GENERAL ASSEMBLY, New York, September 23, 2009

What others said
* * *

What does he actually seek to accomplish, after he's done turning back the waters and healing the planet? The answer is to make government bigger.
SARAH PALIN, accepting the Republican vice-presidential nomination, September 3, 2008

On rightwing Republican attacks on Obama:

I think it's based on racism. There is an inherent feeling among many in this country that an African American should not be president.
JIMMY CARTER, speaking in Atlanta, Georgia, September 2009

Index

* * *

Iran-Contra Scandal 182, 185
Iraq War 195–8, 200–2

J
Jackson, Andrew 38, 41–5, 47–8, 51,
53–4, 56–7, 68–9
Jackson, Rachel *née* Robards 42–3
Jefferson, Martha *née* Skelton 22
Jefferson, Thomas 9, 12, 17, 20–8, 26,
30, 35–6, 42, 44, 47
Johnson, Andrew 81–4
Johnson, Lyndon B. 161, 162–7, 171, 176

K
Kansas-Nebraska Act 1854 65
Kennedy, Jacqueline *née* Lee Bouvier
157, 161
Kennedy, John F. 26, 129, 156–61, 163,
164–5, 169, 171, 191
Kennedy, Joseph 157, 161
Kennedy, Robert 159
Keynes, John Maynard 126
kick, *'You won't have Nixon to kick
around'* (Nixon, R.) 170
kitchen, *'get out of the kitchen'*
(Truman, H. S.) 148
Korean War 147
Ku Klux Klan 86
Kyoto Protocol 195

L
laws, *'repeal of bad or obnoxious laws'*
(Grant, U. S.) 88
LBJ, *'Hey, hey, LBJ'* (Johnson, L. B.) 167
League of Nations 121, 124–5, 128–9, 136
Lee, Robert E. 87
Lend-Lease Act 140
Lewinsky affair 191–2
liberalism 142
liberty 30, 40, 87, 101
'a new nation, conceived in liberty'
(Lincoln, A.) 76
'Liberty ... a plant of rapid growth'
(Washington, G.) 10
'Liberty is to faction what air is to fire'
(Madison, J.) 30
*'Life, liberty and the pursuit of
happiness'* (Jefferson, T.) 23
'tree of liberty must be refreshed'
(Jefferson, T.) 24
lie, *'lie out of both sides of his mouth'*
(Nixon, R.) 171
light, *'a thousand points of light'* (Bush,
G. H. W.) 188
lightning, *'like writing history with
lightning'* (Wilson, W.) 122
Lilacs, *'When lilacs last in the dooryard
bloomed'* (Lincoln, A.) 80
Lincoln, Abraham 12, 57, 60, 68, 71,
72–80, 83–4, 87
Lincoln, *'I am a Ford, not a Lincoln'*
(Ford, G.) 175
lips, *'read my lips, no new taxes'* (Bush,
G. H. W.) 189
Lloyd George, David 126
Lodge, Senator Henry 125
Louisiana Purchase 1803 22, 35, 38
lunatic, *'a lunatic fringe'* (Roosevelt, T.)
115

M
McCain, John 200
McCarthy, Senator Joe 152, 153, 182
McClellan, General George 72, 75
McKinley Tariff Act 1890 107
McKinley, William 106–9, 111, 116, 117
Madison, James 30–3
malice, *'With malice toward none'*
(Lincoln, A.) 78
manifest destiny 56–7, 69
'manifest destiny', (Polk, J. K.) 56
Marshall Plan 147
meaning, *'meaning of the word "is" is'*
(Clinton, B.) 192
Mexican War (1846–8) 57, 59, 65, 72, 86
middle way, *'the middle way is none at
all'* (Adams, J.) 19
military, *'the military-industrial
complex'* (Eisenhower, D. D.) 154
Missouri Compromise 27, 35, 39
Monroe Doctrine 35–6, 38, 113, *see also*
'Roosevelt Cololary'
Monroe, James 34–6
monsters, *'in search of monsters to
destroy'* (Adams, J. Q.) 40
Moon, *'goal ... of landing a man on the
moon'* (Kennedy, J. F.) 159
Moon landings 170
Moran, Edward 63
muckrakes, *'The men with the
muckrakes'* (Roosevelt, T.) 115

N
nation
'Bind up the nation's wounds' (Lincoln,
A.) 78
'No nation is fit to sit in judgement'
(Wilson, W.) 122
'one-third of a nation ill-housed'
(Roosevelt, F. D.) 143
*'this nation, under God, shall have a
new birth of freedom'* (Lincoln, A.)
76
national debt, *'they shall inherit the
national debt'* (Hoover, H.) 138
National Industrial Recovery Act 1933
141
Native Americans 91, 112
NATO 152
negotiate, *'let us never fear to negotiate'*
(Kennedy, J. F.) 158
neighbor, *'policy of the good neighbor'*
(Roosevelt, F. D.) 141
neutral, *'We have stood apart, studiously
neutral'* (Wilson, W.) 123
neutrality, *'Armed neutrality is
ineffectual'* (Wilson, W.) 123
New Deal 136, 140–1, 153, 163, 165, 178
'I pledge myself to a new deal'
(Roosevelt, F. D.) 141
'New Frontier' 157, 158
nightmare, *'Our long national
nightmare is over'* (Ford, G.) 176
9/11 195–6
Nixon Doctrine 170
Nixon, Richard 157, 167, 168–73, 175,
176, 186, 188
Nobel Peace Prize 111
Noriega, Manuel 188

normalcy, *'not nostrums but normalcy'*
(Harding, W.) 129
North American Free Trade
Agreement 191
Nullification Crisis 1832–3 42–3, 53

O
Obama, Barack 80, 186, 198, 199–203
office, *'Public office is a public trust'*
(Cleveland, G.) 100
Oppenheimer, Robert 148
order, *'a new world order'* (Bush,
G. H. W.) 189
O'Sullivan, John L. 56
Oswald, Lee Harvey 157

P
pail, *'from the full dinner pail to the full
garage'* (Hoover, H.) 137
Pan-American Exposition 107
Paris Peace Conference 126
Parker, Rev. Theodore 77
party, *'Party honesty is party expediency'*
(Cleveland, G.) 100
patriotism 134
peace
'a peace between equals' (Wilson, W.)
123
'a peace without victory' (Wilson, W.)
123
'Let us have peace' (Grant, U. S.) 88
'Open covenants of peace' (Wilson, W.)
125
Pearl Harbor 140, 143
pension, *'pension list of the republic a
roll of honor'* (Cleveland, G.) 101
people
'of the people, by the people'
(Lincoln, A.) 76, 92
'people support the government'
(Cleveland, G.) 101
'People who like this sort of thing'
(Lincoln, A.) 78
'You may fool all the people'
(Lincoln, A.) 78
perish, *'shall not perish from the earth'*
(Lincoln, A.) 76
Pierce, Franklin 64–6
plebeian, *'I am a plebeian'* (Johnson, A.)
83
Poles, *'I desire the Poles carnally'*
(Carter, J.) 180
police
*'exercise of an international police
power'* (Roosevelt, T.) 113
*'no mission from God to police the
world'* (Harrison, B) 105
Polk, James K. 53, 55–7, 60, 68–9
poverty, *'unconditional war on poverty'*
(Johnson, L. B.) 164
power
'Balance of power' (Adams, J.) 19
*'Nip the shoots of arbitrary power in the
bud'* (Adams, J.) 19
president
'A president without a party' (Tyler, J.)
54
*'I am the last president of the United
States'* (Buchanan, J.) 70

* * *

Quercus Publishing Plc
21 Bloomsbury Square
London
WC1A 2NS

First published in 2010

A catalogue record of this book is available from the British
Library

ISBN 978-1-84866-045-8

Printed and bound in China

10 9 8 7 6 5 4 3 2 1

PICTURE CREDITS

The publishers would like to thank the following for
permission to reproduce illustrations: Alamy p.194;
iStockphoto p.2-3; Bridgeman Art Library: p.8 Museo
de la Real Academia de Bellas Artes, Madrid, Spain/
Giraudon/The Bridgeman Art Library; p.21 Virginia
Historical Society, Richmond, Virginia, USA/The
Bridgeman Art Library; p.29 © Collection of the New-York
Historical Society, USA/The Bridgeman Art Library; p.37
Private Collection/Peter Newark American Pictures/The
Bridgeman Art Library; p.41 Private Collection/Bridgeman
Art Library; p.52 Private Collection/Roger-Viollet,
Paris/The Bridgeman Art Library; p.67 Credit: James
Buchanan (oil on canvas) by Beck, Augustus J. (19th
century)© Atwater Kent Museum of Philadelphia/Courtesy
of Historical Society of Pennsylvania Collection/The
Bridgeman Art Library; p.89 Private Collection/Bridgeman
Art Library; Corbis pp.16,34,46,49,55,58,64,81,93,96,99,103,
106,117,120,127,131,135,156,199; Getty Images 174; Library of
Congress Brady-Handy Photographic Collection p.61; Press
Association pp.71,85,110,139,146,151,162,177,187;
Rex Features pp.168,181; Topfoto p.190